2nd Workshop on Asian Translation (WAT 2015)

Kyoto, Japan
16 October 2015

ISBN: 978-1-5108-1400-4

Printed from e-media with permission by:

Curran Associates, Inc.
57 Morehouse Lane
Red Hook, NY 12571

Some format issues inherent in the e-media version may also appear in this print version.

Printed by Curran Associates, Inc. (2015)

Association for Computational Linguistics
209 N. Eighth Street
Stroudsburg, Pennsylvania 18360

Phone: 1-570-476-8006
Fax: 1-570-476-0860

acl@aclweb.org

Additional copies of this publication are available from:

Curran Associates, Inc.
57 Morehouse Lane
Red Hook, NY 12571 USA
Phone: 845-758-0400
Fax: 845-758-2634
Email: curran@proceedings.com
Web: www.proceedings.com

Proceedings of the 2nd Workshop on Asian Translation (WAT2015)

Overview of the 2nd Workshop on Asian Translation

Toshiaki Nakazawa
Japan Science and Technology Agency
nakazawa@pa.jst.jp

Hideya Mino
National Institute of Information and Communications Technology
hideya.mino@nict.go.jp

Isao Goto
NHK
goto.i-es@nhk.or.jp

Graham Neubig
Nara Institute of Science and Technology
neubig@is.naist.jp

Sadao Kurohashi
Kyoto University
kuro@i.kyoto-u.ac.jp

Eiichiro Sumita
National Institute of Information and Communications Technology
eiichiro.sumita@nict.go.jp

Abstract

This paper presents the results of the shared tasks from the 2nd workshop on Asian translation (WAT2015) including J↔E, J↔C scientific paper translation subtasks and C→J, K→J patent translation subtasks. For the WAT2015, 12 institutions participated in the shared tasks. About 500 translation results have been submitted to the automatic evaluation server, and selected submissions were manually evaluated.

1 Introduction

The Workshop on Asian Translation (WAT) is a new open evaluation campaign focusing on Asian languages. Following the success of the previous workshop WAT2014(Nakazawa et al., 2014), WAT2015 brings together machine translation researchers and users to try, evaluate, share and discuss brand-new ideas of machine translation. We are working toward the practical use of machine translation among all Asian countries.

For the 2nd WAT, we adopt new translation subtasks "Chinese-to-Japanese and Korean-to-Japanese patent translation" in addition to the subtasks that were conducted in WAT2014.

WAT is unique for the following reasons:

- Open innovation platform
  The test data is fixed and open, so evaluations can be repeated on the same data set to confirm changes in translation accuracy over time. WAT has no deadline for automatic translation quality evaluation (continuous evaluation), so translation results can be submitted at any time.

- Domain and language pairs
  WAT is the world's first workshop that uses scientific papers as the domain, and Chinese↔Japanese and Korean→Japanese as language pairs. In the future, we will add more Asian languages, such as Vietnamese, Indonesian, Thai, Burmese and so on.

- Evaluation method
  Evaluation is done both automatically and manually. For human evaluation, WAT uses crowdsourcing, which is low cost and allows multiple evaluations, as the first-stage evaluation. Also, JPO adequacy evaluation is conducted for the selected submissions according to the crowdsourcing evaluation results.

2 Dataset

WAT uses the Asian Scientific Paper Excerpt Corpus (ASPEC)[1] and JPO Patent Corpus (JPC) [2] as the dataset.

2.1 ASPEC

ASPEC is constructed by the Japan Science and Technology Agency (JST) in collaboration with the National Institute of Information and Communications Technology (NICT). It consists of a Japanese-English scientific paper abstract corpus (ASPEC-JE), which is used for J↔E subtasks, and a Japanese-Chinese scientific paper excerpt corpus (ASPEC-JC), which is used for J↔C subtasks. The statistics for each corpus are described in Table1.

[1] http://lotus.kuee.kyoto-u.ac.jp/ASPEC/
[2] http://lotus.kuee.kyoto-u.ac.jp/WAT/patent/index.html

Proceedings of the 2nd Workshop on Asian Translation (WAT2015), pages 1-28,
Kyoto, Japan, 16th October 2015.

LangPair	Train	Dev	DevTest	Test
ASPEC-JE	3,008,500	1,790	1,784	1,812
ASPEC-JC	672,315	2,090	2,148	2,107

Table 1: Statistics for ASPEC.

2.1.1 ASPEC-JE

The training data for ASPEC-JE was constructed by the NICT from approximately 2 million Japanese-English scientific paper abstracts owned by the JST. Because the abstracts are comparable corpora, the sentence correspondences are found automatically using the method from (Utiyama and Isahara, 2007). Each sentence pair is accompanied by a similarity score and the field symbol. The similarity scores are calculated by the method from (Utiyama and Isahara, 2007). The field symbols are single letters A-Z and show the scientific field for each document[3]. The correspondence between the symbols and field names, along with the frequency and occurrence ratios for the training data, are given in the README file from ASPEC-JE.

The development, development-test and test data were extracted from parallel sentences from the Japanese-English paper abstracts owned by JST that are not contained in the training data. Each data set contains 400 documents. Furthermore, the data has been selected to contain the same relative field coverage across each data set. The document alignment was conducted automatically and only documents with a 1-to-1 alignment are included. It is therefore possible to restore the original documents. The format is the same as for the training data except that there is no similarity score.

2.1.2 ASPEC-JC

ASPEC-JC is a parallel corpus consisting of Japanese scientific papers from the literature database and electronic journal site J-STAGE of JST that have been translated to Chinese with permission from the necessary academic associations. The parts selected were abstracts and paragraph units from the body text, as these contain the highest overall vocabulary coverage.

The development, development-test and test data are extracted at random from documents containing single paragraphs across the entire corpus. Each set contains 400 paragraphs (documents). Therefore, there are no documents sharing the same data across the training, development, development-test and test sets.

[3]http://opac.jst.go.jp/bunrui/index.html

LangPair	Train	Dev	DevTest	Test
JPC-CJ	1,000,000	2,000	2,000	2,000
JPC-KJ	1,000,000	2,000	2,000	2,000

Table 2: Statistics for JPC.

2.2 JPC

JPC was constructed by the Japan Patent Office (JPO). It consists of a Chinese-Japanese patent description corpus (JPC-CJ) and Korean-Japanese patent description corpus (JPC-KJ) with four sections, which are Chemistry, Electricity, Mechanical engineering, and Physics, based on International Patent Classification (IPC). Each corpus is separated into training, development, development-test and test data, which are sentence pairs. This corpus was used for patent subtasks C→J and K→J. The statistics for each corpus are described in Table2.

The Sentence pairs in each data were randomly extracted from a description part of comparable patent documents under the condition that a similarity score between sentences is greater than or equal to the threshold value 0.05. The similarity score was calculated by the method from (Utiyama and Isahara, 2007) as with ASPEC. Document pairs which were used to extract sentence pairs for each data were not used for the other data. Furthermore, the sentence pairs was extracted to be same number among the four sections. The maximize number of sentence pairs which are extracted from one document pair was limited to 60 for training data and 20 for the developent, development-test and test data. The training data for JPC-CJ was made with sentence pairs of Chinese-Japanese patent documents published in 2012. For JPC-KJ, the training data was extracted from sentence pairs of Korean-Japanese patent documents published in 2011 and 2012. The development, development-test and test data for JPC-CJ and JPC-KJ were respectively made with 100 patent documents published in 2013.

3 Baseline Systems

Human evaluations were conducted as pairwise comparisons between the translation results for a specific baseline system and translation results for each participant's system. That is, the specific baseline system was the standard for human evaluation. A phrase-based statistical machine translation (SMT) system was adopted as the specific baseline system at WAT 2015, which is the same system as that at WAT 2014.

In addition to the results for the baseline phrase-based SMT system, we produced results for the baseline systems that consisted of a hierarchical phrase-based SMT system, a string-to-tree syntax-based SMT system, a tree-to-string syntax-based SMT system, seven commercial rule-based machine translation (RBMT) systems, and two online translation systems. The SMT baseline systems consisted of publicly available software, and the procedures for building the systems and for translating using the systems were published on the WAT web page[4]. We used Moses (Koehn et al., 2007; Hoang et al., 2009) as the implementation of the baseline SMT systems. The Berkeley parser (Petrov et al., 2006) was used to obtain syntactic annotations. The baseline systems are shown in Table 3.

The commercial RBMT systems and the online translation systems were operated by the organizers. We note that these RBMT companies and online translation companies did not submit themselves. Because our objective is not to compare commercial RBMT systems or online translation systems from companies that did not themselves participate, the system IDs of these systems are anonymous in this paper.

3.1 Training Data

We used the following data for training the SMT baseline systems.

- Training data for the language model: All of the target language sentences in the parallel corpus.
- Training data for the translation model: Sentences that were 40 words or less in length. (For Japanese–English training data, we only used train-1.txt, which consists of one million parallel sentence pairs with high similarity scores.)
- Development data for tuning: All of the development data.

3.2 Common Settings for Baseline SMT

We used the following tools for tokenization.

- Juman version 7.0[5] for Japanese segmentation.
- Stanford Word Segmenter version 2014-01-04[6] (Chinese Penn Treebank (CTB) model) for Chinese segmentation.
- The Moses toolkit for English tokenization.
- Mecab-ko[7] for Korean segmentation.

To obtain word alignments, GIZA++ and grow-diag-final-and heuristics were used. We used 5-gram language models with modified Kneser-Ney smoothing, which were built using a tool in the Moses toolkit (Heafield et al., 2013).

3.3 Phrase-based SMT

We used the following Moses configuration for the phrase-based SMT system.

- distortion-limit = 20 except for KJ and distortion-limit = 0 for KJ
- msd-bidirectional-fe lexicalized reordering
- Phrase score option: GoodTuring

The default values were used for the other system parameters.

3.4 Hierarchical Phrase-based SMT

We used the following Moses configuration for the hierarchical phrase-based SMT system.

- max-chart-span = 1000
- Phrase score option: GoodTuring

The default values were used for the other system parameters.

3.5 String-to-Tree Syntax-based SMT

We used the Berkeley parser to obtain target language syntax. We used the following Moses configuration for the string-to-tree syntax-based SMT system.

- max-chart-span = 1000
- Phrase score option: GoodTuring
- Phrase extraction options: MaxSpan = 1000, MinHoleSource = 1, and NonTermConsecSource.

The default values were used for the other system parameters.

[4] http://lotus.kuee.kyoto-u.ac.jp/WAT/

[5] http://nlp.ist.i.kyoto-u.ac.jp/EN/index.php?JUMAN

[6] http://nlp.stanford.edu/software/segmenter.shtml

[7] https://bitbucket.org/eunjeon/mecab-ko/

System ID	System	Type	ASPEC				JPC	
			JE	EJ	JC	CJ	CJ	KJ
SMT Phrase	Moses' Phrase-based SMT	SMT	✓	✓	✓	✓	✓	✓
SMT Hiero	Moses' Hierarchical Phrase-based SMT	SMT	✓	✓	✓	✓	✓	✓
SMT S2T	Moses' String-to-Tree Syntax-based SMT and Berkeley parser	SMT	✓		✓			
SMT T2S	Moses' Tree-to-String Syntax-based SMT and Berkeley parser	SMT		✓		✓	✓	
RBMT X	The Honyaku V15 (Commercial system)	RBMT	✓	✓				
RBMT X	ATLAS V14 (Commercial system)	RBMT	✓	✓				
RBMT X	PAT-Transer 2009 (Commercial system)	RBMT	✓	✓				
RBMT X	J-Beijing 7 (Commercial system)	RBMT			✓	✓	✓	
RBMT X	Hohrai 2011 (Commercial system)	RBMT			✓	✓	✓	
RBMT X	J Soul 9 (Commercial system)	RBMT						✓
RBMT X	Korai 2011 (Commercial system)	RBMT						✓
Online X	Google translate (August, 2015)	(SMT)	✓	✓	✓	✓	✓	✓
Online X	Bing translator (August and September, 2015)	(SMT)	✓	✓	✓	✓	✓	✓

Table 3: Baseline Systems

3.6 Tree-to-String Syntax-based SMT

We used the Berkeley parser to obtain source language syntax. We used the following Moses configuration for the baseline tree-to-string syntax-based SMT system.

- max-chart-span = 1000
- Phrase score option: GoodTuring
- Phrase extraction options: MaxSpan = 1000, MinHoleSource = 1, MinWords = 0, NonTermConsecSource, and AllowOnlyUnalignedWords.

The default values were used for the other system parameters.

4 Automatic Evaluation

4.1 Procedure for Calculating Automatic Evaluation Score

We calculated automatic evaluation scores for the translation results by applying two popular metrics: BLEU (Papineni et al., 2002) and RIBES (Isozaki et al., 2010). BLEU scores were calculated using *multi-bleu.perl* distributed with the Moses toolkit (Koehn et al., 2007); RIBES scores were calculated using *RIBES.py* version 1.02.4 [8]. All scores for each task were calculated using one reference. Before the calculation of the automatic evaluation scores, the translation results were tokenized with word segmentation tools for each language.

For Japanese segmentation, we used three different tools: Juman version 7.0 (Kurohashi et al., 1994), KyTea 0.4.6 (Neubig et al., 2011) with Full SVM model [9] and MeCab 0.996 (Kudo, 2005) with IPA dictionary 2.7.0 [10]. For Chinese segmentation we used two different tools: KyTea 0.4.6 with Full SVM Model in MSR model and Stanford Word Segmenter version 2014-06-16 with Chinese Penn Treebank (CTB) and Peking University (PKU) model [11] (Tseng, 2005). For Korean segmentation we used mecab-ko [12]. For English segmentation we used tokenizer.perl [13] in the Moses toolkit.

Detailed procedures for the automatic evaluation are shown on the WAT2015 evaluation web page [14].

4.2 Automatic Evaluation System

The participants submit translation results via an automatic evaluation system deployed on the WAT2015 web page, which automatically gives evaluation scores for the uploaded results. Figure 1 shows the submission interface for participants. The system requires participants to provide the following information when they upload translation results:

- Subtask:
  - Scientific papers subtask ($J \leftrightarrow E$, $J \leftrightarrow C$);
  - Patents subtask ($C \rightarrow J$, $K \rightarrow J$);
- Method (SMT, RBMT, SMT and RBMT, EBMT, Other);

[8] http://www.kecl.ntt.co.jp/icl/lirg/ribes/index.html

[9] http://www.phontron.com/kytea/model.html

[10] http://code.google.com/p/mecab/downloads/detail?name=mecab-ipadic-2.7.0-20070801.tar.gz

[11] http://nlp.stanford.edu/software/segmenter.shtml

[12] https://bitbucket.org/eunjeon/mecab-ko/

[13] https://github.com/moses-smt/mosesdecoder/tree/RELEASE-2.1.1/scripts/tokenizer/tokenizer.perl

[14] http://lotus.kuee.kyoto-u.ac.jp/WAT/evaluation/index.html

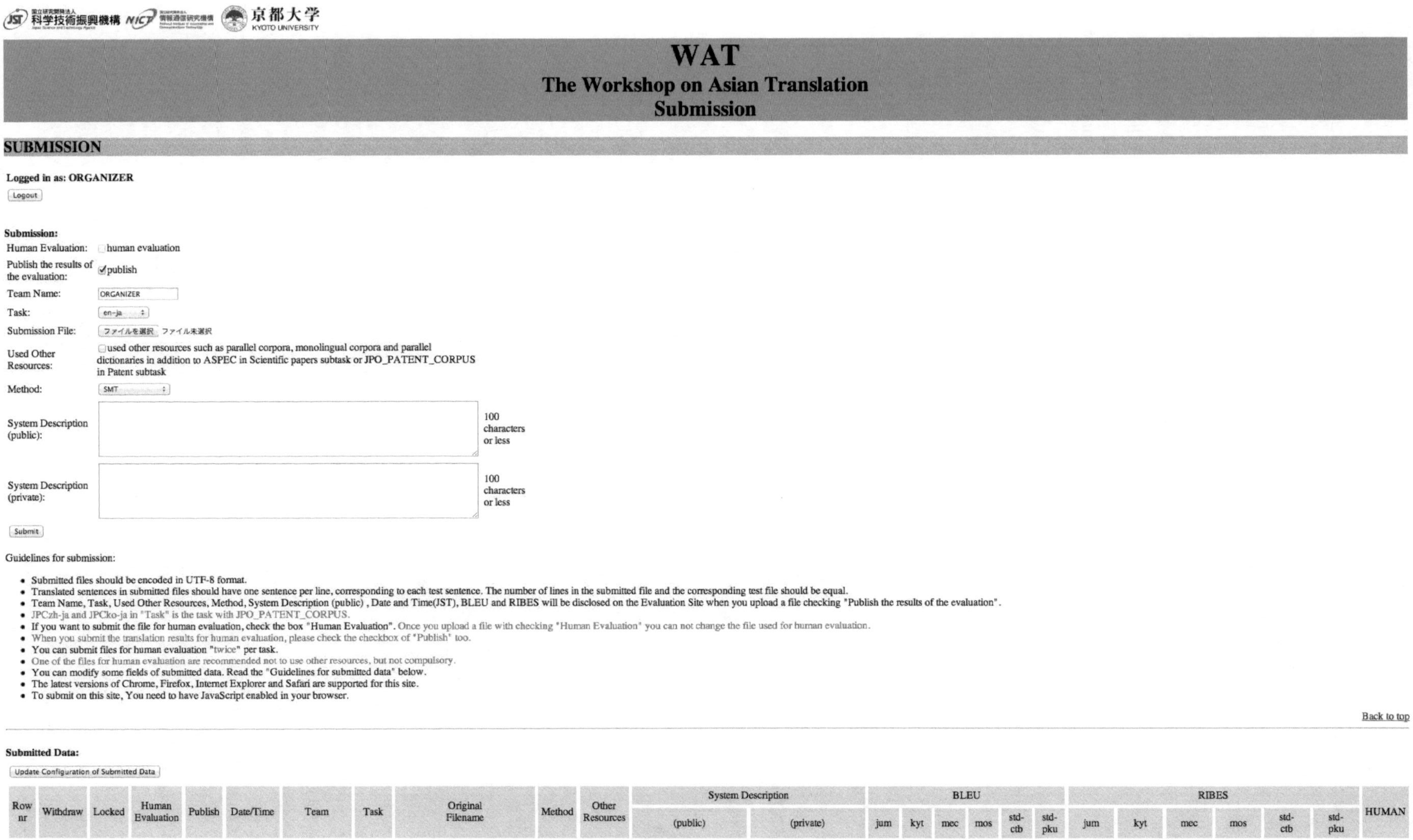

Figure 1: The submission web page for participants

- Use of other resources in addition to ASPEC or JPC;
- Permission to publish the automatic evaluation scores on the WAT2015 web page.

The server for the system stores all submitted information, including translation results and scores, although participants can confirm only the information that they uploaded. Information about translation results that participants permit to be published is disclosed on the web page. In addition to submitting translation results for automatic evaluation, participants submit the results for human evaluation using the same web interface. This automatic evaluation system will remain available even after WAT2015. Anybody can register to use the system on the registration web page [15].

5 Human Evaluation

In WAT2015, we conducted 2 kinds of human evaluations: *pairwise crowdsourcing evaluation* and *JPO adequacy evaluation*.

5.1 Pairwise Crowdsourcing Evaluation

The pairwise crowdsourcing evaluation is the same as the last year. We used Lancers as the crowdsourcing platform. There are two reasons of choosing Lancers. One is that we can set the category of the crowdsourcing task ('Translation' in this case). We can reach the appropriate workers by choosing the appropriate categories. The other reason is that we can assign the task to identity-verified workers. This function guaranteed the quality of the workers. These two advantages ensure a high evaluation quality.

We used the same sentences as the last year for the pairwise crowdsourcing evaluation. We randomly chose *documents* from the Test set from the ASPEC data, for a total of 400 sentence pairs for JE and JC. We excluded documents containing sentences longer than 100 Japanese characters. Each submission is compared with the baseline translation (Phrase-based SMT, described in Section 3) and given a *Crowd* score[16].

5.1.1 Pairwise Evaluation of Sentences

We conducted pairwise evaluation of each of the 400 test sentences. The input sentence and two translations (the baseline and a submission) are shown to the workers, and the workers are asked to judge which of the translation is better, or if they are of the same quality. The order of the two translations are at random. Figure 2 illustrates the evaluation.

[15] http://lotus.kuee.kyoto-u.ac.jp/WAT/registration/index.html

[16] It was called HUMAN score in WAT2014.

5.1.2 Voting

The crowdsourcing workers are not specialists, and thus the quality of the judgments are not necessarily precise. To guarantee the quality of the evaluations, each sentence is evaluated by 5 different workers and the final decision is made depending on the 5 judgements[17]. We define each judgement $j_i (i = 1, \cdots, 5)$ as:

$$j_i = \begin{cases} 1 & \text{if better than the baseline} \\ -1 & \text{if worse than the baseline} \\ 0 & \text{if the quality is the same} \end{cases}$$

The final decision D is defined as follows using $S = \sum j_i$:

$$D = \begin{cases} win & (S \geq 2) \\ loss & (S \leq -2) \\ tie & (otherwise) \end{cases}$$

5.1.3 Crowd Score Calculation

Suppose that W is the number of *wins* compared to the baseline, L is the number of *losses* and T is the number of *ties*. The Crowd score can be calculated by the following formula:

$$Crowd = 100 \times \frac{W - L}{W + L + T}$$

From the definition, the Crowd score ranges between -100 and 100.

5.1.4 Confidence Interval Estimation

There are several ways to estimate a confidence interval. We chose to use bootstrap resampling (Koehn, 2004) to estimate the 95% confidence interval. The procedure is as follows:

1. randomly select 300 sentences from the 400 human evaluation sentences, and calculate the Crowd score of the selected sentences
2. iterate the previous step 1000 times and get 1000 Crowd scores
3. sort the 1000 scores and estimate the 95% confidence interval by discarding the top 25 scores and the bottom 25 scores

[17] We used 3 judgements in WAT2014.

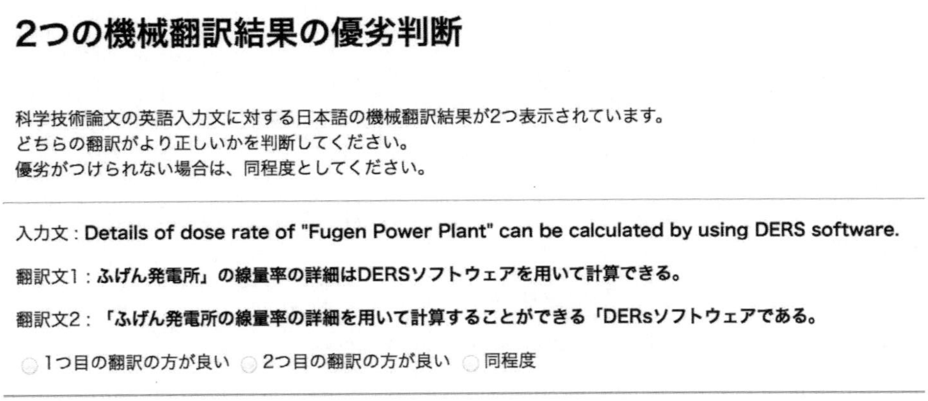

Figure 2: Illustration of the crowdsourcing evaluation. The workers are asked to judge which translation is better, or the same.

5.1.5 Cost

A major benefit of using crowdsourcing is that it reduces the cost of evaluations. In WAT2015, one judgment costs 5 JPY. The evaluation of a submission requires 5 (judgments) $\times$ 400 (sentence pairs) = 2,000 judgments and costs 5 $\times$ 2,000 = 10,000 JPY. The time for the evaluation differs depending on the translation direction. On average, one evaluation takes a couple of days.

5.2 JPO Adequacy Evaluation

The participants' systems, which achieved the top 3 highest scores among the pairwise crowdsourcing evaluation results of each subtask, were also evaluated with the JPO adequacy evaluation. The JPO adequacy evaluation was carried out by translation experts with a quality evaluation criterion for translated patent documents which the Japanese Patent Office (JPO) decided. In addition to the top 3 systems, the Sense 1 system of the JPC-KJ subtask, which was the lower score on the pairwise crowdsourcing evaluation despite the high score on the automatic evaluation, was evaluated exceptionally. For each system, two annotators evaluate the test sentences to guarantee the quality.

5.2.1 Evaluation of Sentences

The number of test sentences for the JPO adequacy evaluation is 200. The 200 test sentences were randomly selected from the 400 test sentences of the pairwise evaluation. The test sentence include the input sentence, the submitted system's translation and the reference translation.

5	All important information is transmitted correctly. (100%)
4	Almost all important information is transmitted correctly. (80%–)
3	More than half of important information is transmitted correctly. (50%–)
2	Some of important information is transmitted correctly. (20%–)
1	Almost all important information is NOT transmitted correctly. (–20%)

Table 4: The JPO adequacy criterion

5.2.2 Evaluation Criterion

Table 4 shows the JPO adequacy criterion from 5 to 1. The evaluation is performed subjectively. "Important information" represents the technical factors and their relationships. The degree of importance of each element is also considered to evaluate. The percentages in each grade are rough indications for the transmission degree of the source sentence meanings. The detailed criterion can be found on the JPO document (in Japanese) [18].

6 Participants List

Table 5 shows the list of participants for WAT2015. This includes not only Japanese organizations, but also some organizations from outside Japan. 12 teams submitted one or more translation results to the both automatic evaluation server and human evaluation.

[18]http://www.jpo.go.jp/shiryou/toushin/chousa/tokkyohonyaku_hyouka.htm

Team ID	Organization	ASPEC				JPC	
		JE	EJ	JC	CJ	CJ	KJ
NAIST (Neubig et al., 2015)	Nara Institute of Science and Technology	✓	✓	✓	✓		
Kyoto-U (Richardson et al., 2015)	Kyoto University	✓	✓	✓	✓	✓	
WEBLIO_MT (Zhu, 2015)	Weblio, Inc.		✓				
TMU (Matsuo et al., 2015)	Tokyo Metropolitan University	✓					
BJTUNLP (Shan et al., 2015)	Beijing Jiaotong University				✓		
Sense (Tan et al., 2015)	Saarland University & Nanyang Technological University	✓	✓				✓
NICT (Ding et al., 2015)	National Institute of Information and Communication Technology	✓					✓
TOSHIBA (Sonoh and Kinoshita, 2015)	Toshiba Corporation	✓	✓	✓	✓	✓	✓
WASUIPS (Yang et al., 2015)	Waseda University					✓	
naver (Lee et al., 2015)	NAVER Corporation		✓				✓
EHR (Ehara, 2015)	Ehara NLP Research Laboratory		✓		✓	✓	✓
ntt (Sudoh and Nagata, 2015)	NTT Communication Science Laboratories					✓	

Table 5: List of participants who submitted translation results to WAT2015 and their participation in each subtasks.

7 Evaluation Results

In this section, the evaluation results for WAT2015 are reported from several perspectives. Some of the results for both automatic and human evaluations are also accessible at the WAT2015 website[19].

7.1 Official Automatic Evaluation Results

Figures 3 and 4 show the official automatic evaluation results for the representative submissions and baseline systems. The automatic evaluation results for all the submissions are shown in Section Appendix A.

7.2 Official Crowdsourcing Evaluation Results

Crowd Score

Figure 5 shows the official crowdsourcing evaluation results. The error bars in the figures show the 95% confidence interval (see Section 5.1.4). Note that overlapping error bars between two submissions do not necessarily mean that there is no significant difference. If an error bar crosses the x-axis (Crowd score = 0), it means that there is no significant difference between the submission and the baseline (SMT Phrase).

Statistical Significance Testing between Submissions

Tables 6, 7, 8, 9, 10 and 11 show the results of statistical significance testing for the JE, EJ, JC and CJ translations respectively where all the pairs of submissions are tested. $\ggg$, $\gg$ and $>$ mean that the system in the row is *better* than the system in the column at a significance level of $p < 0.01, 0.05$ and 0.1 respectively. Testing is also done by the bootstrap resampling as follows:

1. randomly select 300 sentences from the 400 crowdsourcing evaluation sentences, and calculate the Crowd scores on the selected sentences for both systems

2. iterate the previous step 1000 times and count the number of wins (W), losses (L) and ties (T)

3. calculate $p = \frac{L}{W+L}$

Inter-annotator Agreement

To assess the reliability of agreement between the crowdsourcing workers, we calculated the Fleiss' κ (Fleiss and others, 1971) values. The results are shown in Table 12. We can see that the κ values are larger for X $\rightarrow$ J translations than for J $\rightarrow$ X translations. This may be because we used a Japanese crowdsourcing service for the evaluation and so the majority of the crowdsourcing workers are Japanese, and the evaluation of one's mother tongue is much easier than for other languages in general. Also, K $\rightarrow$ J evaluations seem to be more consistent than the other directions. This may be because the quality of K $\rightarrow$ J translations are much better than the other directions.

Correlation between Automatic and Crowdsourcing Evaluations

Figure 6 and 7 show the correlations between the automatic evaluation measures (BLEU/RIBES) and the Crowd score.

[19] http://lotus.kuee.kyoto-u.ac.jp/WAT/evaluation/index.html

	Kyoto-U 2	TOSHIBA 2	TOSHIBA 1	RBMT D	Kyoto-U 1	NICT 1	NAIST 2	SMT S2T	NICT 2	Online D	Sense 1	Sense 2	TMU
NAIST 1	-	⋙	⋙	⋙	⋙	⋙	⋙	⋙	⋙	⋙	⋙	⋙	⋙
Kyoto-U 2		⋙	⋙	⋙	⋙	⋙	⋙	⋙	⋙	⋙	⋙	⋙	⋙
TOSHIBA 2			≫	⋙	⋙	⋙	⋙	⋙	⋙	⋙	⋙	⋙	⋙
TOSHIBA 1				≫	≫	≫	⋙	⋙	⋙	⋙	⋙	⋙	⋙
RBMT D					-	-	≫	⋙	⋙	⋙	⋙	⋙	⋙
Kyoto-U 1						-	≫	⋙	⋙	⋙	⋙	⋙	⋙
NICT 1							≫	⋙	⋙	⋙	⋙	⋙	⋙
NAIST 2								≫	≫	⋙	⋙	⋙	⋙
SMT S2T									-	≫	⋙	⋙	⋙
NICT 2										≫	⋙	⋙	⋙
Online D											⋙	⋙	⋙
Sense 1												≫	⋙
Sense 2													⋙

Table 6: Statistical significance testing of the ASPEC-JE Crowd scores.

	WEBLIO_MT 1	naver 2	Kyoto-U 2	NAIST 2	naver 1	WEBLIO MT 2	Kyoto-U 1	TOSHIBA	Online A	EHR	SMT T2S	RBMT B	Sense 2	Sense 1
NAIST 1	⋙	⋙	⋙	⋙	⋙	⋙	⋙	⋙	⋙	⋙	⋙	⋙	⋙	⋙
WEBLIO_MT 1		-	>	≫	⋙	⋙	⋙	⋙	⋙	⋙	⋙	⋙	⋙	⋙
naver 2			-	>	⋙	⋙	⋙	⋙	⋙	⋙	⋙	⋙	⋙	⋙
Kyoto-U 2				-	>	⋙	⋙	⋙	⋙	⋙	⋙	⋙	⋙	⋙
NAIST 2					-	⋙	⋙	⋙	⋙	⋙	⋙	⋙	⋙	⋙
naver 1						≫	⋙	⋙	⋙	⋙	⋙	⋙	⋙	⋙
WEBLIO_MT 2							>	>	⋙	⋙	⋙	⋙	⋙	⋙
Kyoto-U 1								-	⋙	⋙	⋙	⋙	⋙	⋙
TOSHIBA									⋙	⋙	⋙	⋙	⋙	⋙
Online A										-	≫	⋙	⋙	⋙
EHR											-	⋙	⋙	⋙
SMT T2S												⋙	⋙	⋙
RBMT B													⋙	⋙
Sense 2														⋙

Table 7: Statistical significance testing of the ASPEC-EJ Crowd scores.

7.3 Chronological Evaluation

Figure 8 shows the chronological evaluation results of ASPEC. The x-axis indicates the BLEU score and the y-axis indicates the Crowd score. Note that the first 3 annotations among 5 by the crowdsourcing were used, and the decision for each sentence is made by the same criteria in WAT2014 for calculating the Crowd score of WAT2015 submissions.

7.4 Official JPO Adequacy Evaluation Results

Table 13 and Figure 9 show the JPO Adequacy Evaluation results for the selected submissions. The weights for the weighted κ (Cohen, 1968) is defined as $|Evaluation1 - Evaluation2|/4$.

As described in Section 5.2, we selected top 3 teams per subtask for the JPO adequacy evaluation according to the pairwise crowdsourcing evaluation results. However, for JPC K $\rightarrow$ J, we exceptionally selected 4 teams including the top 3 teams and the Sense team. This is because the Sense team achieved notably better automatic evaluation scores, but got the worst crowdsourcing evaluation result, and we thought this is a very interesting case.

Figure 10 shows the summary of automatic and human evaluations for the selected submissions. We can see that all of Crowd, BLEU and RIBES scores partially correlate to the JPO adequacy score, but none of them perfectly correlates. Especially, for JPC-KJ, both BLEU and RIBES failed to correctly evaluate the quality of Sense team.

	Kyoto-U 1	Kyoto-U 2	SMT S2T	NAIST 1	NAIST 2	TOSHIBA 1	RBMT B	Online D
TOSHIBA 2	-	$\gg$	$\ggg$	$\ggg$	$\ggg$	$\ggg$	$\ggg$	$\ggg$
Kyoto-U 1		$>$	$\ggg$	$\ggg$	$\ggg$	$\ggg$	$\ggg$	$\ggg$
Kyoto-U 2			$\gg$	$\gg$	$\ggg$	$\ggg$	$\ggg$	$\ggg$
SMT S2T				-	$\gg$	$\gg$	$\ggg$	$\ggg$
NAIST 1					$\gg$	$\gg$	$\ggg$	$\ggg$
NAIST 2						-	$\ggg$	$\ggg$
TOSHIBA 1							$\ggg$	$\ggg$
RBMT B								$>$

Table 8: Statistical significance testing of the ASPEC-JC Crowd scores.

	NAIST 2	EHR	Kyoto-U 2	TOSHIBA 1	SMT T2S	Kyoto-U 1	BJTUNLP	TOSHIBA 2	Online A	RBMT A
NAIST 1	$\ggg$	$\ggg$	$\ggg$	$\ggg$	$\ggg$	$\ggg$	$\ggg$	$\ggg$	$\ggg$	$\ggg$
NAIST 2		-	$\ggg$	$\ggg$	$\ggg$	$\ggg$	$\ggg$	$\ggg$	$\ggg$	$\ggg$
EHR			$\ggg$	$\ggg$	$\ggg$	$\ggg$	$\ggg$	$\ggg$	$\ggg$	$\ggg$
Kyoto-U 2				-	-	-	$\ggg$	$\ggg$	$\ggg$	$\ggg$
TOSHIBA 1					-	-	$\ggg$	$\ggg$	$\ggg$	$\ggg$
SMT T2S						-	$\ggg$	$\ggg$	$\ggg$	$\ggg$
Kyoto-U 1							$\ggg$	$\ggg$	$\ggg$	$\ggg$
BJTUNLP								$\ggg$	$\ggg$	$\ggg$
TOSHIBA 2									$\ggg$	$\ggg$
Online A										$\ggg$

Table 9: Statistical significance testing of the ASPEC-CJ Crowd scores.

From the evaluation results, the following can be observed (see Figure 10):

- Neural Network based re-ranking is effective (NAIST, Kyoto-U, naver).
- The top SMT outperformed RBMT for CJ and KJ patent translation.
- K→J patent translation achieved high scores for automatic and human evaluations.
- A new problem of automatic evaluation was found in the KJ evaluation.

8 Submitted Data

The number of published automatic evaluation results for the twelve teams exceeded 400 before the start of WAT2015, and 56 translation results for pairwise crowsdourcing evaluation were submitted by twelve teams. Furthermore, we selected 3 translation results from each subtask and evaluated them for JPO adequacy evaluation. We will organize the all of the submitted data for human evaluation and make this public.

9 Conclusion and Future Perspective

This paper summarizes the WAT2015 machine translation evaluation campaign. We had 12 participants worldwide, and collected a large number of useful submissions for improving the current machine translation systems by analyzing the submissions and identifying the issues.

For the next WAT workshop, we plan to conduct context-aware MT evaluations. The test data for WAT are prepared using the paragraphs as the unit, while almost all other evaluation campaigns use the sentences as the unit. Therefore, it is suitable to investigate the importance of context in translation.

We would also be very happy to include other languages if the resources are available.

Appendix A Submissions

Tables 14, 15, 16, 17, 18, 19, summarize all the submissions listed in the automatic evaluation server at the time of the WAT2015 workshop (16th, October, 2015). The OTHER RESOURCES column shows the use of resources such as parallel corpora, monolingual corpora and

	TOSHIBA 2	EHR 1	SMT T2S	ntt 1	TOSHIBA 1	Kyoto-U 1	EHR 2	ntt 2	Online A	WASUIPS	RBMT A
Kyoto-U 2	-	$\gg$	$\ggg$	$\ggg$	$\ggg$	$\ggg$	$\ggg$	$\ggg$	$\ggg$	$\ggg$	$\ggg$
TOSHIBA 2		-	$>$	$\ggg$	$\ggg$	$\ggg$	$\ggg$	$\ggg$	$\ggg$	$\ggg$	$\ggg$
EHR 1			-	$\ggg$	$\ggg$	$\ggg$	$\ggg$	$\ggg$	$\ggg$	$\ggg$	$\ggg$
SMT T2S				$\gg$	$\ggg$	$\ggg$	$\ggg$	$\ggg$	$\ggg$	$\ggg$	$\ggg$
ntt 1					-	-	$\ggg$	$\ggg$	$\ggg$	$\ggg$	$\ggg$
TOSHIBA 1						-	$\ggg$	$\ggg$	$\ggg$	$\ggg$	$\ggg$
Kyoto-U 1							$\gg$	$\ggg$	$\ggg$	$\ggg$	$\ggg$
EHR 2								-	$\ggg$	$\ggg$	$\ggg$
ntt 2									$\ggg$	$\ggg$	$\ggg$
Online A										$\gg$	$\ggg$
WASUIPS											$\ggg$

Table 10: Statistical significance testing of the JPC-CJ Crowd scores.

	naver 2	NICT 2	EHR 1	NICT 1	naver 1	EHR 2	TOSHIBA 2	Sense 2	TOSHIBA 1	SMT Hiero	RBMT A	Sense 1
Online A	$\ggg$	$\ggg$	$\ggg$	$\ggg$	$\ggg$	$\ggg$	$\ggg$	$\ggg$	$\ggg$	$\ggg$	$\ggg$	$\ggg$
naver 2		$\gg$	$\gg$	$\ggg$	$\ggg$	$\ggg$	$\ggg$	$\ggg$	$\ggg$	$\ggg$	$\ggg$	$\ggg$
NICT 2			-	$>$	$\gg$	$\gg$	$\ggg$	$\ggg$	$\ggg$	$\ggg$	$\ggg$	$\ggg$
EHR 1				-	$\gg$	$\gg$	$\ggg$	$\ggg$	$\ggg$	$\ggg$	$\ggg$	$\ggg$
NICT 1					-	-	$\gg$	$\ggg$	$\ggg$	$\ggg$	$\ggg$	$\ggg$
naver 1						-	$>$	$\gg$	$\gg$	$\gg$	$\ggg$	$\ggg$
EHR 2							-	$>$	$\gg$	$>$	$\ggg$	$\ggg$
TOSHIBA 2								-	-	-	$\ggg$	$\ggg$
Sense 2									-	-	$\ggg$	$\ggg$
TOSHIBA 1										-	$\ggg$	$\ggg$
SMT Hiero											$\ggg$	$\ggg$
RBMT A												$\ggg$

Table 11: Statistical significance testing of the JPC-KJ Crowd scores.

parallel dictionaries in addition to ASPEC or JPC.

ASPEC-JE	
SYSTEM ID	κ
NAIST 1	0.104
Kyoto-U 2	0.070
TOSHIBA 2	0.076
TOSHIBA 1	0.080
RBMT D	0.070
Kyoto-U 1	0.112
NICT 1	0.118
NAIST 2	0.109
SMT S2T	0.046
NICT 2	0.078
Online D	0.044
Sense 1	0.077
Sense 2	0.073
TMU	0.065
ave.	0.080

ASPEC-EJ	
SYSTEM ID	κ
NAIST 1	0.243
WEBLIO_MT 1	0.216
naver 2	0.170
Kyoto-U 2	0.219
NAIST 2	0.187
naver 1	0.193
WEBLIO_MT 2	0.170
Kyoto-U 1	0.208
TOSHIBA	0.221
Online A	0.170
EHR	0.196
SMT T2S	0.206
RBMT B	0.171
Sense 2	0.200
Sense 1	0.140
ave.	0.194

ASPEC-JC	
SYSTEM ID	κ
TOSHIBA 2	0.159
Kyoto-U 1	0.022
Kyoto-U 2	-0.042
SMT S2T	-0.013
NAIST 1	0.004
NAIST 2	0.021
TOSHIBA 1	0.072
RBMT B	-0.031
Online D	0.019
ave.	0.023

ASPEC-CJ	
SYSTEM ID	κ
NAIST 1	0.116
NAIST 2	0.066
EHR	0.155
Kyoto-U 2	0.078
TOSHIBA 1	0.171
SMT T2S	0.169
Kyoto-U 1	0.043
BJTUNLP	0.115
TOSHIBA 2	0.095
Online A	0.076
RBMT A	0.094
ave.	0.107

JPC-CJ	
SYSTEM ID	κ
Kyoto-U 2	0.087
TOSHIBA 2	0.117
EHR 1	0.111
SMT T2S	0.109
ntt 1	0.114
TOSHIBA 1	0.105
Kyoto-U 1	0.057
EHR 2	0.148
ntt 2	0.042
Online A	0.027
WASUIPS	0.044
RBMT A	0.054
ave.	0.084

JPC-KJ	
SYSTEM ID	κ
Online A	0.142
naver 2	0.248
NICT 2	0.317
EHR 1	0.221
NICT 1	0.295
naver 1	0.388
EHR 2	0.213
TOSHIBA 2	0.305
Sense 2	0.323
TOSHIBA 1	0.304
SMT Hiero	0.246
RBMT A	0.125
Sense 1	0.200
ave.	0.255

Table 12: The Fleiss' kappa values for the crowdsourcing evaluation results.

ASPEC-JE SYSTEM ID	Annotator A average	Annotator B average	all average	κ	weighted κ
NAIST 1	3.605	4.055	3.830	0.250	0.439
Kyoto-U 2	3.495	3.805	3.650	0.296	0.475
TOSHIBA 2	3.450	3.755	3.600	0.269	0.459

ASPEC-EJ SYSTEM ID	Annotator A average	Annotator B average	all average	κ	weighted κ
NAIST 1	3.865	4.220	4.043	0.377	0.535
naver 2	3.760	4.240	4.000	0.371	0.544
WEBLIO_MT 1	3.585	4.040	3.813	0.356	0.535

ASPEC-JC SYSTEM ID	Annotator A average	Annotator B average	all average	κ	weighted κ
NAIST 1	3.600	2.740	3.170	0.151	0.296
Kyoto-U 1	3.330	2.400	2.865	0.162	0.319
TOSHIBA 2	3.220	2.275	2.748	0.112	0.287

ASPEC-CJ SYSTEM ID	Annotator A average	Annotator B average	all average	κ	weighted κ
NAIST 1	3.970	3.785	3.878	0.247	0.417
Kyoto-U 2	3.785	3.700	3.743	0.292	0.433
EHR	3.250	3.245	3.248	0.199	0.418

JPC-CJ SYSTEM ID	Annotator A average	Annotator B average	all average	κ	weighted κ
Kyoto-U 2	3.570	3.245	3.408	0.287	0.513
EHR 1	3.410	3.225	3.318	0.351	0.531
TOSHIBA 2	3.405	3.095	3.250	0.349	0.557

JPC-KJ SYSTEM ID	Annotator A average	Annotator B average	all average	κ	weighted κ
naver 2	4.900	4.655	4.778	0.329	0.333
NICT 2	4.905	4.610	4.758	0.186	0.218
Online A	4.735	4.315	4.525	0.183	0.300
Sense 1	4.445	4.195	4.320	0.367	0.528

Table 13: JPO adequacy evaluation results.

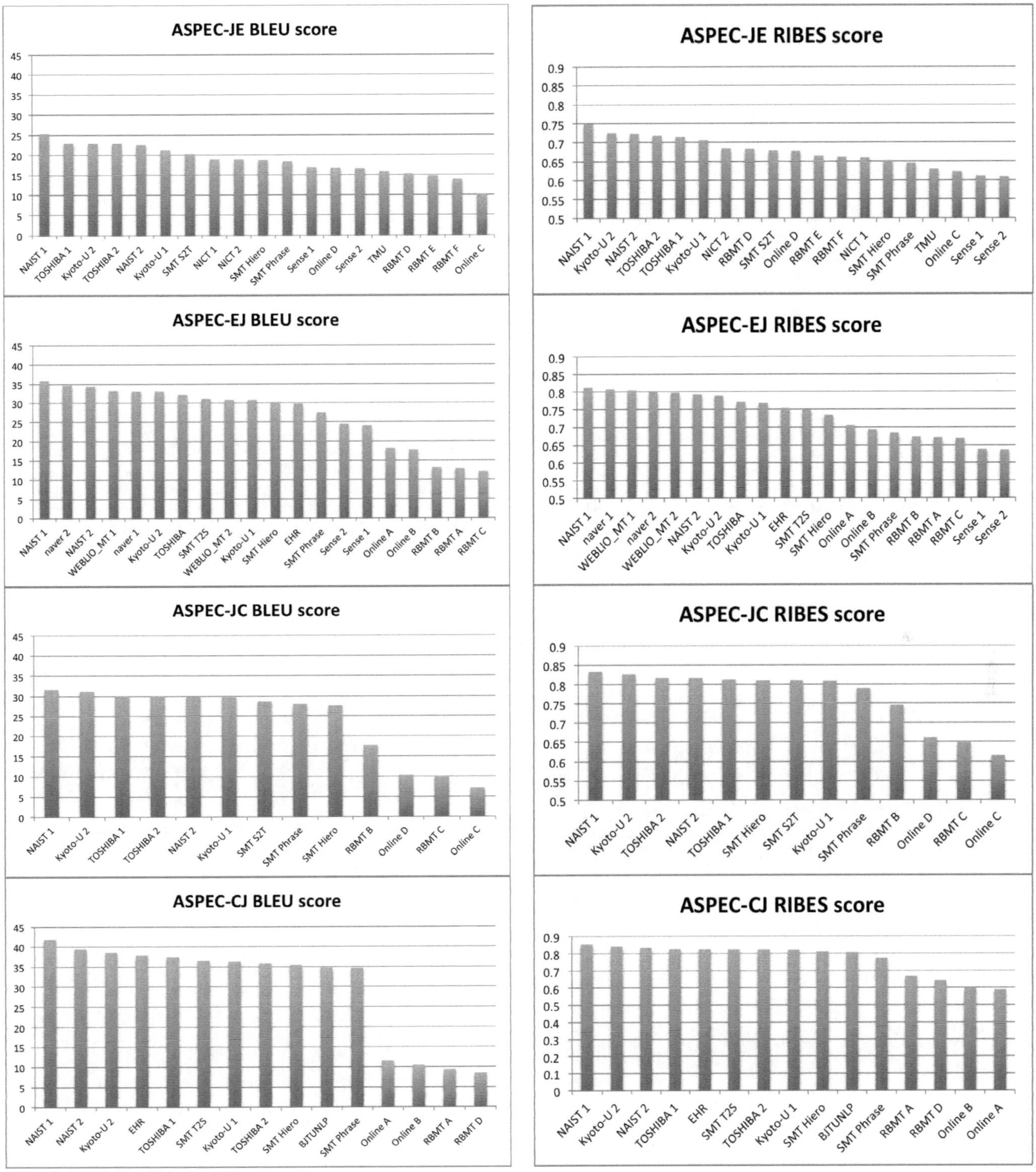

Figure 3: Official automatic evaluation results of ASPEC.

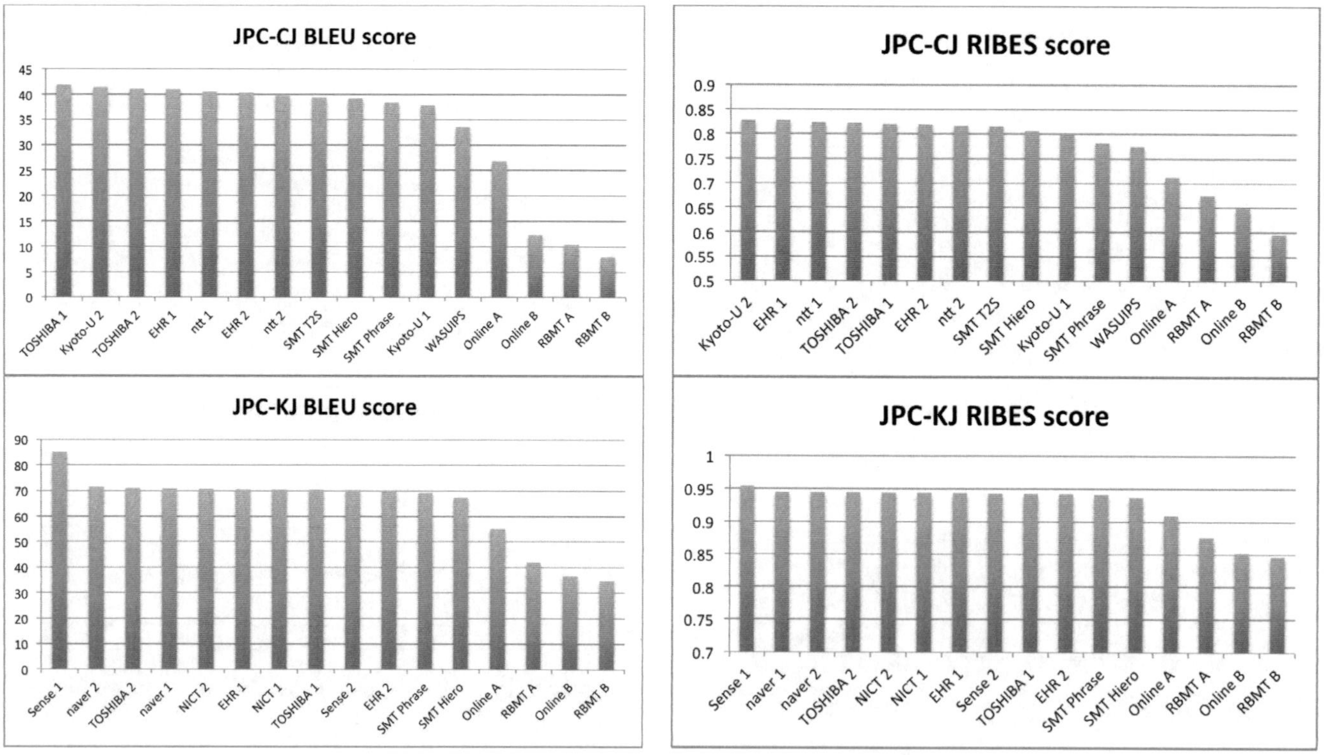

Figure 4: Official automatic evaluation results of JPC.

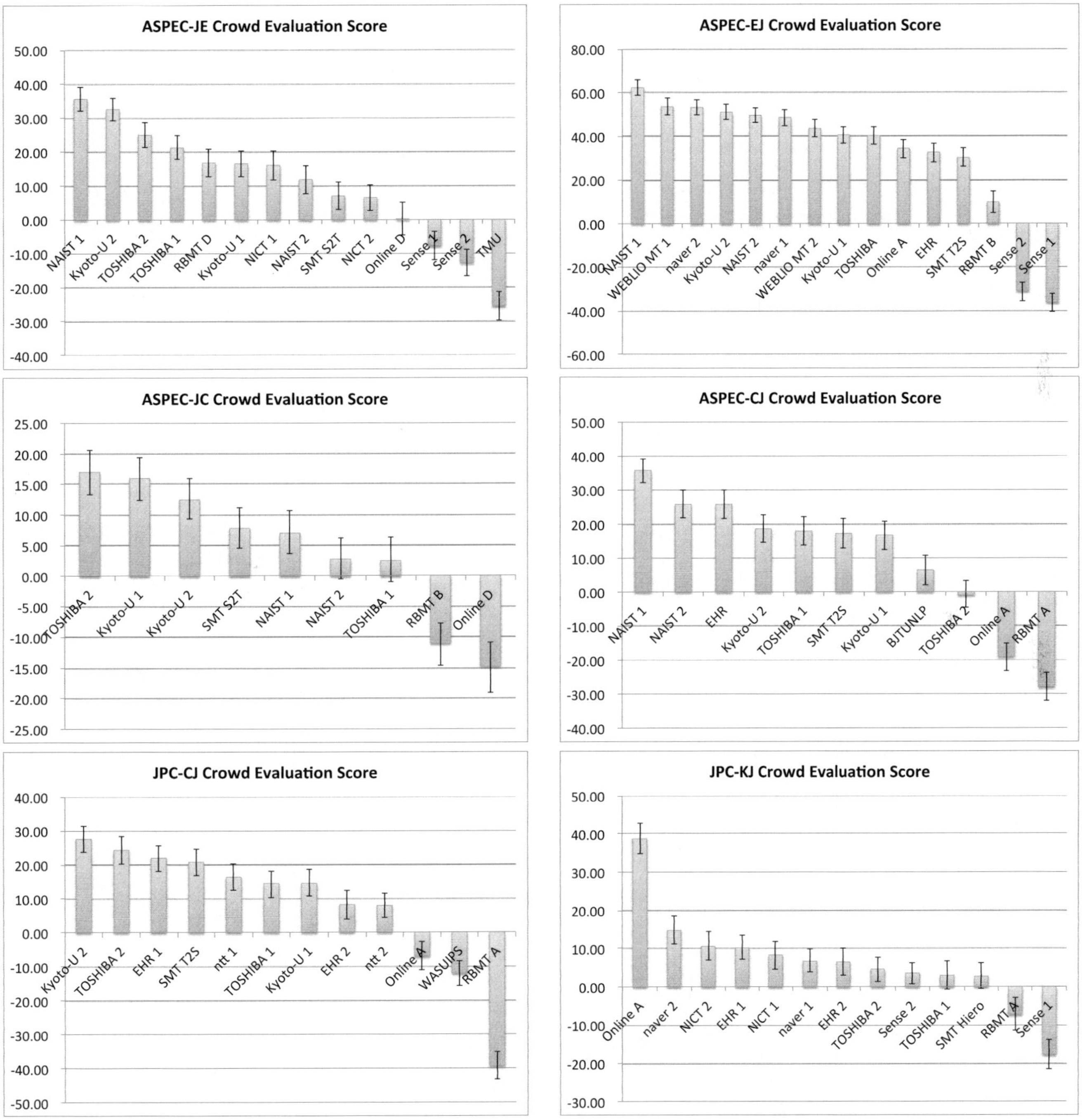

Figure 5: Official pairwise crowdsourcing evaluation results.

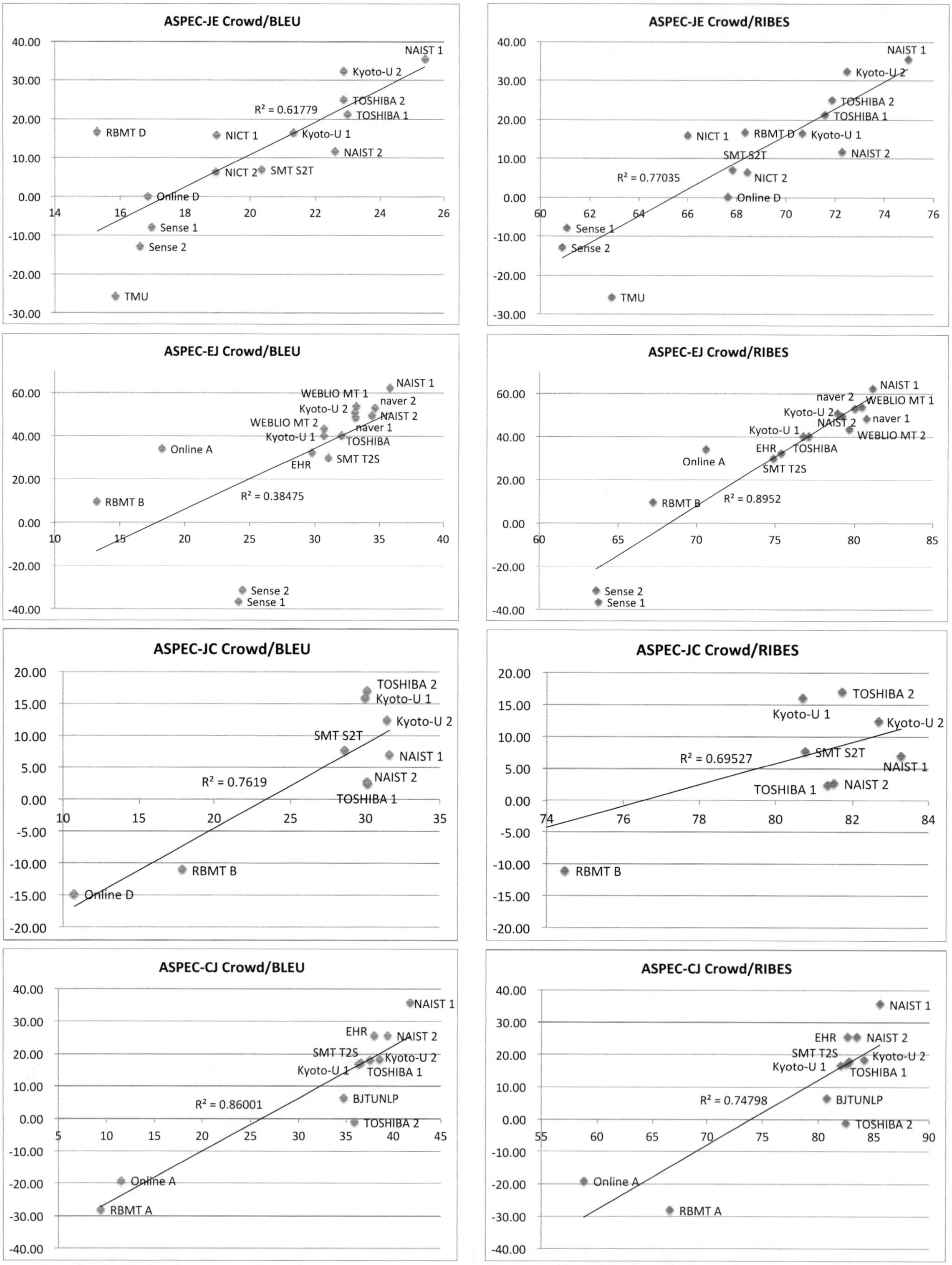

Figure 6: The correlations between the BLEU/RIBES and Crowd scores of ASPEC.

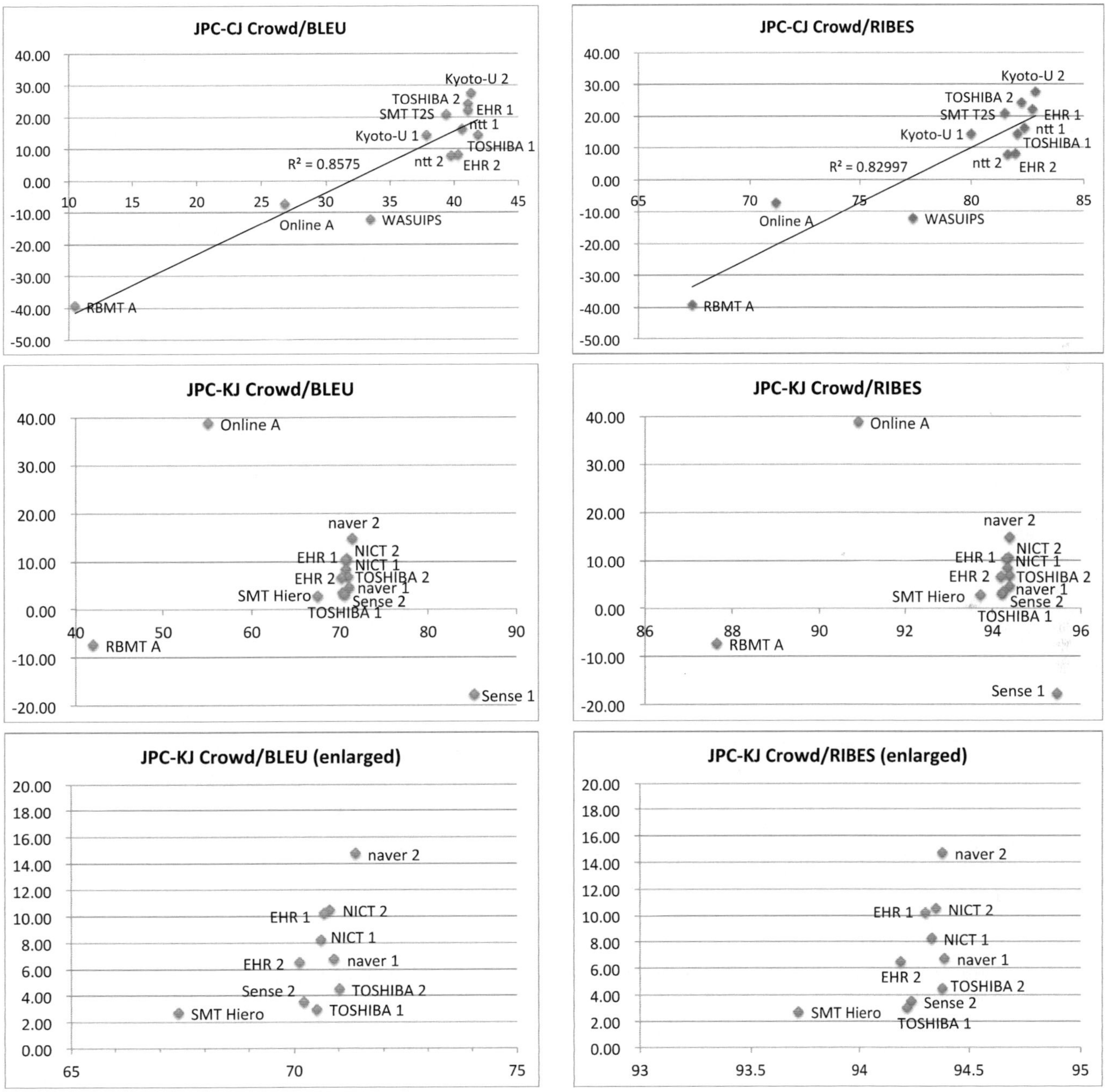

Figure 7: The correlations between the BLEU/RIBES and Crowd scores of JPC.

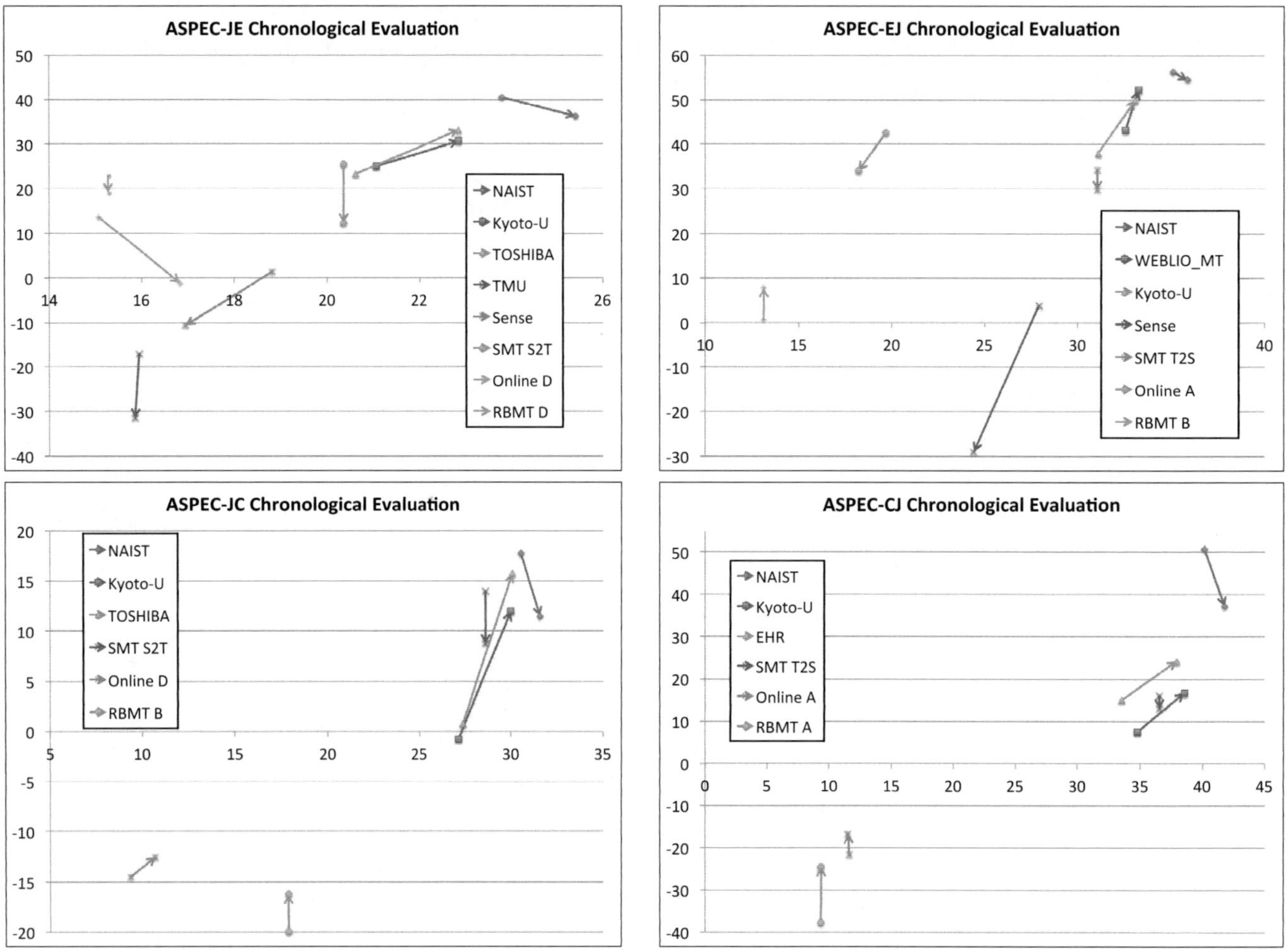

Figure 8: The chronological evaluation results of ASPEC. (The x-axis indicates the BLEU score and the y-axis indicates the Crowd score.)

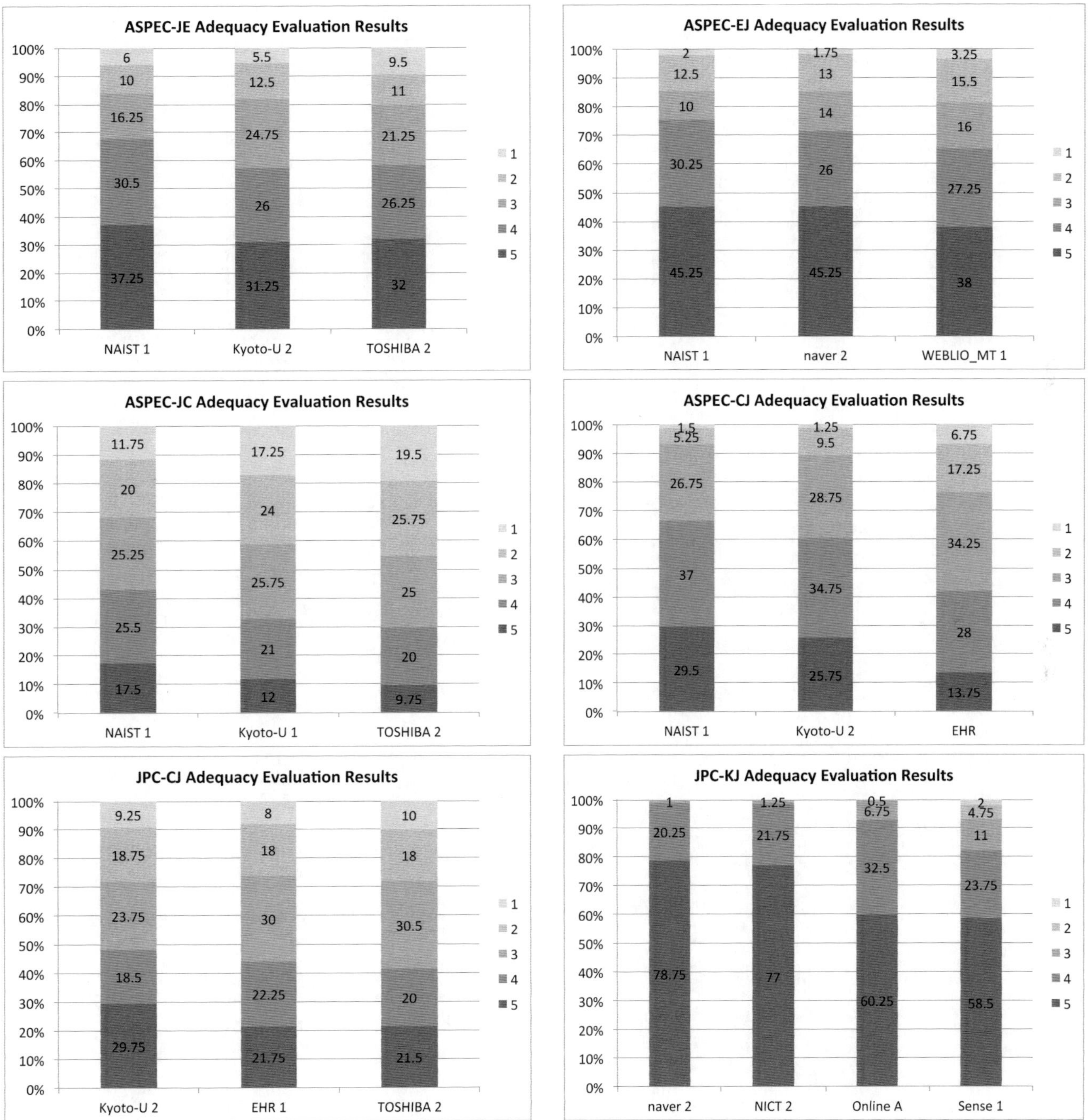

Figure 9: Distribution of JPO adequacy evaluations.

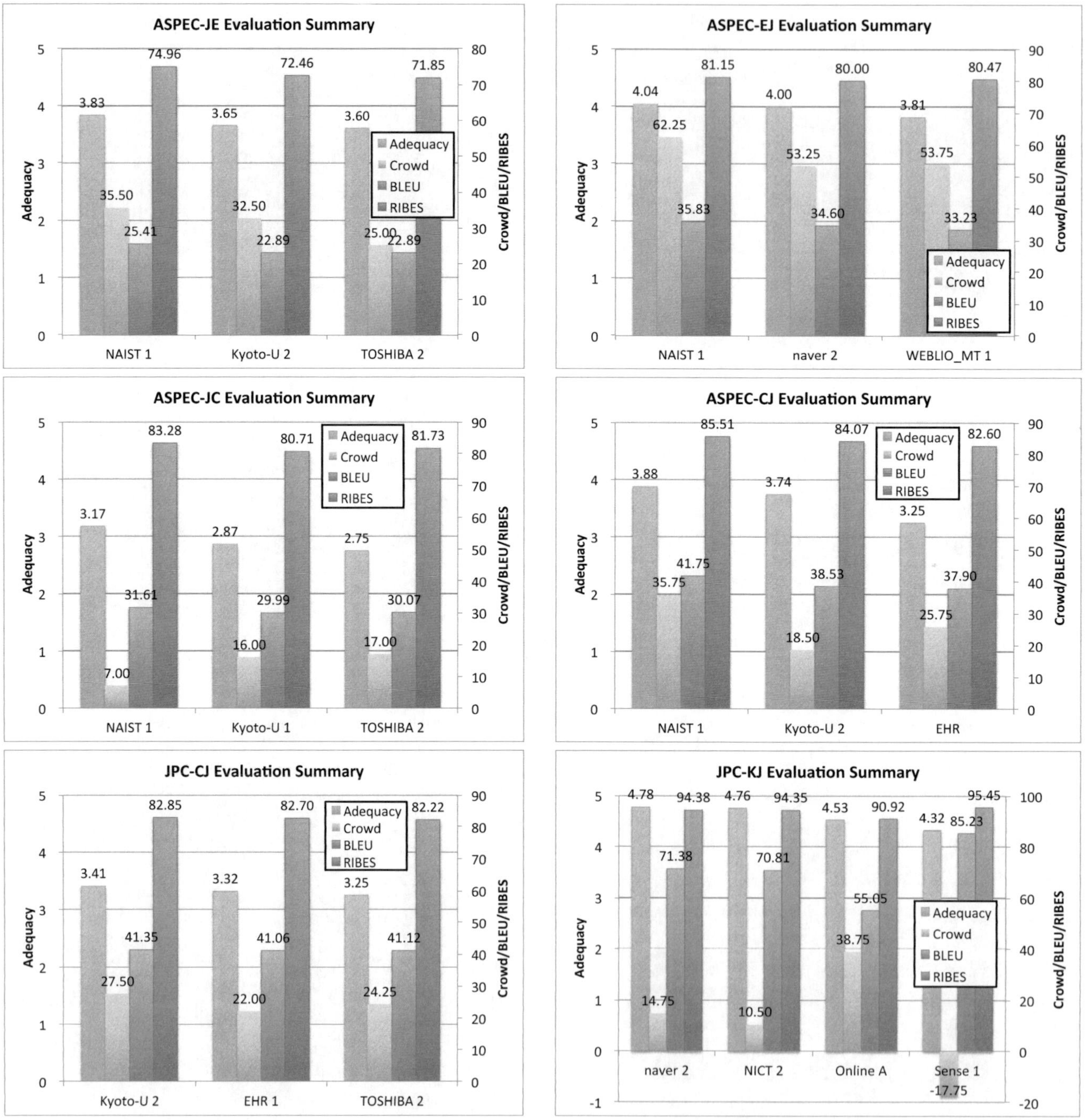

Figure 10: Summary of automatic and human evaluations.

SYSTEM ID	ID	METHOD	OTHER RESOURCES	BLEU	RIBES	Crowd	SYSTEM DESCRIPTION
SMT Hiero	2	SMT	NO	18.72	0.651066	+7.75	Hierarchical Phrase-based SMT (2014)
SMT Phrase	6	SMT	NO	18.45	0.645137	—	Phrase-based SMT
SMT S2T	9	SMT	NO	20.36	0.678253	+25.50	String-to-Tree SMT (2014)
RBMT E	76	Other	YES	14.82	0.663851	—	RBMT E
RBMT F	79	Other	YES	13.86	0.661387	—	RBMT F
Online D	775	Other	YES	16.85	0.676609	+0.25	Online D (2015)
SMT S2T	877	SMT	NO	20.36	0.678253	+7.00	String-to-Tree SMT (2015)
RBMT D	887	Other	YES	15.29	0.683378	+16.75	RBMT D (2015)
Online C	892	Other	YES	10.29	0.622564	—	Online C (2015)
NAIST 1	655	SMT	NO	25.41	0.749573	+35.50	Travatar System with NeuralMT Reranking and Parser Self Training
NAIST 2	766	SMT	NO	22.62	0.722798	+11.75	Travatar System with Parser Self Training
Kyoto-U 1	796	EBMT	NO	21.31	0.706480	+16.50	KyotoEBMT system without reranking
Kyoto-U 2	829	EBMT	NO	22.89	0.724555	+32.50	KyotoEBMT system with bilingual RNNLM reranking
TMU	847	SMT	NO	15.85	0.628897	-25.50	PBSMT with dependency based phrase segmentation
Sense 1	860	SMT	YES	16.96	0.610775	-7.75	Passive JSTx1
Sense 2	861	SMT	YES	16.61	0.609008	-12.75	Pervasive JSTx1
NICT 1	488	SMT	NO	18.98	0.659883	+16.00	our baseline (DL=6) + dependency-based pre-reordering [Ding+ 2015]
NICT 2	492	SMT	NO	18.96	0.684485	+6.50	our baseline (DL=9) + reverse pre-reordering [Katz-Brown & Collins 2008]
TOSHIBA 1	506	SMT and RBMT	YES	23.00	0.715795	+21.25	System combination SMT and RBMT(SPE) with RNNLM language model
TOSHIBA 2	529	SMT and RBMT	YES	22.89	0.718540	+25.00	RBMT with SPE(Statistical Post Editing) system

Table 14: ASPEC-JE submissions

SYSTEM ID	ID	METHOD	OTHER RESOURCES	BLEU			RIBES			Crowd	SYSTEM DESCRIPTION
				juman	kytea	mecab	juman	kytea	mecab		
SMT Phrase	5	SMT	NO	27.48	29.80	28.27	0.683735	0.691926	0.695390	—	Phrase-based SMT
SMT T2S	12	SMT	NO	31.05	33.44	32.10	0.748883	0.758031	0.760516	+34.25	Tree-to-String SMT (2014)
RBMT A	68	Other	YES	12.86	14.43	13.16	0.670167	0.676464	0.678934	—	RBMT A
RBMT C	95	Other	YES	12.19	13.32	12.14	0.668372	0.672645	0.676018	—	RBMT C
SMT Hiero	367	SMT	NO	30.19	32.56	30.94	0.734705	0.746978	0.747722	+31.50	Hierarchical Phrase-based SMT (2014)
Online A	774	Other	YES	18.22	19.77	18.46	0.705882	0.713960	0.718150	+34.25	Online A (2015)
SMT T2S	875	SMT	NO	31.05	33.44	32.10	0.748883	0.758031	0.760516	+30.00	Tree-to-String SMT (2015)
RBMT B	883	Other	YES	13.18	14.85	13.48	0.671958	0.680748	0.682683	+9.75	RBMT B (2015)
Online B	889	Other	YES	17.80	19.52	18.11	0.693359	0.701966	0.703859	—	Online B (2015)
NAIST 1	761	SMT	NO	35.83	38.17	36.61	0.811479	0.813827	0.820337	+62.25	Travatar System with NeuralMT Reranking
NAIST 2	763	SMT	NO	34.38	36.58	35.16	0.792447	0.796489	0.802228	+49.75	Travatar System Baseline
Kyoto-U 1	805	EBMT	NO	30.69	33.25	31.71	0.767778	0.776672	0.778358	+40.50	KyotoEBMT system without reranking
Kyoto-U 2	832	EBMT	NO	33.06	35.57	33.99	0.789514	0.797182	0.799979	+51.00	KyotoEBMT system with bilingual RNNLM reranking
WEBLIO_MT 1	786	SMT	NO	33.23	36.21	34.05	0.804722	0.809065	0.814337	+53.75	NMT, LSTM Search, 5 ensembles, beam size 20, UNK replacing, System Combination with NMT score (Pick top-1k results from NMT)
WEBLIO_MT 2	813	Other	NO	30.72	34.19	31.57	0.796863	0.802666	0.807186	+43.50	NMT, LSTM Search, Beam Size 20, Ensemble of 2 models, UNK replacing
Sense 1	700	SMT	NO	24.13	26.24	24.96	0.637378	0.642789	0.647831	-36.25	Baseline-dictmt
Sense 2	715	SMT	YES	24.43	26.58	25.36	0.635933	0.641517	0.646682	-31.00	Passive JSTx3
TOSHIBA	524	SMT and RBMT	YES	32.06	34.17	32.76	0.770989	0.778570	0.780467	+40.25	RBMT with SPE(Statistical Post Editing) system
naver 1	836	SMT	NO	33.14	35.75	33.93	0.807280	0.811487	0.817343	+48.50	NMT only
naver 2	837	SMT	NO	34.60	36.14	35.30	0.799966	0.803154	0.808787	+53.25	SMT t2s + Spell correction + NMT reranking
EHR	742	SMT	NO	29.78	32.36	30.71	0.753576	0.766044	0.768105	+32.50	Phrase based SMT with preordering.

Table 15: ASPEC-EJ submissions

SYSTEM ID	ID	METHOD	OTHER RESOURCES	BLEU kytea	BLEU stanford (ctb)	BLEU stanford (pku)	RIBES kytea	RIBES stanford (ctb)	RIBES stanford (pku)	Crowd	SYSTEM DESCRIPTION
SMT Hiero	3	SMT	NO	27.71	27.70	27.35	0.809128	0.809561	0.811394	+3.75	Hierarchical Phrase-based SMT (2014)
SMT Phrase	7	SMT	NO	27.96	28.01	27.68	0.788961	0.790263	0.790937	—	Phrase-based SMT
SMT S2T	10	SMT	NO	28.65	28.65	28.35	0.807606	0.809457	0.808417	+14.00	String-to-Tree SMT (2014)
RBMT C	244	RBMT	NO	9.62	9.96	9.59	0.642278	0.648758	0.645385	—	RBMT C
Online D	777	Other	YES	10.73	10.33	10.08	0.660484	0.660847	0.660482	-14.75	Online D (2015)
SMT S2T	881	SMT	NO	28.65	28.65	28.35	0.807606	0.809457	0.808417	+7.75	String-to-Tree SMT (2015)
RBMT B	886	Other	YES	17.86	17.75	17.49	0.744818	0.745885	0.743794	-11.00	RBMT B (2015)
Online C	891	Other	YES	7.44	7.05	6.75	0.611964	0.615048	0.612158	—	Online C (2015)
NAIST 1	838	SMT	NO	31.61	31.59	31.42	0.832765	0.834245	0.833721	+7.00	Travatar System with NeuralMT Reranking
NAIST 2	839	SMT	NO	30.06	29.92	29.73	0.815084	0.816624	0.816462	+2.75	Travatar System Baseline
Kyoto-U 1	778	EBMT	NO	29.99	29.76	29.81	0.807083	0.808275	0.808010	+16.00	KyotoEBMT system without reranking
Kyoto-U 2	793	EBMT	NO	31.40	31.26	31.23	0.826986	0.826919	0.827190	+12.50	KyotoEBMT system with bilingual RNNLM reranking
TOSHIBA 1	505	SMT and RBMT	YES	30.17	30.15	29.89	0.813490	0.813233	0.813441	+2.50	SPE(Statistical Post Editing) System
TOSHIBA 2	676	SMT and RBMT	YES	30.07	30.14	29.83	0.817294	0.816984	0.816981	+17.00	System combination SMT and RBMT(SPE) with RNNLM language model + post-processing

Table 16: ASPEC-JC submissions

SYSTEM ID	ID	METHOD	OTHER RESOURCES	BLEU			RIBES			Crowd	SYSTEM DESCRIPTION
				juman	kytea	mecab	juman	kytea	mecab		
SMT Hiero	4	SMT	NO	35.43	35.91	35.64	0.810406	0.798726	0.807665	+4.75	Hierarchical Phrase-based SMT (2014)
SMT Phrase	8	SMT	NO	34.65	35.16	34.77	0.772498	0.766384	0.771005	—	Phrase-based SMT
SMT T2S	13	SMT	NO	36.52	37.07	36.64	0.825292	0.820490	0.825025	+16.00	Tree-to-String SMT (2014)
RBMT D	242	RBMT	NO	8.39	8.70	8.30	0.641189	0.626400	0.633319	—	RBMT D
Online A	776	Other	YES	11.53	12.82	11.68	0.588285	0.590393	0.592887	-19.00	Online A (2015)
SMT T2S	879	SMT	NO	36.52	37.07	36.64	0.825292	0.820490	0.825025	+17.25	Tree-to-String SMT (2015)
RBMT A	885	Other	YES	9.37	9.87	9.35	0.666277	0.652402	0.661730	-28.00	RBMT A (2015)
Online B	890	Other	YES	10.41	11.03	10.36	0.597355	0.592841	0.597298	—	Online B (2015)
NAIST 1	834	SMT	NO	41.75	42.95	41.93	0.855089	0.847746	0.854587	+35.75	Travatar System with NeuralMT Reranking
NAIST 2	835	SMT	NO	39.36	40.51	39.47	0.834388	0.827148	0.834130	+25.75	Travatar System Baseline
Kyoto-U 1	844	EBMT	NO	36.30	37.22	36.44	0.819743	0.814581	0.818794	+16.75	KyotoEBMT system without reranking
Kyoto-U 2	845	EBMT	NO	38.53	39.41	38.66	0.840681	0.834451	0.839063	+18.50	KyotoEBMT system with bilingual RNNLM reranking
BJTUNLP	862	SMT	NO	34.72	34.87	34.79	0.807012	0.792488	0.802430	+6.50	a dependency-to-string model for SMT
TOSHIBA 1	508	SMT and RBMT	YES	37.47	37.44	37.34	0.827291	0.817395	0.825472	+18.00	System combination SMT and RBMT(SPE) with RNNLM language model
TOSHIBA 2	525	SMT and RBMT	YES	35.85	36.02	35.73	0.824740	0.815388	0.822423	-1.00	RBMT with SPE(Statistical Post Editing) system
EHR	720	SMT and RBMT	YES	37.90	38.68	37.98	0.826003	0.818620	0.824806	+25.75	System combination of RBMT with user dictionary plus SPE and phrase based SMT with preordering. Candidate selection by language model score.

Table 17: ASPEC-CJ submissions

SYSTEM ID	ID	METHOD	OTHER RESOURCES	BLEU			RIBES			Crowd	SYSTEM DESCRIPTION
				juman	kytea	mecab	juman	kytea	mecab		
SMT Hiero	430	SMT	NO	39.22	39.52	39.14	0.806058	0.802059	0.804523	—	Hierarchical Phrase-based SMT
SMT Phrase	431	SMT	NO	38.34	38.51	38.22	0.782019	0.778921	0.781456	—	Phrase-based SMT
SMT T2S	432	SMT	NO	39.39	39.90	39.39	0.814919	0.811350	0.813595	+20.75	Tree-to-String SMT (2015)
Online A	647	Other	YES	26.80	27.81	26.89	0.712242	0.707264	0.711273	-7.00	Online A (2015)
Online B	648	Other	YES	12.33	12.72	12.44	0.648996	0.641255	0.648742	—	Online B (2015)
RBMT A	759	RBMT	NO	10.49	10.72	10.35	0.674060	0.664098	0.667349	-39.25	RBMT A (2015)
RBMT B	760	RBMT	NO	7.94	8.07	7.73	0.596200	0.581837	0.586941	—	RBMT B
Kyoto-U 1	781	EBMT	NO	37.87	38.62	37.71	0.799730	0.797700	0.798979	+14.50	Baseline w/o reranking
Kyoto-U 2	864	EBMT	NO	41.35	41.92	41.16	0.828543	0.824199	0.827230	+27.50	KyotoEBMT system with bilingual RNNLM reranking (only character-base model)
TOSHIBA 1	504	SMT and RBMT	YES	41.82	41.90	41.60	0.820568	0.813536	0.817614	+14.50	Combination of phrase-based SMT and SPE systems.
TOSHIBA 2	526	SMT and RBMT	YES	41.12	40.87	40.59	0.822268	0.814249	0.818981	+24.25	RBMT with SPE(Statistical Post Editing) system
WASUIPS	853	SMT	NO	33.48	34.55	33.55	0.773985	0.771099	0.772202	-12.00	Combining sampling-based alignment and bilingual hierarchical sub-sentential alignment methods.
EHR 1	671	SMT and RBMT	YES	41.06	42.24	41.15	0.826987	0.821983	0.825056	+22.00	System combination of RBMT with user dictionary plus SPE and phrase based SMT with preordering. Candidate selection by language model score.
EHR 2	828	SMT and RBMT	YES	40.35	40.16	39.92	0.819516	0.812982	0.816743	+8.25	RBMT with user dictionary plus SPE
ntt 1	736	SMT	NO	40.60	41.10	40.63	0.823436	0.820252	0.822026	+16.25	A pre-ordering-based PBMT with patent-tuned dependency parsing and phrase table smoothing.
ntt 2	811	SMT	NO	39.77	40.08	39.88	0.816288	0.811911	0.815543	+8.00	A pre-ordering-based PBMT with patent-tuned dependency parsing, learning-based pre-ordering, and phrase table smoothing.

Table 18: JPC-CJ submissions

SYSTEM ID	ID	METHOD	OTHER RESOURCES	BLEU			RIBES			Crowd	SYSTEM DESCRIPTION
				juman	kytea	mecab	juman	kytea	mecab		
SMT Phrase	438	SMT	NO	69.22	70.36	69.73	0.941302	0.939729	0.940756	—	Phrase-based SMT
SMT Hiero	439	SMT	NO	67.41	68.65	68.00	0.937162	0.935903	0.936570	+2.75	Hierarchical Phrase-based SMT (2015)
Online B	651	Other	YES	36.41	38.72	37.01	0.851745	0.852263	0.851945	—	Online B (2015)
Online A	652	Other	YES	55.05	56.84	55.46	0.909152	0.909385	0.908838	+38.75	Online A (2015)
RBMT A	653	Other	YES	42.00	43.97	42.45	0.876396	0.873734	0.875146	-7.25	RBMT A (2015)
RBMT B	654	Other	YES	34.74	37.51	35.54	0.845712	0.849014	0.846228	—	RBMT B
Sense 1	657	SMT	NO	85.23	85.20	85.23	0.954506	0.954448	0.954435	-17.75	Unicode2String with devtest MERT run2
Sense 2	833	SMT	NO	70.23	71.11	70.51	0.942415	0.940887	0.941687	+3.50	Baseline with only train.ja/ko
NICT 1	501	SMT	NO	70.62	71.52	70.92	0.943348	0.942402	0.942748	+8.25	our baseline: character-based / PB SMT in MOSES (DL=0, max-phrase-len=9, no lex-reordering) / SRILM (9-gram)
NICT 2	513	SMT	NO	70.81	71.70	71.11	0.943463	0.942519	0.942904	+10.50	our baseline + post-processing of bracket balancing
TOSHIBA 1	554	SMT and RBMT	YES	70.51	70.84	70.71	0.942183	0.939545	0.941471	+3.00	System combination SMT, SPE and RBMT with RNNLM + post-processing
TOSHIBA 2	568	SMT	YES	71.01	71.44	71.26	0.943794	0.941287	0.943181	+4.50	Phrase-based SMT with RNNLM reranking + post-processing
naver 1	630	SMT	NO	70.91	71.76	71.18	0.943928	0.942800	0.943376	+6.75	combined two phrase-based systems, post-processing
naver 2	816	SMT	NO	71.38	72.27	71.68	0.943814	0.942805	0.943584	+14.75	SMT PB + NMT reranking
EHR 1	500	SMT and RBMT	YES	70.67	71.52	70.93	0.943040	0.941893	0.942771	+10.25	System combination of RBMT with user dictionary plus SPE and phrase based SMT. Candidate selection by language model score.
EHR 2	831	SMT and RBMT	YES	70.13	70.86	70.35	0.941887	0.940341	0.941517	+6.50	RBMT with user dictionary plus SPE

Table 19: JPC-KJ submissions

References

Jacob Cohen. 1968. Weighted kappa: Nominal scale agreement with provision for scaled disagreement or partial credit. *Psychological Bulletin*, 70(4):213 – 220.

Chenchen Ding, Masao Utiyama, and Eiichiro Sumita. 2015. NICT at WAT 2015. In *Proceedings of the 2nd Workshop on Asian Translation (WAT2015)*, pages 42–47, Kyoto, Japan, October.

Terumasa Ehara. 2015. System Combination of RBMT plus SPE and Preordering plus SMT. In *Proceedings of the 2nd Workshop on Asian Translation (WAT2015)*, pages 29–34, Kyoto, Japan, October.

J.L. Fleiss et al. 1971. Measuring nominal scale agreement among many raters. *Psychological Bulletin*, 76(5):378–382.

Kenneth Heafield, Ivan Pouzyrevsky, Jonathan H. Clark, and Philipp Koehn. 2013. Scalable modified kneser-ney language model estimation. In *Proceedings of the 51st Annual Meeting of the Association for Computational Linguistics (Volume 2: Short Papers)*, pages 690–696, Sofia, Bulgaria, August. Association for Computational Linguistics.

Hieu Hoang, Philipp Koehn, and Adam Lopez. 2009. A unified framework for phrase-based, hierarchical, and syntax-based statistical machine translation. In *Proceedings of the International Workshop on Spoken Language Translation*, pages 152–159.

Hideki Isozaki, Tsutomu Hirao, Kevin Duh, Katsuhito Sudoh, and Hajime Tsukada. 2010. Automatic evaluation of translation quality for distant language pairs. In *Proceedings of the 2010 Conference on Empirical Methods in Natural Language Processing*, EMNLP '10, pages 944–952, Stroudsburg, PA, USA. Association for Computational Linguistics.

Philipp Koehn, Hieu Hoang, Alexandra Birch, Chris Callison-Burch, Marcello Federico, Nicola Bertoldi, Brooke Cowan, Wade Shen, Christine Moran, Richard Zens, Chris Dyer, Ondrej Bojar, Alexandra Constantin, and Evan Herbst. 2007. Moses: Open source toolkit for statistical machine translation. In *Annual Meeting of the Association for Computational Linguistics (ACL), demonstration session*.

Philipp Koehn. 2004. Statistical significance tests for machine translation evaluation. In Dekang Lin and Dekai Wu, editors, *Proceedings of EMNLP 2004*, pages 388–395, Barcelona, Spain, July. Association for Computational Linguistics.

T. Kudo. 2005. Mecab : Yet another part-of-speech and morphological analyzer. *http://mecab.sourceforge.net/*.

Sadao Kurohashi, Toshihisa Nakamura, Yuji Matsumoto, and Makoto Nagao. 1994. Improvements of Japanese morphological analyzer JUMAN. In *Proceedings of The International Workshop on Sharable Natural Language*, pages 22–28.

Hyoung-Gyu Lee, JaeSong Lee, Jun-Seok Kim, and Chang-Ki Lee. 2015. NAVER Machine Translation System for WAT 2015. In *Proceedings of the 2nd Workshop on Asian Translation (WAT2015)*, pages 69–73, Kyoto, Japan, October.

Junki Matsuo, Kenichi Ohwada, and Mamoru Komachi. 2015. Source Phrase Segmentation and Translation for Japanese-English Translation Using Dependency Structure. In *Proceedings of the 2nd Workshop on Asian Translation (WAT2015)*, pages 99–104, Kyoto, Japan, October.

Toshiaki Nakazawa, Hideya Mino, Isao Goto, Sadao Kurohashi, and Eiichiro Sumita. 2014. Overview of the 1st Workshop on Asian Translation. In *Proceedings of the 1st Workshop on Asian Translation (WAT2014)*, pages 1–19, Tokyo, Japan, October.

Graham Neubig, Yosuke Nakata, and Shinsuke Mori. 2011. Pointwise prediction for robust, adaptable japanese morphological analysis. In *Proceedings of the 49th Annual Meeting of the Association for Computational Linguistics: Human Language Technologies: Short Papers - Volume 2*, HLT '11, pages 529–533, Stroudsburg, PA, USA. Association for Computational Linguistics.

Graham Neubig, Makoto Morishita, and Satoshi Nakamura. 2015. Neural Reranking Improves Subjective Quality of Machine Translation: NAIST at WAT2015. In *Proceedings of the 2nd Workshop on Asian Translation (WAT2015)*, pages 35–41, Kyoto, Japan, October.

Kishore Papineni, Salim Roukos, Todd Ward, and Wei-Jing Zhu. 2002. Bleu: a method for automatic evaluation of machine translation. In *ACL*, pages 311–318.

Slav Petrov, Leon Barrett, Romain Thibaux, and Dan Klein. 2006. Learning accurate, compact, and interpretable tree annotation. In *Proceedings of the 21st International Conference on Computational Linguistics and 44th Annual Meeting of the Association for Computational Linguistics*, pages 433–440, Sydney, Australia, July. Association for Computational Linguistics.

John Richardson, Raj Dabre, Fabien Cromières, Toshiaki Nakazawa, and Sadao Kurohashi. 2015. KyotoEBMT System Description for the 2nd Workshop on Asian Translation. In *Proceedings of the 2nd Workshop on Asian Translation (WAT2015)*, pages 54–60, Kyoto, Japan, October.

Hua Shan, Yujie Zhang, Lu Bai, and Te Luo. 2015. A Dependency-to-String Model for Chinese-Japanese SMT System. In *Proceedings of the 2nd Workshop on Asian Translation (WAT2015)*, pages 82–86, Kyoto, Japan, October.

Satoshi Sonoh and Satoshi Kinoshita. 2015. Toshiba MT System Description for the WAT2015 Workshop. In *Proceedings of the 2nd Workshop on Asian*

Translation (WAT2015), pages 48–53, Kyoto, Japan, October.

Katsuhito Sudoh and Masaaki Nagata. 2015. Chinese-to-Japanese Patent Machine Translation based on Syntactic Pre-ordering forWAT 2015. In *Proceedings of the 2nd Workshop on Asian Translation (WAT2015)*, pages 95–98, Kyoto, Japan, October.

Liling Tan, Jon Dehdari, and Josef van Genabith. 2015. An Awkward Disparity between BLEU / RIBES Scores and Human Judgements in Machine Translation. In *Proceedings of the 2nd Workshop on Asian Translation (WAT2015)*, pages 74–81, Kyoto, Japan, October.

Huihsin Tseng. 2005. A conditional random field word segmenter. In *In Fourth SIGHAN Workshop on Chinese Language Processing*.

Masao Utiyama and Hitoshi Isahara. 2007. A japanese-english patent parallel corpus. In *MT summit XI*, pages 475–482.

Wei Yang, Zhongwen Zhao, Baosong Yang, and Yves Lepage. 2015. Sampling-based Alignment and Hierarchical Sub-sentential Alignment in Chinese-Japanese Translation of Patents. In *Proceedings of the 2nd Workshop on Asian Translation (WAT2015)*, pages 87–94, Kyoto, Japan, October.

Zhongyuan Zhu. 2015. Evaluating Neural Machine Translation in English-Japanese Task. In *Proceedings of the 2nd Workshop on Asian Translation (WAT2015)*, pages 61–68, Kyoto, Japan, October.

System Combination of RBMT plus SPE and Preordering plus SMT

Terumasa EHARA
Ehara NLP Research Laboratory
Seijo, Setagaya, Tokyo, JAPAN

eharate @ gmail.com

Abstract

System architecture, experimental settings and evaluation results of EHR group in the en-ja, zh-ja, JPCzh-ja and JPCko-ja tasks are described. Our system concept is combination of a rule based method and a statistical method. System combination of rule-based machine translation (RBMT), RBMT plus statistical post-editing (SPE) and preordering plus statistical machine translation (SMT) is conducted. From the multiple outputs of three systems, candidate selection part selects the best output by language model score. For JPCzh-ja task devtest data translation, SPE improves BLEU score by 17.81, preordering improves BLEU score by 1.89 and system combination improves BLEU score by 0.26.

1 Introduction

Two main processes of machine translation are lexical transfer and structural transfer. Machine translation techniques and related techniques are classified in terms of these two processes as shown in Table 1.

Technique	Lex. Trans.	Struct. Trans.
RBMT	✔	✔
SMT	✔	✔
Monotone SPE	✔	
Preordering		✔
Monotone SMT	✔	

Table 1: Classification of MT and related techniques.

RBMT and SMT conduct lexical transfer and structural transfer simultaneously. On the other hand, monotone SPE and monotone SMT, which are technically the same process, conduct lexical transfer only. Preordering conducts structural transfer only.

We have made researches combining a rule based method and a statistical method that is RBMT plus SPE (Ehara, 2014). This year, we add preordering plus SMT part to our system for WAT2015. This new system is also the combination of rule based method (RBMT and preordering) and statistical method (SPE and SMT).

2 System architecture

Our basic system architecture is shown in Figure 1.

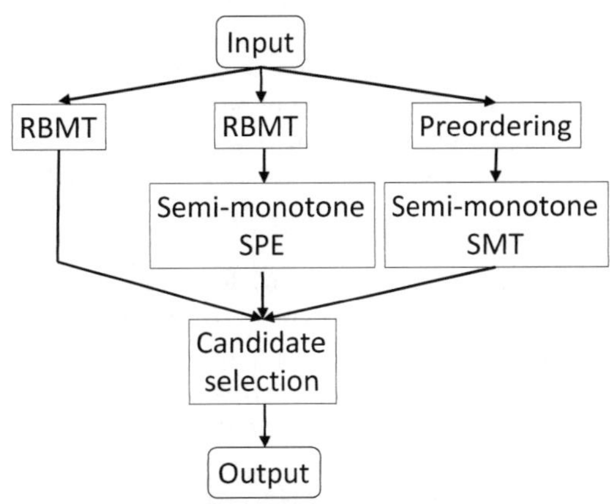

Figure 1: Basic system architecture.

Input sentence is fed to RBMT system, RBMT plus SPE system and Preordering plus SMT system[1]. From outputs of three systems, candidate selection part selects best output as the system output. Here, our SPE and SMT are semi-monotone,

[1] For JPCko-ja task, we don't use preordering part.

Proceedings of the 2nd Workshop on Asian Translation (WAT2015), pages 29-34,
Kyoto, Japan, 16th October 2015.

because distortion limit of decoder is set to 6 instead of 0. We will explain details of the each part of the system in the following subsections.

2.1 RBMT part

We use a commercial based RBMT system for the RBMT part. We, also, use user terminology dictionaries for zh-ja, JPCzh-ja and JPCko-ja tasks. For zh-ja and JPCzh-ja tasks, we use a part of Chinese to Japanese technical term dictionary of JPO (Japan Patent Office) (Japio, 2015)[2]. Original JPO's dictionary includes 2,210,294 words (nouns and verbs). We filter out all verbs and the nouns which have identical Japanese translations with the commercial based RBMT outputs. As the result, we select 1,463,265 terms for the user dictionary for JPCzh-ja and zh-ja tasks. For JPCko-ja task, we make a user dictionary from the training corpus of the task. We get 434,334 terms for the user dictionary for the JPCko-ja task. For en-ja task, we don't use any user dictionary.

We also use sentence pattern dictionary for JPCzh-ja task. We use only 13 sentence patterns for the task.

2.2 SPE part

SPE part intends to improve the translation quality of the output of the RBMT part. All target languages of the tasks are Japanese. So SPE part translates Japanese to Japanese. We use phrase based Moses (Koehn et al., 2003) with default options as the SPE engine. Word segmenter for Japanese is Juman ver.7.01 (Kurohashi et al., 1994).

Translation models (TM) of each task is built from RBMT output and reference translation of the training corpus of each task. Training corpus size (number of sentence pairs) will be listed in Table 3.

Language model (LM) is built from the following monolingual corpora. LM for en-ja task and zh-ja task is built from target side of the training corpora both of the en-ja task and zh-ja task (3.6M sentences). LM is built by lmplz tool in Moses (KenLM) with order 6. LM for JPCko-ja task and JPCzh-ja task is built from target side of the training corpora both of the JPCko-ja task and JPCzh-ja task and also Japanese side of NTCIR-10's training corpora of PatentMT task EJ subtask (Goto et al. 2013)[3]. Total number of sentences for this LM training is 5M. This LM is also built by lmplz with order 6.

Distortion limit (DL) of the decoder is set to 6. Usual setting of DL between Japanese and English or between Japanese and Chinese is 10 or over. So we call our SPE part semi-monotone SPE.

2.3 Preordering part

Preordering is one of the effective technique to improve structural transfer accuracy (Isozaki, 2010). Our preordering method uses context free parsing rules with reordering rules. Figure 2 shows examples of parsing rules with reordering rules and example of parsed phrases[4]. First example is English grammar rule with reordering rule. The right hand side of the parsing rule "ADVP VBN PP" is reordered to "PP ADVP VBN" by the reordering rule "2 0 1[5]." Second example is Chinese grammar rule with reordering rule. Reordering rules are built by a heuristic algorithm.

VP ⇒ ADVP VBN PP 2 0 1 (widely utilized in many fields)
VP ⇒ VV NP IP 1 2 0 (使 各个 电动机 13 旋转 驱动)

Figure 2: Example of parsing rules and reordering rules with examples

Parsing accuracy directly affects preordering accuracy. We use Stanford Chinese word segmenter (Tseng et al., 2005; Chang et al., 2008) and Berkeley parser (Petrov et al., 2006) as the parsing engine of our preordering part. Two improvements for the parsing are conducted. First one is grammar improvement for Chinese grammar. For en-ja task, we use the original English grammar of the Berkeley parser, eng_sm6.gr. For JPCko-ja task, we don't conduct preordering because of the similarity of word order of Korean and Japanese. For zh-ja task and JPCzh-ja task, we improve the original Chinese grammar, chn_sm5.gr. It will be explained in section 2.3.1. Second improvement of parsing is reranking of k-best parse trees that will be explained in section 2.3.2.

---

[2] https://alaginrc.nict.go.jp/resources/jpo-info/jpo-list.html

[3] Dev, devtest and test data of JPCko-ja task and JPCzh-ja task are extracted from Japanese patent documents published in 2013. On the other hand, NTCIR-10's training corpora is extracted from Japanese patent documents published in 1990 to 2005. They are not overlapped.

[4] All sample sentences and phrases in this paper are from ASPEC Corpora or JPO Patent Corpora provided by the workshop organizer.

[5] Reordering rule "2 0 1" means that position of right hand side tags permutates from "0 1 2" to "2 0 1". Then, "ADVP VBN PP" is reordered to "PP ADVP VBN".

2.3.1 Grammar improvement

The idea for grammar improvement is to use word alignment of JPCzh-ja bilingual training corpus. Firstly, word alignment is conducted from JPCzh-ja training corpus (1M sentence pairs) by GIZA++ (Och and Ney, 2003). For each sentence pairs, we decide sentence head word both for Japanese and Chinese using word alignment. Since Japanese is a typical head final language, head word of Japanese sentence is positioned at the end of the sentence. So it is easy to find the sentence head word for Japanese sentences. We find Chinese sentence head word as the aligned word to the Japanese sentence head word. For example, in the ja-zh sentence pair shown in Figure 3, Japanese sentence head word "発生する" is aligned to Chinese word "产生". So "产生" is decided as the head word of this Chinese sentence. We consider it as the gold standard head word.

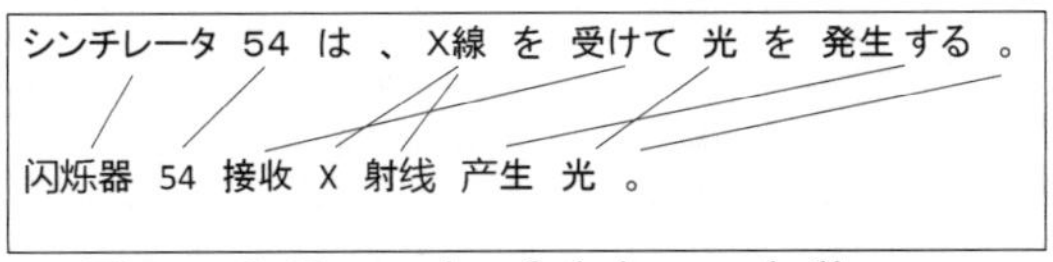

Figure 3: Example of zh-ja word alignment.

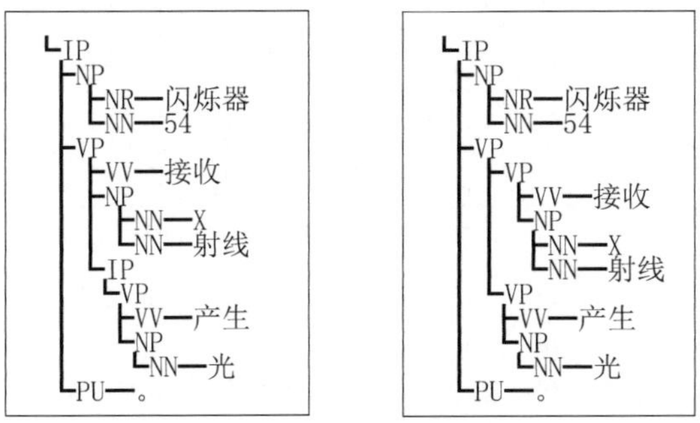

(a) top ranked tree (b) second ranked tree

Figure 4: Parsed trees.

Next step is to make a tree bank. Chinese sentences of training corpus are parsed by the original grammar i.e. chn_sm5.gr, and we get k-best parse trees for each sentence (k is set to 100). Then we select the best parse, in which the sentence head word is same as the gold standard head word. For example, the Chinese sentence in Figure 3 is k-best parsed shown in Figure 4. The top ranked tree has "接收" as the sentence head word and the second ranked tree has "产生" as the sentence head word, which is same as the gold standard. So we put the second ranked tree to our tree bank in this case.

From 1M JPCzh-ja training corpus, the number of second or lower ranked tree is selected is about 151K. Re-training Berkeley Chinese grammar using this 151K tree bank, we get new grammar named chn_jpo.gr. Comparing original chn_sm5.gr and chn_jpo.gr, the agreement rate of sentence head word of top ranked parse tree and gold standard for devtest data is shown in Table 2[6].

Agreement rate rises about 13%.

Grammar	Agreement rate (%)
chn_sm5.gr	50.5
chn_jpo.gr	63.0

Table 2: Agreement rate of sentence head word for the devtest data

2.3.2 Reranking of k-best parse trees

Another improvement of preordering part is reranking of k-best parse trees. For the training corpus, reordered source sentence is compared to gold standard reordered source sentence. Here, gold standard reordered source sentence is determined using alignment to a target sentence. For example, Chinese sentence shown in Figure 3 "闪烁器 54 接收 X 射线 产生 光 。" is gold standard reordered to "闪烁器 54 X 射线 接收 光 产生 。" using alignment to the target sentence. This comparison is measured by word error rate and select the parse tree which has the minimum word error rate in the k-best parse trees as the best parse tree. The parse tree shown in Figure 4 (a) is reordered to "闪烁器 54 X 射线 光 产生 接收 。" and the parse tree shown in Figure 4 (b) is reordered to "闪烁器 54 X 射线 接收 光 产生 。". Then, Figure 4 (b) is selected as the best parse tree in this case.

For the dev, devtest and test sets, we use LM based reranking to select the best parse tree. Firstly, we make reordered source sentence corpus from the training corpus by the above method and build LM using this corpus. Next, we select the best parse tree which has the maximum LM score in the k-best reordered sentences in dev, devtest and test sets. Here, LM score of a sentence is a score calculated by the tool "query" in Moses divided by the number of words in the sentence.

[6] Devtest data is not included in the training data for the grammar improvement. Gold standard of Chinese sentence head for devtest data is determined by the method described above.

2.4 SMT part

SMT part uses phrase based Moses same as SPE part. For JPCko-ja task, SMT part translates source sentences to target sentences as the usual phrase based SMT. As the segmenter for Korean, we use MeCab-ko[7]. For JPCzh-ja task, zh-ja task and en-ja task, SMT part translates reordered source sentences to the target. Reordering is made by the method described in 2.3. Distortion limit is set to 6 both JPCko-ja task and other tasks. So, we call our SMT semi-monotone SMT. LM for SMT is same as LM for SPE. TM is trained from the training corpus provided by the workshop organizer. Training corpus sizes (number of sentence pairs) are listed in Table 3.

Task	Corpus size
JPCko-ja	994,998
JPCzh-ja	995,385
zh-ja	668,468
en-ja	2,351,575

Table 3: Training corpus size

2.5 Candidate selection part

The last part of our translation system is a candidate selection part. This part select the candidate which has the maximum LM score from the outputs of RBMT part, RBMT+SPE part and Preordering+SMT part. Here, LM score is calculated from the LM for SMT part by the method described in section 2.3.2.

2.6 Other ad-hoc processing

For JPCko-ja task, we conduct an ad-hoc preprocessing for Korean source sentences of the train, dev, devtest and test corpora and their RBMT outputs. It is deletion of brackets surrounding the number, because the use of brackets between Korean and Japanese is different shown in Figure 5. In Korean sentence, number "2" is surrounded by the brackets. However, in Japanese sentence, number " 2 " is not surrounded by the brackets. So we delete brackets surrounding the number in Korean side to improve alignment accuracy of brackets.

또한, 산화피막(2)이 존재하는 경우에는, ・・・
また、酸化皮膜2が存在する場合には、・・・

Figure 5: Different bracket usage in Korean and Japanese.

[7] https://bitbucket.org/eunjeon/mecab-ko/

Another ad-hoc processing is to convert all half width characters in RBMT and SMT outputs to full width characters, because Japanese document tend to use full width characters.

2.7 Issues for context-aware machine translation

We have no consideration for context-awareness in our system.

3 Experimental results

3.1 Translation results

Table 4 shows the official evaluation results of the translation of the test data (Nakazawa et al., 2015). In all cases, BLEU and RIBES are calculated using Japanese segmenter Juman.

Task	System	BLEU	RIBES	HUMAN
JPCko-ja	RBMT+SPE	70.13	0.9419	6.500
	SMT	70.81	0.9430	--
	Combination	70.67	0.9430	10.250
JPCzh-ja	RBMT+SPE	40.35	0.8195	8.250
	Preordering+SMT	40.70	0.8243	--
	Combination	41.06	0.8270	22.000
zh-ja	RBMT+SPE	35.59	0.8158	--
	Preordering+SMT	39.43	0.8377	--
	Combination	37.90	0.8260	25.750
en-ja	RBMT+SPE	30.46	0.7685	--
	Preordering+SMT	29.78	0.7536	32.500
	Combination	30.88	0.7657	--

Table 4: Evaluation results of the translation

In JPCko-ja task and JPCzh-ja task, system combination using candidate selection by LM score is more accurate than RBMT+SPE system both in automatic and human evaluation. In zh-ja task, Preordering+SMT system has higher BLEU and RIBES than system combination. However, we don't have human score for preordering+SMT system for the zh-ja task.

3.2 Candidate selection results

Table 5 shows the candidate selection results. Most of outputs of RBMT part are not selected. Outputs of RBMT+SPE part and outputs of preordering+SMT part are selected about half and half.

Task	RBMT	RBMT+SPE	Preordering +SMT	Total
JPCko-ja	25	1177	798	2000
JPCzh-ja	2	875	1123	2000
zh-ja	9	1270	828	2107
en-ja	5	658	1149	1812

Table 5: The number of each system outputs selected by the candidate selection part.

To confirm effectiveness of candidate selection process, we compare LM scores and human evaluation scores for JPCzh-ja task. Table 6 shows human evaluation score of SPE[8] outputs and SMT outputs when the case of LM score for SMT output exceeds LM score for SPE output.

SMT＼SPE	-1	0	1
-1	6	4	2
0	25	101	26
1	8	32	18

Table 6: The number of human evaluation scores for SPE outputs and SMT outputs when the case of LM score of SMT output exceeds LM score of SPE output.

From the Table 6, we can see this candidate selection process makes human score better in 65 cases (SMT > SPE) and worse in 32 cases (SPE > SMT). The number of tie cases is 125.

To investigate worsen cases, we show several translation examples. Table 7 shows SMT output and SPE output, baseline (BASE) output, reference (REF) and source (SRC) of two translation examples. In these cases, LM score of SMT output is greater than LM score of SPE output. But human score of SMT output (-1) is less than human score of SPE output (1).

In the first example, the word "オートコリメータ" is less general than the word "コリメータ". Actually, LM score of the former word is -5.61676 and LM score of the latter word is -4.12944. Then LM score of the former sentence is less than LM score of the latter sentence.

In the second example, "アノード４１０と陰極４１５" is less general than "アノード４１５とカソード４１０" in our LM. Actually, LM score of SMT output sentence is -66.1355 and the LM score of the sentence which is converted the term "アノード４１５とカソード４１０" of SMT output to "アノード４１０とカソード４１５" is -71.1855. These two examples indicate the limitation of LM score based candidate selection method.

SMT	図5は、コリメータ装置による調整動作を説明するための概略図である。
SPE	図5は、オートコリメータ装置による調整動作を説明するための概略図である。
BASE	図5は、自動コリメータ装置による調整動作を説明するための概略図である。
REF	図5は、オートコリメータ装置による調整動作を説明するための概略図である。
SRC	图5是用于说明由自动准直仪装置进行的调整操作的概略图。

SMT	図4は、名称からアノード415とカソード410との間に挟まれた発光層405のOLED400とを含む第1の例示的な実施の形態について説明する。
SPE	図4は、概念上からアノード410と陰極415との間の発光層405のOLED400の第1の例示的実施形態を含むと説明する。
BASE	図4は、陽極410とカソード415との間の発光層405のOLED400の第1で概念的に説明は、例示的な実施形態が挟まれている。
REF	図4は、アノード410とカソード415とに挟まれた発光層405を含むOLED400の第1実施例の概念図である。
SRC	图4从概念上说明包括夹在阳极410与阴极415之间的发射层405的OLED 400的第一示例性实施方案。

Table 7: Example of candidate selection part making worse output.

3.3 Other results

Table 8 shows other evaluation results for JPCzh-ja task on devtest data translation.

System	Additional feature	BLEU	RIBES
RBMT		16.55	0.7192
RBMT	User dictionary	23.54	0.7510
RBMT+SPE	User dictionary	41.35	0.8203
SMT	(DL=10)	40.86	0.8071
Preordering+SMT	original grammar	40.15	0.8164
Preordering+SMT	improved grammar	41.84	0.8218
Preordering+SMT	improved grammar + reranking of parse trees	42.75	0.8237
System combination		43.01	0.8265

Table 8: Evaluation results for JPCzh-ja devtest data translation

User dictionary, SPE and preordering greatly improve RIBES score. Improving of grammar, reranking of parse trees and system combination slightly improve RIBES score. For BLEU score,

[8] In this section, the term "SPE" is used for RBMT+SPE and the term "SMT" is used for preordering+SMT for the simplicity.

results are almost similar as RIBES case. However, preordering with original grammar makes BLEU score worse compared with simple SMT. RBMT+SPE with user dictionary improves BLEU score by 17.81 compared with simple RBMT. Preordering+SMT with the improved grammar and reranking of parse trees improves BLEU score by 1.89 compared with simple SMT with DL 10. System combination improves BLEU score by 0.26 compared with preordering+SMT.

4 Conclusion

System architecture, experimental settings and evaluation results of the EHR group in the WAT2015 tasks are described. Our system design concept is combining of rule-based method and statistical method and it gives the good effect to the translation accuracy. One of the future issues is to improve parsing accuracy both in RBMT part and preordering part.

Reference

Pi-Chuan Chang, Michel Galley and Chris Manning. 2008. Optimizing Chinese Word Segmentation for Machine Translation Performance. *Proceedings of the Third Workshop on Statistical Machine Translation,* pages 224-232.

Terumasa Ehara. 2014. A machine translation system combining rule-based machine translation and statistical post-editing, *Proceedings of the 1st Workshop on Asian Translation* (*WAT2014*), pages 50-54.

Isao Goto, Ka Po Chow, Bin Lu, Eiichiro Sumita and Benjamin K. Tsou. 2013. Overview of the Patent Machine Translation Task at the NTCIR-10 Workshop, *Proceedings of the 10th NTCIR Conference*, pages 260-286.

Hideki Isozaki, Katsuhito Sudoh, Hajime Tsukada and Kevin Duh. 2010. Head finalization: A simple reordering rule for SOV languages. *Proceedings of the Joint 5th Workshop on Statistical Machine Translation and MetricsMATR*, pages 244-251.

Japio (Japan Patent Information Organization). 2015. Investigation report of dictionary improvement and quality evaluation of machine translation for Chinese patent documents (in Japanese).

Philipp Koehn, Franz J. Och and Daniel Marcu. 2003. Statistical Phrase-Based Translation, *Proceedings of HLT-NAACL 2003*, pages 48-54.

Sadao Kurohashi, Toshihisa Nakamura, Yuji Matsumoto and Makoto Nagao. 1994. Improvements of Japanese morphological analyzer JUMAN. *Proceedings of The International Workshop on Sharable Natural Language Resources,* pages 22-28.

Toshiaki Nakazawa, Hideya Mino, Isao Goto, Graham Neubig, Sadao Kurohashi and Eiichiro Sumita. 2015. Overview of the 2nd Workshop on Asian Translation, *Proceedings of the 2nd Workshop on Asian Translation (WAT2015).*

Franz Josef Och, Hermann Ney. 2003. A Systematic Comparison of Various Statistical Alignment Models, *Computational Linguistics,* volume 29, number 1, pages 19-51.

Slav Petrov, Leon Barrett, Romain Thibaux and Dan Klein. 2006. Learning Accurate, Compact, and Interpretable Tree Annotation, *Proceedings of COLING-ACL 2006,* pages 433-440.

Huihsin Tseng, Pichuan Chang, Galen Andrew, Daniel Jurafsky and Christopher Manning. 2005. A Conditional Random Field Word Segmenter. In *Fourth SIGHAN Workshop on Chinese Language Processing.*

Neural Reranking Improves Subjective Quality of Machine Translation: NAIST at WAT2015

Graham Neubig, Makoto Morishita, Satoshi Nakamura
Graduate School of Information Science
Nara Institute of Science and Technology
8916-5 Takayama-cho, Ikoma-shi, Nara, Japan
{neubig,morishita.makoto.mb1,s-nakamura}@is.naist.jp

Abstract

This year, the Nara Institute of Science and Technology (NAIST)'s submission to the 2015 Workshop on Asian Translation was based on syntax-based statistical machine translation, with the addition of a reranking component using neural attentional machine translation models. Experiments re-confirmed results from previous work stating that neural MT reranking provides a large gain in objective evaluation measures such as BLEU, and also confirmed for the first time that these results also carry over to manual evaluation. We further perform a detailed analysis of reasons for this increase, finding that the main contributions of the neural models lie in improvement of the grammatical correctness of the output, as opposed to improvements in lexical choice of content words.

1 Introduction

Neural network models for machine translation (MT) (Kalchbrenner and Blunsom, 2013; Sutskever et al., 2014; Bahdanau et al., 2015), while still in a nascent stage, have shown impressive results in a number of translation tasks. Specifically, a number of works have demonstrated gains in BLEU score (Papineni et al., 2002) over state-of-the-art non-neural systems, both when using the neural MT model standalone (Luong et al., 2015a; Jean et al., 2015; Luong et al., 2015b), or to rerank the output of more traditional systems phrase-based MT systems (Sutskever et al., 2014).

However, despite these impressive results with regards to automatic measures of translation quality, there has been little examination of the effect that these gains have on the subjective impressions of human users. Because BLEU generally has some correlation with translation quality,[1] it is fair to hypothesize that these gains will carry over to gains in human evaluation, but empirical evidence for this hypothesis is still scarce. In this paper, we attempt to close this gap by examining the gains provided by using neural MT models to rerank the hypotheses a state-of-the-art non-neural MT system, both from the objective and subjective perspectives.

Specifically, as part of the Nara Institute of Science and Technology (NAIST) submission to the Workshop on Asian Translation (WAT) 2015 (Nakazawa et al., 2015), we generate reranked and non-reranked translation results in four language pairs (Section 2). Based on these translation results, we calculate scores according to automatic evaluation measures BLEU and RIBES (Isozaki et al., 2010), and a manual evaluation that involves comparing hypotheses to a baseline system (Section 3). Next, we perform a detailed analysis of the cases in which subjective impressions improved or degraded due to neural MT reranking, and identify major areas in which neural reranking improves results, and areas in which reranking is less helpful (Section 4). Finally, as an auxiliary result, we also examine the effect that the size of the n-best list used in reranking has on the improvement of translation results (Section 5).

2 Generation of Translation Results

2.1 Baseline System

All experiments are performed on WAT2015 translation task from Japanese (ja) to/from English (en) and Chinese (zh). As a baseline, we used the NAIST system for WAT 2014 (Neubig, 2014), a state-of-the-art system that achieved the highest accuracy on all four tracks in the last year's eval-

[1] Particularly when comparing similar systems, such as the case of when neural MT is used for reranking existing system results.

Proceedings of the 2nd Workshop on Asian Translation (WAT2015), pages 35-41,
Kyoto, Japan, 16th October 2015.

uation.[2] The details of construction are described in Neubig (2014), but we briefly outline it here for completeness.

The system is based on the Travatar toolkit (Neubig, 2013), using tree-to-string statistical MT (Graehl and Knight, 2004; Liu et al., 2006), in which the source is first syntactically parsed, then subtrees of the input parse are converted into strings on the target side. This translation paradigm has proven effective for translation between syntactically distant language pairs such as those handled by the WAT tasks. In addition, following our findings in Neubig and Duh (2014), to improve the accuracy of translation we use forest-based encoding of many parse candidates (Mi et al., 2008), and a supervised alignment technique for ja-en and en-ja (Riesa and Marcu, 2010).

To train the systems, we used the ASPEC corpus provided by WAT. For the zh-ja and ja-zh systems, we used all of the data, amounting to 672k sentences. For the en-ja and ja-en systems, we used all 3M sentences for training the language models, and the first 2M sentences of the training data for training the translation models.

For English, Japanese, and Chinese, tokenization was performed using the Stanford Parser (Klein and Manning, 2003), the KyTea toolkit (Neubig et al., 2011), and the Stanford Segmenter (Tseng et al., 2005) respectively. For parsing, we use the Egret parser,[3] which implements the latent variable parsing model of (Petrov et al., 2006).[4]

For all systems, we trained a 6-gram language model smoothed with modified Kneser-Ney smoothing (Chen and Goodman, 1996) using KenLM (Heafield et al., 2013). To optimize the parameters of the log-linear model, we use standard minimum error rate training (MERT; Och (2003)) with BLEU as an objective.

2.2 Neural MT Models

As our neural MT model, we use the attentional model of Bahdanau et al. (2015). The model first encodes the source sentence $\boldsymbol{f}$ using bidirectional long short-term memory (LSTM; Hochreiter and Schmidhuber (1997)) recurrent networks. This results in an encoding vector $\boldsymbol{h}_j$ for each word f_j in $\boldsymbol{f}$. The model then proceeds to generate the target translation $\hat{e}$ one word at a time, at each time step calculating soft alignments $\boldsymbol{a}_i$ that are used to generate a context vector $\boldsymbol{g}_i$, which is referenced when generating the target word

$$\boldsymbol{g}_i = \sum_{j=1}^{|\boldsymbol{f}|} a_{i,j} \boldsymbol{h}_j. \tag{1}$$

Attentional models have a number of appealing properties, such as being theoretically able to encode variable length sequences without worrying about memory constraints imposed by the fixed-size vectors used in encoder-decoder models. These advantages are confirmed in empirical results, with attentional models performing markedly better on longer sequences (Bahdanau et al., 2015).

To train the neural MT models, we used the implementation provided by the lamtram toolkit.[5] The forward and reverse LSTM models each had 256 nodes, and word embeddings were also set to size 256. For ja-en and en-ja models we chose the first 500k sentences in the training corpus, and for ja-zh and zh-ja models we used all 672k sentences. Training was performed using stochastic gradient descent (SGD) with an initial learning rate of 0.1, which was halved every epoch in which the development likelihood decreased.

For each language pair, we trained two models and ensembled the probabilities by linearly interpolating between the two probability distributions.[6] These probabilities were used to rerank unique 1,000-best lists from the baseline model. To perform reranking, the log likelihood of the neural MT model was added as an additional feature to the standard baseline model features, and the weight of this feature was decided by running MERT on the dev set.

3 Experimental Results

First, we calculate overall numerical results for our systems with and without the neural MT reranking model. As automatic evaluation we use the standard BLEU (Papineni et al., 2002) and reordering-oriented RIBES (Isozaki et al., 2010) metrics. In

[2] Scripts to reproduce the system are available at `http://phontron.com/project/wat2014`.

[3] `https://github.com/neubig/egret`

[4] In addition, for ja-en translation, we make one modification to the parser used in the previous year's submission, performing parser self-training (McClosky et al., 2006) using sentences from the training data that had a BLEU score greater than 0.8, and selecting the tree corresponding to the 500-best hypothesis that had the best score according to BLEU+1 (Lin and Och, 2004).

[5] `http://github.com/neubig/lamtram`

[6] More standard log-linear interpolation resulted in similar, or slightly inferior results.

System	en-ja B	en-ja R	en-ja H	ja-en B	ja-en R	ja-en H	zh-ja B	zh-ja R	zh-ja H	ja-zh B	ja-zh R	ja-zh H
Base	36.6	79.6	49.8	22.6	72.3	11.8	40.5	83.4	25.8	30.1	81.5	2.8
Rerank	**38.2**	**81.4**	**62.3**	**25.4**	**75.0**	**35.5**	**43.0**	**84.8**	**35.8**	**31.6**	**83.3**	7.0

Table 1: Overall BLEU, RIBES, and HUMAN scores for our baseline system and system with neural MT reranking. Bold indicates a significant improvement according to bootstrap resampling at $p < 0.05$ (Koehn, 2004).

manual evaluation, we use the WAT "HUMAN" evaluation score (Nakazawa et al., 2015), which is essentially related to the number of wins over a baseline phrase-based system. In the case that the system beats the baseline on all sentences, the HUMAN score will be 100, and if it loses on all sentences the score will be -100.

From the results in Table 1, we can first see that adding the neural MT reranking resulted in a significant increase in the evaluation scores for all language pairs under consideration, except for the manual evaluation in ja-zh translation.[7] It should be noted that these gains are achieved even though the original baseline was already quite strong (outperforming most other WAT2015 systems without a neural component). While neural MT reranking has been noted to improve traditional systems with respect to BLEU score in previous work (Sutskever et al., 2014), to our knowledge this is the first work that notes that these gains also carry over convincingly to human evaluation scores. In the following section, we will examine the results in more detail and attempt to explain exactly what is causing this increase in translation quality.

4 Analysis

To perform a deeper analysis, we manually examined the first 200 sentences of the ja-en part of the official WAT2015 human evaluation set. Specifically, we (1) compared the baseline and reranked outputs, and decided whether one was better or if they were of the same quality and (2) in the case that one of the two was better, classified the example by the type of error that was fixed or caused by the reranking leading to this change in subjective impression. Specifically, when annotating the type of error, we used a simplified version of

[7]The overall scores for ja-zh are lower than others, perhaps a result of word-order between Japanese and Chinese being more similar than Japanese and English, the parser for Japanese being weaker than that of the other languages, and less consistent evaluation scores for the Chinese output (Nakazawa et al., 2014).

Type	Impr.	Degr.	% Impr.
Reordering	55	9	86%
Deletion	20	10	67%
Insertion	19	2	90%
Substitution	15	11	58%
Conjugation	8	1	89%
Total	117	33	78%

Table 2: A summary of the improvements and degradations caused by neural reranking.

the error typology of Vilar et al. (2006) consisting of *insertion*, *deletion*, *word conjugation*, *word substitution*, and *reordering*, as well as subcategories of each of these categories (the number of sub-categories totalled approximately 40). If there was more than one change in the sentence, only the change that we subjectively felt had the largest effect on the translation quality was annotated.

The number of improvements and degradations afforded by neural MT reranking is shown in Table 2. From this figure, we can see that overall, neural reranking caused an improvement in 117 sentences, and a degradation in 33 sentences, corroborating the fact that the reranking process is giving consistent improvements in accuracy. Further breaking down the changes, we can see that improvements in word reordering are by far the most prominent, slightly less than three times the number of improvements in the next most common category. This demonstrates that the neural MT model is successfully capturing the overall structure of the sentence, and effectively disambiguating reorderings that could not be appropriately scored in the baseline model.

Next in Table 3 we show examples of the four most common sub-categories of errors that were fixed by the neural MT reranker, and note the total number of improvements and degradations of each. The first subcategory is related to the general reordering of phrases in the sentence. As there

1. Reordering of Phrases (+26, -4)	
In.	症例２においては，直腸がんの肝転移に対する化学療法中に，発赤，硬結，皮膚潰ようを生じた。
Ref.	In case 2, reddening, induration, and skin ulcer appeared during chemical therapy for liver metastasis of rectal cancer.
Base.	In case 2, occurred during chemotherapy for liver metastasis of rectal cancer, flare, induration, skin ulcer.
Rerank	In case 2, the flare, induration, skin ulcer was produced during the chemotherapy for hepatic metastasis of rectal cancer.
2. Insertion/Deletion of Auxiliary Verbs (+15, -0)	
In.	これにより得られる支配方程式は壁面乱流のようなせん断乱流にも有用である。
Ref.	Governing equation derived by this method is useful for turbulent shear flow like turbulent flow near wall.
Base.	The governing equation **is** obtained by this is also useful for such as wall turbulence shear flow.
Rerank	The governing equation obtained by this is also useful for shear flow such as wall turbulence.
3. Reordering of Coordinate Structures (+13, -2)	
In.	レーザー加工は高密度光束による局所的な加熱とアブレーションにより行う。
Ref.	Laser work is done by local heating and ablation with high density light flux.
Base.	The laser processing is carried out by local heating by high-density luminous flux and ablation.
Rerank	The laser processing is carried out by local heating and ablation by high-density flux.
4. Conjugation of Verb Agreement (+6, -0)	
In.	ラングミュア‐ブロジェット法や包接化にも触れた。
Ref.	Langmuir-Blodgett method and inclusion compounds are mentioned.
Base.	Langmuir-Blodgett method and inclusion is also discussed.
Rerank	Langmuir-Blodgett method and inclusion are also mentioned.

Table 3: An example of more common varieties of improvements caused by the neural MT reranking.

is a large amount of reordering involved in translating from Japanese to English, mistaken long-distance reordering is one of the more common causes for errors, and the neural MT model was effective at fixing these problems, resulting in 26 improvements and only 4 degradations. In the sentence shown in the example, the baseline system swaps the verb phrase and subject positions, making it difficult to tell that the list of conditions are what "occurred," while the reranked system appropriately puts this list as the subject of "occurred."

The second subcategory includes insertions or deletions of auxiliary verbs, for which there were 15 improvements and not a single degradation. The reason why these errors occurred in the first place is that when a transitive verb, for example "obtained," occurs on its own, it is often translated as "X was obtained by Y,"[8] but when it occurs as a relative clause decorating the noun X it will be translated as "X obtained by Y," as shown in the example. The baseline system does not include any explicit features to make this distinction between whether a verb is part of a relative clause or not, and thus made a number of mistakes of this variety. However, it is evident that the neural MT model has learned to make this distinction, greatly reducing the number of these errors.

The third subcategory is similar to the first, but explicitly involves the correct interpretation of coordinate structures. It is well known that syntactic parsers often make mistakes in their interpretation of coordinate structures (Kummerfeld et al., 2012). Of course, the parser used in our syntax-based MT system is no exception to this rule, and parse errors often cause coordinate phrases to be broken apart on the target side, as is the case in the example's "local heating and ablation." The fact that the neural MT models were able to correct a large number of errors related to these structures suggests that they are able to successfully determine whether two phrases are coordinated or not, and keep them together on the target side.

The final sub-category of the top four is related to verb conjugation agreement. Many of the examples related to verb conjugation, including the one shown in Table 3, were related to when two singular nouns were connected by a conjunction. In this case, the local context provided by a standard n-gram language model is not enough to resolve the ambiguity, but the longer context handled by the neural MT model is able to resolve this easily.

What is notable about these four categories is that they all are related to improving the correctness of the output from a grammatical point of view, as opposed to fixing mistakes in lexical choice or terminology. In fact, neural MT reranking had an overall negative effect on choice of terminology with only 2 improvements at the cost of 4 degradations. This was due to the fact that the neural MT model tended to prefer more com-

[8]This passivization is somewhat of a trait of the scientific paper material used as material for this analysis.

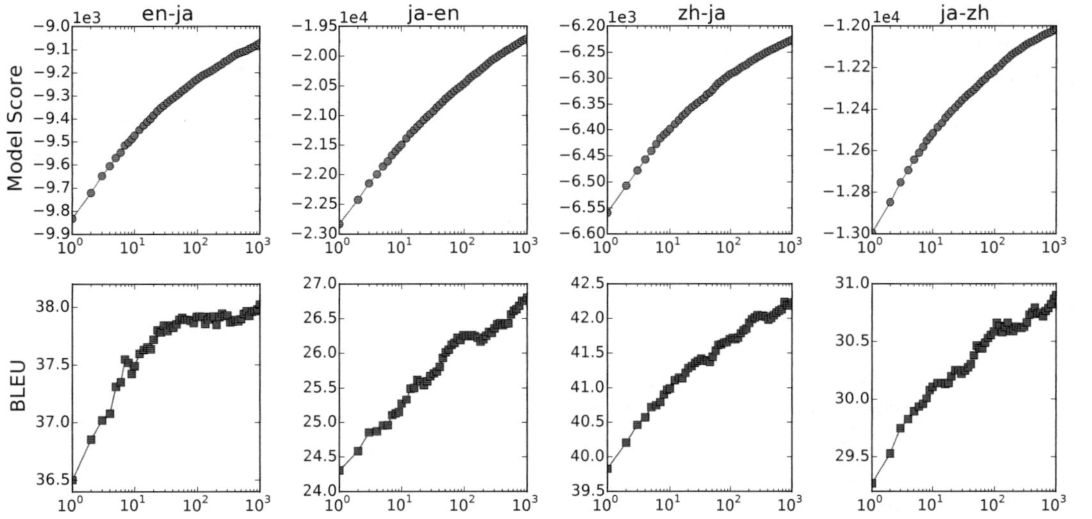

Figure 1: Model and BLEU scores after neural MT reranking for each n-best list size (log scale).

mon words, mistaking "radiant heat" as "radiation heat" or "slipring" as "ring." While these tendencies will be affected by many factors such as the size of the vocabulary or the number and size of hidden layers of the net, we feel it is safe to say that neural MT reranking can be expected to have a large positive effect on syntactic correctness of output, while results for lexical choice are less conclusive.

5 Effect of n-best Size on Reranking

In the previous sections, we confirmed the effectiveness of n-best list reranking using neural MT models. However, reranking using n-best lists (like other search methods for MT) is an approximate search method, and its effectiveness is limited by the size of the n-best list used. In order to quantify the effect of this inexact search, we performed experiments to examine the post-reranking automatic evaluation scores of the MT results for all n-best list sizes from 1 to 1000. Figure 1 shows the results of this examination, with the x-axis referring to the log-scaled number of hypotheses in the n-best list, and the y-axis referring to the quality of the translation, either with regards to model score (for the model including the neural MT likelihood as a feature) or BLEU score.[9]

From these results we can note several interesting points. First, we can see that the improvement in scores is very slightly sub-linear in the log number of hypotheses in the n-best list. In other words, every time we double the n-best list size we will see an improvement in accuracy that is slightly smaller than the last time we doubled the size. Second, we can note that in most cases this trend continues all the way up to our limit of 1000-best lists, indicating that gains are not saturating, and we can likely expect even more improvements from using larger lists, or perhaps directly performing decoding using neural models (Alkhouli et al., 2015). The en-ja results, however, are an exception to this rule, with BLEU gains more or less saturating around the 50-best list point.

6 Conclusion

In this paper we described results applying neural MT reranking to a baseline syntax-based machine translation system in 4 languages. In particular, we performed an in-depth analysis of what kinds of translation errors were fixed by neural MT reranking. Based on this analysis, we found that the majority of the gains were related to improvements in the accuracy of transfer of correct grammatical structure to the target sentence, with the most prominent gains being related to errors regarding reordering of phrases, insertion/deletion of copulas, coordinate structures, and verb agreement. We also found that, within the neural MT reranking framework, accuracy gains scaled ap-

[9]The BLEU scores differ slightly from Table 1 due to differences in tokenization standards between these experiments and the official evaluation server.

proximately log-linearly with the size of the n-best list, and in most cases were not saturated even after examining 1000 unique hypotheses.

Acknowledgments:

This work was supported by JSPS KAKENHI Grant Number 25730136.

References

Tamer Alkhouli, Felix Rietig, and Hermann Ney. 2015. Investigations on phrase-based decoding with recurrent neural network language and translation models. In *Proc. WMT*, pages 294–303.

Dzmitry Bahdanau, Kyunghyun Cho, and Yoshua Bengio. 2015. Neural machine translation by jointly learning to align and translate. In *Proc. ICLR*.

Stanley F. Chen and Joshua Goodman. 1996. An empirical study of smoothing techniques for language modeling. In *Proc. ACL*, pages 310–318.

Jonathan Graehl and Kevin Knight. 2004. Training tree transducers. In *Proc. HLT*, pages 105–112.

Kenneth Heafield, Ivan Pouzyrevsky, Jonathan H. Clark, and Philipp Koehn. 2013. Scalable modified Kneser-Ney language model estimation. In *Proc. ACL*, pages 690–696.

Sepp Hochreiter and Jürgen Schmidhuber. 1997. Long short-term memory. *Neural computation*, 9(8):1735–1780.

Hideki Isozaki, Tsutomu Hirao, Kevin Duh, Katsuhito Sudoh, and Hajime Tsukada. 2010. Automatic evaluation of translation quality for distant language pairs. In *Proc. EMNLP*, pages 944–952.

Sébastien Jean, Kyunghyun Cho, Roland Memisevic, and Yoshua Bengio. 2015. On using very large target vocabulary for neural machine translation. In *Proc. ACL*, pages 1–10.

Nal Kalchbrenner and Phil Blunsom. 2013. Recurrent continuous translation models. In *Proc. EMNLP*, pages 1700–1709.

Dan Klein and Christopher D. Manning. 2003. Accurate unlexicalized parsing. In *Proc. ACL*, pages 423–430.

Philipp Koehn. 2004. Statistical significance tests for machine translation evaluation. In *Proc. EMNLP*, pages 388–395.

Jonathan K Kummerfeld, David Hall, James R Curran, and Dan Klein. 2012. Parser showdown at the wall street corral: an empirical investigation of error types in parser output. In *Proc. EMNLP*, pages 1048–1059.

Chin-Yew Lin and Franz Josef Och. 2004. Orange: a method for evaluating automatic evaluation metrics for machine translation. In *Proc. COLING*, pages 501–507.

Yang Liu, Qun Liu, and Shouxun Lin. 2006. Tree-to-string alignment template for statistical machine translation. In *Proc. ACL*, pages 609–616.

Minh-Thang Luong, Ilya Sutskever, Quoc Le, Oriol Vinyals, and Wojciech Zaremba. 2015a. Addressing the rare word problem in neural machine translation. In *Proc. ACL*, pages 11–19.

Thang Luong, Hieu Pham, and Christopher D. Manning. 2015b. Effective approaches to attention-based neural machine translation. In *Proc. EMNLP*, pages 1412–1421.

David McClosky, Eugene Charniak, and Mark Johnson. 2006. Effective self-training for parsing. In *Proc. HLT*, pages 152–159.

Haitao Mi, Liang Huang, and Qun Liu. 2008. Forest-based translation. In *Proc. ACL*, pages 192–199.

Toshiaki Nakazawa, Hideki Mino, Isao Goto, Sadao Kurohashi, and Eiichiro Sumita. 2014. Overview of the 1st Workshop on Asian Translation. In *Proc. WAT*.

Toshiaki Nakazawa, Hideya Mino, Isao Goto, Graham Neubig, Sadao Kurohashi, and Eiichiro Sumita. 2015. Overview of the 2nd Workshop on Asian Translation. In *Proc. WAT*.

Graham Neubig and Kevin Duh. 2014. On the elements of an accurate tree-to-string machine translation system. In *Proc. ACL*, pages 143–149.

Graham Neubig, Yosuke Nakata, and Shinsuke Mori. 2011. Pointwise prediction for robust, adaptable Japanese morphological analysis. In *Proc. ACL*, pages 529–533.

Graham Neubig. 2013. Travatar: A forest-to-string machine translation engine based on tree transducers. In *Proc. ACL Demo Track*, pages 91–96.

Graham Neubig. 2014. Forest-to-string SMT for Asian language translation: NAIST at WAT2014. In *Proc. WAT*.

Franz Josef Och. 2003. Minimum error rate training in statistical machine translation. In *Proc. ACL*, pages 160–167.

Kishore Papineni, Salim Roukos, Todd Ward, and Wei-Jing Zhu. 2002. BLEU: a method for automatic evaluation of machine translation. In *Proc. ACL*, pages 311–318.

Slav Petrov, Leon Barrett, Romain Thibaux, and Dan Klein. 2006. Learning accurate, compact, and interpretable tree annotation. In *Proc. ACL*, pages 433–440.

Jason Riesa and Daniel Marcu. 2010. Hierarchical search for word alignment. In *Proc. ACL*, pages 157–166.

Ilya Sutskever, Oriol Vinyals, and Quoc VV Le. 2014. Sequence to sequence learning with neural networks. In *Proc. NIPS*, pages 3104–3112.

Huihsin Tseng, Pichuan Chang, Galen Andrew, Daniel Jurafsky, and Christopher Manning. 2005. A conditional random field word segmenter for SIGHAN bakeoff 2005. In *Proc. SIGHAN*.

David Vilar, Jia Xu, Luis Fernando d ' Haro, and Hermann Ney. 2006. Error analysis of statistical machine translation output. In *Proc. LREC*, pages 697–702.

NICT at WAT 2015

Chenchen Ding, Masao Utiyama, Eiichiro Sumita
Multilingual Translation Laboratory
National Institute of Information and Communications Technology
3-5 Hikaridai, Seikacho, Sorakugun, Kyoto, 619-0289, Japan
{chenchen.ding, mutiyama, eiichiro.sumita}@nict.go.jp

Abstract

Translation systems of our NICT team at *the 2nd Workshop on Asian Translation* (WAT 2015) are described in this paper. We participated in two translation tasks: Japanese-to-English (JE) and Korean-to-Japanese (KJ). A baseline phrased-based (PB) statistical machine translation (SMT) system in Moses was used. On JE translation, two pre-reordering approaches were applied: a simple *reverse preordering* and a dependency-based approach. On KJ translation, the processing was purely conducted on character-level. Evaluation results show that even simple approaches can improve JE and KJ PB SMT significantly. These techniques can be easily applied in practice because of the simplicity.

1 Introduction

Statistical machine translation (SMT) techniques have been well developed and widely applied in practice. Linguistic knowledge-free SMT frameworks, such as phrase-based (PB) SMT (Koehn et al., 2003) and hierarchical phrase-based SMT (HIERO) (Chiang, 2007), handle many translation tasks efficiently as long as sufficient training data prepared. Further, sophisticated syntactically-driven approaches (Neubig, 2013) give better performance than PB SMT and HIERO on difficult translation tasks (Neubig, 2014).

At *the 2nd Workshop on Asian Translation* (WAT 2015) (Nakazawa et al., 2015), our intention is to test the efficiency of several simple techniques for Japanese-to-English (JE) and Korean-to-Japanese (KJ) translation, specifically, pre-reordering approaches for JE translation and character-based processing for KJ translation. On JE translation, we found the simple *reverse preordering* approach proposed by Katz-Brown and Collins (2008) performed as well as a well-designed dependency-based approach, in improving a PB SMT baseline. Considering the simplicity of the *reverse preordering*, we think the approach should be used more widely for JE translation. On KJ translation, we found even a pure character-based approach outperformed the organizer's baseline a lot, due to the similarity of the two languages on their vocabularies and syntaxes. We give descriptions of the approaches in the following sections.

2 Pre-reordering for JE Translation

As Japanese and English have dramatically different word orders, the performance of *word reordering* affects translation results significantly. Among different lines of researches, *pre-reordering* has been widely applied in practice and still studied in recent researches (de Gispert et al., 2015; Hoshino et al., 2015).

For the JE translation task of WAT 2015, we test two pre-reordering approaches. The first one is the *reverse preordering* (REV-REO) proposed by Katz-Brown and Collins (2008) for the NTCIR-7 JE Patent MT translation task. Another one is a recently proposed dependency-based approach (DEP-REO) (Ding et al., 2015)[1] with well-designed rules. We select the two approaches because they are on two extremes, that REV-REO is an approach needs no syntactic analysis at all, while the DEP-REO makes a good use of the dependency structure of Japanese sentences. As both approaches have been described in detail in their original papers, We do not give repeated descriptions but just state several details in experiments.

For DEP-REO, the processes were completely identical to the experiments in Ding et al. (2015), where the tool chain of `MeCab`[2] and `CaboCha`[3]

[1] A non-refereed version in Japanese is Ding et al. (2014a).
[2] `http://taku910.github.io/mecab/`
[3] `http://taku910.github.io/cabocha/`

Proceedings of the 2nd Workshop on Asian Translation (WAT2015), pages 42-47,
Kyoto, Japan, 16th October 2015.

(Kudo and Matsumoto, 2002) based on IPA system for Japanese morphemes was used. For REV-REO, an important point is to **avoid the reordering across punctuations**[4]. In the experiments, we used four marks to compose the punctuation set: `U+002C`[5], `U+FF0C`[6], `U+3001`[7], and `U+3002`[8]. For the Japanese topic marker *wa*, which plays the key role of the approach, we did not judge it only by the surface form, but also referred to the specific tag *joshi, kakarijoshi*[9].

3 Character-based KJ Translation

As Korean and Japanese share so many similar features, we tried a purely character-based approach in WAT 2015. The process was identical to Ding et al. (2014b). Specifically, no morphological analysis or text normalization[10] were conducted except (unicode) characters were separated using spaces. The original space is replaced by a `<sp>` tag and the original tab is replaced by a `<tab>` tag[11]. The processes were applied consistently on training and test sets.

We found even the above-mentioned trivial process led to satisfactory performance on KJ translation. We further found a post-processing of bracket balancing (because the data contain many brackets) could give a slight improvement in performance. We will describe the process in the following Section 4.

4 Experiment and Evaluation

We used the PB SMT system in `Moses`[12] (Koehn et al., 2007) for JE and KJ translation tasks. Basically, we used identical settings as the organizer used in the baseline. However, there were several differences as follows.

- We used `SRILM`[13] (Stolcke, 2002) for language model training (interpolated modified Kneser-Ney discounting; 5-gram on English for JE translation and 9-gram on Japanese for KJ translation).

- We used `MeCab` (IPA) and `CaboCha` to process Japanese sentences in JE translation.

- We used no tools for Korean and Japanese morphological analysis in KJ translation, instead, the *max-phrase-length* were set to 9 in translation model training.

We selected the optimal distortion limit (DL) in PB SMT decoding by indoor experiments[14] and used the selected setting in the final submissions.

Table 1 shows the experimental results of DEP-REO and REV-REO on JE devtest set. The excellent performance of REV-REO is impressive. However, REV-REO needs a proper DL to reach its best performance, while DEP-REO has a more

	DL	BLEU	RIBES
BASELINE	20	16.95	.6356
+DEP-REO	0	17.77	.6512
	3	17.54	.6520
	6	**17.80**	**.6545**
	9	17.60	.6488
	12	17.79	.6497
	15	17.74	.6499
+REV-REO	0	15.16	.6556
	3	16.08	.6586
	6	17.58	.6707
	9	**18.02**	**.6751**
	12	17.78	.6733
	15	17.54	.6691

Table 1: Devtest set BLEU score and RIBES on JE translation.

	DL	BLEU	RIBES
+Lex.-Reo.	0	66.79	.9222
	3	66.64	.9221
	6	66.80	.9228
−Lex.-Reo.	0	66.74	.9221
+ Bracket Balanc.	0	**66.98**	**.9224**

Table 2: Devtest set BLEU score and RIBES on KJ translation (morpheme level, by `MeCab`).

[4] otherwise the reordering will become excessive.

[5] i.e., the ordinary comma.

[6] "fullwidth comma", the Chinese comma.

[7] "ideographic comma", the Japanese *tōten*.

[8] "ideographic full stop", the Japanese *kuten*.

[9] Because the DEP-REO is totally based on the IPA system, we also used the system for REV-REO. Actually 100% of the surface form *wa* were tagged as *joshi, kakarijoshi* by `MeCab` in our experiments.

[10] We only introduce the minimum rewriting to replace the "|", "[", "]" to full-width characters for Moses' decoder.

[11] The spaces mainly appeared on the Korean side due to its orthography. Those occasional spaces on the Japanese side were also replaced with tags.

[12] `http://www.statmt.org/moses/`

[13] `http://www.speech.sri.com/projects/srilm/`

[14] In KJ translation, we measured the results on morpheme-level by applying `MeCab` on outputs (after `<sp>` and `<tab>` tags recovered).

	Local Evaluation		Organizer Evaluation		
	BLEU	RIBES	BLEU	RIBES	HUMAN
BASELINE $_{\text{organizer, DL=20}}$	–	–	18.45	.6451	–
BASELINE $_{\text{indoor, DL=20}}$	18.09	.6435	18.09	.6397	–
BASELINE $_{\text{indoor}}$ + DEP-REO $_{\text{DL=6}}$	18.99	.6644	18.98	.6599	+16.000
BASELINE $_{\text{indoor}}$ + REV-REO $_{\text{DL=9}}$	18.96	.6870	18.96	.6845	+6.500

Table 3: Evaluation of our submission on JE translation compared with the organizer's PB SMT baseline.

	Local Evaluation		Organizer Evaluation		
	BLEU	RIBES	BLEU	RIBES	HUMAN
BASELINE $_{\text{organizer, DL=0, +Lex.-Reo.}}$	–	–	69.73	.9408	–
BASELINE $_{\text{indoor, DL=0, −Lex.-Reo.}}$	70.94	.9428	70.92	.9427	+8.250
+ Bracket Balancing	71.12	.9429	71.11	.9429	+10.500

Table 4: Evaluation of our submission on KJ translation compared with the organizer's PB SMT baseline.

stable performance across different DLs. The phenomenon is in agree to Ding et al. (2015).

Table 2 shows the experimental results on KJ translation results. We tested different DLs of 0, 3, and 6 with the lexicalized orientation reordering model (+Lex.-Reo.). The performance has only quite slight changes under different DLs. We also tested the monotone translation (DL $= 0$) without reordering model (−Lex.-Reo.). The change on performance is still insignificant. So a pure monotone translation is enough for KJ and a reordering model helps little. The phenomenon is in agree to Ding et al. (2014b).

We have observed there are many brackets in the data of KJ translation task. The translations of brackets are not consistent in training data and PB SMT cannot handle bracket pairs well in decoding. We used a simple post-processing for bracket balancing according to the following steps.

1. Getting $1,000$-best list for each output[15];
2. Selecting the m-th candidate, where m is $\min(\arg\min_n |\#L_n - \#R_n|)$; $\#L_n$ and $\#R_n$ are counts of "(" and ")" in the n-th candidate;
3. Inserting untranslated source-side ")" to the selected candidate after the translated parts of its preceding character[16], when
   (a) its paired "(" on source side is translated to a "(" on target side;
   (b) it has no paired "(" on source side but follows numbers / alphabets.

The described brackets balancing brought a gain about $+0.2$ BLEU scores on devtest set, which is larger than the effect of DL and reordering models. We consider specific post-processing will improve KJ translation more.

The evaluation results of our submission are listed in Table 3 and Table 4. Our local evaluation on automatic measures had slight but not significant differences compared with the organizer's in cases. On JE translation, our baseline was a little lower than the organizer's baseline, as the experimental settings were not totally identical to the organizer's ones, we think the difference is acceptable. Both REV-REO and DEP-REO improved the baseline (ours) approximately one point on BLEU score, but REV-REO gave a larger improvement on RIBES. On KJ translation, the listed scores are all based on the `MeCab`'s analysis. Our baseline, i.e., a character-based one, outperformed the organizer's baseline more than one BLEU score and the bracket balancing still gave a further improvement around $+0.2$ BLEU scores.

As to the human evaluations, our approaches still have stable improvement. On JE translation, the DEP-REO has a more obvious improvement than REV-REO, although the BLEU scores of the two approaches are nearly the same. We consider the using of specific syntactic information in DEP-REO brings benefits in human evaluation. On KJ translation, the automatic and human evaluations have consistent results, that our character-based

[15] We used the *distinct* options of Moses, so there were less than $1,000$ candidates.

[16] based on the alignment information given by `Moses`.

baseline performs better than organizer's baseline and post-processing gives further improvement.

5 Discussion

From the evaluation results, we have observed that simple (or, naïve) approaches can give satisfactory improvement for a PB SMT baseline. We show examples of REV-REO and DEP-REO in Fig. 1 and Fig. 2, respectively. JE and KJ translation examples are shown in Table 5 and Fig. 3, respectively.

On JE translation, in our opinion, the REV-REO approach should be used as a new baseline in future, due to its simplicity and efficiency. The REV-REO only needs morphological analysis, which is needed after all for a general SMT task. As the Japanese topic marker *wa* is available across different POS systems[17], the REV-REO is actually an approach with strong ability of generalization[18].

On KJ translation, we illustrated character-based processing led to good performance due to the similarity of the two languages. Actually, our approach is more like a transliteration process rather than a translation process. Although an SMT system gives satisfactory performance on KJ translation, we would like to state several issues for KJ SMT in practice.

- Although the syntaxes are similar between Korean and Japanese, there are differences in collocations of verbs and postpositions (case markers)[19]. Specific process or stronger models are needed for correct translation if such a collocation is over a long-range.

- Negation is purely realized by suffixes[20] in Japanese, but can be realized by both suffixes[21] and prefixes[22] in Korean. So, reordering is needed when a Korean negative prefix is translated into Japanese, unless we have a translation table covering all the negation forms of all the verbs. Specific process is also needed for this phenomenon.

- Specific named entity recognition / translation modules are needed for correct translation of proper nouns.

6 Conclusion

We have described the translation systems of NICT team for JE and KJ translation task at WAT 2015). Although the approaches we used are very simple, their efficiency has been proved by the evaluation. We expect these techniques to be more widely applied in the community of Asian NLP.

References

David Chiang. 2007. Hierarchical phrase-based translation. *Computational Linguistics*, 33(2):201–228.

Adrià de Gispert, Gonzalo Iglesias, and Bill Byrne. 2015. Fast and accurate preordering for SMT using neural networks. In *Proc. of NAACL-HLT*, pages 1012–1017.

Chenchen Ding, Keisuke Sakaushi, Hirona Touji, and Mikio Yamamoto. 2014a. Dependency tree-based pre-reordering rules for statistical Japanese-to-English machine translation. In *Proc. of ANLP*, pages 963–966. (In Japanese).

Chenchen Ding, Masao Utiyama, Mitsuo Yoshida, and Mikio Yamamoto. 2014b. Model learning form parallel documents: Korean-japanese smt. In *Proc. of ANLP*, pages 820–823. (In Japanese).

Chenchen Ding, Keisuke Sakanushi, Hirona Touji, and Mikio Yamamoto. 2015. Inter-, intra-, and extra-chunk pre-reordering for statistical Japanese-to-English machine translation. *ACM Transactions on Asian Language Information Processing*, x(x):x. (Accepted, to appear).

Sho Hoshino, Yusuke Miyao, Katsuhito Sudoh, Katsuhiko Hayashi, and Masaaki Nagata. 2015. Discriminative preordering meets Kendall's Tau maximization. In *Proc. of ACL (Short Papers)*, pages 139–144.

Jason Katz-Brown and Michael Collins. 2008. Syntactic reordering in preprocessing for Japanese → English translation: MIT system description for NTCIR-7 patent translation task. In *Proc. of NTCIR*, pages 409–414.

Philipp Koehn, Franz Josef Och, and Daniel Marcu. 2003. Statistical phrase-based translation. In *Proc. of HTL-NAACL*, pages 48–54.

[17] Of course, the specific tag is different.

[18] We believe (although we have not done experiments) the REV-REO should work for Korean-to-English translation task as well because Korean has a topic marker *(n)eun* which is very similar to Japanese *wa*.

[19] Here are examples for some common verbs. Japanese *noru* and Korean *tada*, both have the meaning of *to ride*; *noru* requires a dative marker *ni* but *tada* requires an accusative marker *(r)eul* (the equivalent Japanese accusative marker is *wo*). Japanese *naru* and Korean *toeda*, both have the meaning of *to become*; *naru* requires a dative marker *ni* but *toeda* requires a nominative marker *i / ga* (the equivalent Japanese nominative marker is *ga*).

[20] Analyzed as auxiliary verbs, e.g., *nai*, *nu*, *mai*, etc.

[21] Analyzed as auxiliary verbs, e.g., *anta*, *anida*, etc.

[22] Analyzed as adverbs, e.g., *an* and *mot*.

[24] For convenience, we just use *kanji* here instead of *hanja*.

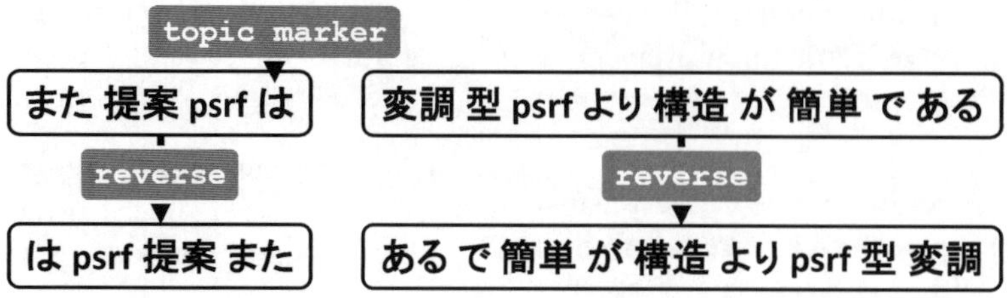

Figure 1: Example of REV-REO. The original Japanese sentence at the top is segmented after the topic marker and the morphemes within each segment are reversed.

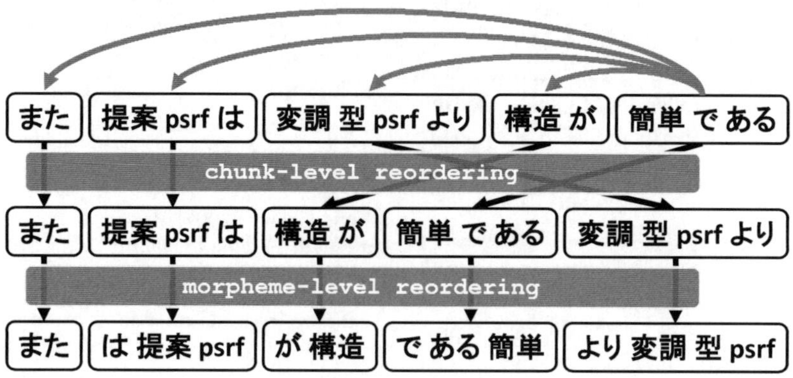

Figure 2: Example of DEP-REO. The original Japanese sentence at the top is reordered on both chunk- and morpheme-level based on its dependency structure.

BASELINE	*the proposed psrf psrf modulation type than the simple structure*
REV-REO	*the proposed psrf is simple structure than psrf modulation type*
DEP-REO	*the proposed psrf structure is simpler than psrf modulation type*
REFERENCE	*and , the proposed psrf has simpler structure than that of modulated psrf*

Table 5: JE translation examples. The inputs for BASELINE, REV-REO, and DEP-REO are the original Japanese sentence at the top of Fig. 1 (and Fig. 2), reordered Japanese sentence at the bottom of Fig. 1, and reordered sentence at the bottom of Fig. 2, respectively.

Figure 3: KJ translation example on a part of a Korean sentence. The gray blocks show the spaces used in Korean orthography. The characters[24] above hanguls show the Sino-Korean morphemes. The Japanese sentence at the bottom is the output by the character-level translation; the alignment between input and output is also shown. The output is nearly identical to the reference translation except an insignificantly redundant *tōten* (underlined).

Philipp Koehn, Hieu Hoang, Alexandra Birch, Chris Callison-Burch, Marcello Federico, Nicola Bertoldi, Brooke Cowan, Wade Shen, Christine Moran, Richard Zens, Chris Dyer, Ondrej Bojar, Alexandra Constantin, and Evan Herbst. 2007. Moses: Open source toolkit for statistical machine translation. In *Proc. of ACL*, pages 177–180.

Taku Kudo and Yuji Matsumoto. 2002. Japanese dependency analysis using cascaded chunking. In *Proc. of CoNLL*, pages 63–69.

Toshiaki Nakazawa, Hideya Mino, Isao Goto, Graham Neubig, Sadao Kurohashi, and Eiichiro Sumita. 2015. Overview of the 2nd workshop on Asian translation. In *Proc. of WAT*.

Graham Neubig. 2013. Travatar: A forest-to-string machine translation engine based on tree transducers. In *Proc. of ACL (Conference System Demonstrations)*, pages 91–96.

Graham Neubig. 2014. Forest-to-string SMT for Asian language translation: NAIST at WAT 2014. In *Proc. of WAT*, pages 20–25.

Andreas Stolcke. 2002. SRILM–an extensible language modeling toolkit. In *Proc. of ICSLP 2002*, pages 901–904.

Toshiba MT System Description for the WAT2015 Workshop

Satoshi Sonoh and Satoshi Kinoshita

Knowledge Media Laboratory, Corporate Research & Development Center,
Toshiba Corporation.
1, Komukai Toshiba-cho, Saiwai-ku, Kawasaki 212-8582, JAPAN
{satoshi.sonoo,satoshi.kinoshita}@toshiba.co.jp

Abstract

This paper provides the system description of Toshiba Machine Translation System for the 2nd Workshop on Asian Translation (WAT2015). We participated in all tasks that consist of "scientific papers subtask" and "patents subtask". We submitted statistically post edited translation (SPE) results based on our rule based translation system and SMT for each language pair. In addition, we submitted system combination results between SPE and SMT with a recurrent neural language model (RNNLM). In experimental results, the system combination achieved higher BLEU scores than single system with reranking. We also obtained improvements in Chinese translation in crowdsourcing evaluations.

1 Introduction

Recently, statistical machine translation (SMT) has been broadly developed and successfully used in the portion of practicable systems. However, it is costly to make a large volume of parallel corpora in a wide range of domains for commercial use. For this reason, we have developed rule based machine translation (RBMT) system using a monolingual corpus in the target language. For example, target word selection is possible based on co-occurrence relationship extracted from a monolingual corpus (Suzuki et al., 2005). Furthermore, we have developed a word sense disambiguation based on a monolingual corpus in the target domain, and it has been applied to Japanese-Korean and Korean-Japanese translation systems (Kumano 2013, Tanaka et al., 2014). On the other hand, open Asian parallel corpora including ASPEC [1], NTCIR PatentMT[2] and JPO Patent Corpus[3] are available for the research of machine translation systems. By using the parallel corpora, we have confirmed advantages which apply statistical post editing (SPE) to RBMT in domain adaptation (Suzuki, 2011).

In the last workshop (Nakazawa et al., 2014), we participated in Japanese-English and Japanese-Chinese tasks with SPE approach and obtained higher evaluation results than RBMT. Meanwhile, RBMT showed better performance than SPE in the direct and relative comparison (Sonoh et al., 2014). In this workshop (WAT2015), we participated in all tasks including Japanese-English (ja-en), English-Japanese (en-ja), Japanese-Chinese (ja-zh) and Chinese-Japanese (zh-ja) for "scientific paper subtask", and Chinese-Japanese (JPCzh-ja) and Korean-Japanese (JPCko-ja) for "patents subtask". Patents subtask is newly added, and its parallel corpus has 4 sections (Chemistry, Electricity, Mechanical Engineering and Physics).

In all the tasks, we submitted SPE translation results based on our RBMT and SMT. In addition, we submitted system combination results between SPE and SMT with recurrent neural language model (RNNLM; Mikolov el al., 2010).

Section 2 and 3 describe the overview of our systems and some pre/post processing. The experimental results and official results are shown in Section 4 and 5. The analysis for the official results is discussed in Section 6 and finally, Section 7 concludes this paper. As for a context-aware translation, the description was omitted because our baseline system is the same as the last workshop (see Sonoh et al., 2014).

---

[1] http://lotus.kuee.kyoto-u.ac.jp/ASPEC/
[2] http://research.nii.ac.jp/ntcir/permission/ntcir-10/perm-en-PatentMT.html
[3] http://lotus.kuee.kyoto-u.ac.jp/WAT/patent/

Proceedings of the 2nd Workshop on Asian Translation (WAT2015), pages 48-53,
Kyoto, Japan, 16th October 2015.

2 Overview of Toshiba System

2.1 RBMT System

Our RBMT system is basically a transfer-based machine translation (Izuha et al., 2008). The core framework consists of morphological analysis, syntactic/semantic analysis, target word selection, structural transfer, syntactic generation and morphological generation. Furthermore, huge amount of rules as translation knowledge including word dictionaries can realize both high translation performance and flexibility of customization. As for Japanese-Korean translation, syntactic analysis and transfer are omitted because the languages are grammatically similar.

2.2 Statistical Post Editing

SPE using phrase-based SMT has been proposed and it is an efficient framework which is able to adapt translation output to target domains (Michel et al., 2007).

We first translated source sentences of training data in ASPEC and JPO Patent Corpus by RBMT. Then we trained phrase-based model between translated sentences and reference sentences using Moses toolkit (Kohen et al., 2007). In the training, we used 1M sentences for ja-en, en-ja, JPCzh-ja and JPCko-ja, 0.67M for ja-zh and zh-ja in the training data. Japanese sentences were tokenized by JUMAN[4], and Moses tokenizer for English, and Kytea (Neubig et. al, 2011) for Chinese. We also trained 5-gram language models using KenLM (Heafield et al., 2013). In tuning and decoding, we set distortion limit to 0 for JPOko-ja in consideration of grammatical similarity and 6 for other language pairs.

2.3 System Combination using RNNLM

Although both SPE and SMT are based on a statistical model from the given corpora, they generate different translation candidates because SPE has some features from RBMT. If a better system can be selected from the candidates in each translation, we can get a better translation result.

Thus, we realized a system combination between SPE and SMT as n-best reranking using a RNNLM. The n-best reranking can be achieved using both basic features and RNNLM score. In tuning, we combined 100-best candidates of both SPE and SMT for dev-set, and ran MERT tuning by adding the RNNLM score to the basic features. In decoding, we re-ranked combined candidates by product-sum of the features including RNNLM score and tuned weights.

For ja-en, en-ja, ja-zh and zh-ja, we used RNNLMs trained by the first 500k sentences in the training data of ASPEC. For JPOzh-ja and JPOko-ja, we used 500k sentences which were evenly extracted from 4 sections in JPO Patent Corpus. All RNNLMs were trained with 500 hidden layers and 50 classes by RNNLM toolkit[5].

3 Tuning RBMT and pre/post-processing

3.1 Technical Term Dictionaries

As the preparation for each task, we selected technical term dictionaries by the same principle in the last workshop (Sonoh el al., 2014). For JPOzh-ja, we used an additional patent dictionary, which is extracted from JPO Chinese-Japanese dictionary[6]. Furthermore, for JPOko-ja, we used n-gram probability dictionary, which was made from monolingual patent resources, in order to resolve word sense disambiguation (Tanaka et al., 2014).

3.2 English Word Correction

To improve translation of sentences including misspelled words in English, we applied correction processing based on an edited distance. We replaced the word considered as misspelling with a word which had the smallest edited distance in the training data. However, because SMT and SPE basically have robustness to the misspelling, we confined words to be replaced to words which remain as unknown words in SMT and SPE results.

3.3 Japanese KATAKANA Normalization

In the case where a target language is Japanese; we applied normalization of KATAKANA notation. In advance of translation, we counted the frequency of KATAKANA notation, which has fluctuations of prolonged sound mark, in the

[4] http://nlp.ist.i.kyoto-u.ac.jp/index.php?JUMAN

[5] http://www.fit.vutbr.cz/~imikolov/rnnlm/

[6] https://alaginrc.nict.go.jp/resources/jpo-info/jpo-outline.html#jpo-dic-zh

Table 1: Overall BLEU and RIBES scores for "scientific papers subtask".

System	Rerank	ja-en		en-ja		ja-zh		zh-ja	
		BLEU	RIBES	BLEU	RIBES	BLEU	RIBES	BLEU	RIBES
RBMT	No	15.31	0.677	14.78	0.685	19.51	0.767	15.39	0.723
SMT	No	17.41	0.620	25.17	0.642	28.20	**0.810**	36.34	0.815
	Yes	17.85	0.619	25.37	0.643	28.46	0.809	36.69	0.815
SPE	No	22.65	0.717	31.10	0.767	29.48	0.809	35.76	0.822
	Yes	22.92	**0.718**	31.73	**0.770**	29.49	0.809	36.06	0.823
COMB	Yes	**23.00**	0.716	**31.82**	**0.770**	**29.60**	**0.810**	**37.47**	**0.827**

Table 2: Overall BLEU and RIBES scores for "patents subtask".

System	Rerank	JPOzh-ja		JPOko-ja	
		BLEU	RIBES	BLEU	RIBES
RBMT	No	25.81	0.764	51.28	0.902
SMT	No	38.77	0.802	70.17	0.943
	Yes	39.18	0.805	**70.89**	**0.944**
SPE	No	39.01	**0.813**	68.47	0.940
	Yes	39.30	0.811	68.76	0.940
COMB	Yes	**40.23**	**0.813**	70.40	0.942

target sentences of the training data. In the translation results, KATAKANA fluctuations were replaced with those of highly-frequent notations, such as "from スクリュ to スクリュー" and "from サーバー to サーバ". By applying normalization, we got improvements of about 0.5 BLEU in RBMT.

Furthermore, we replaced the ideographic comma "、" in number expression with a normal comma "," for translation results in Japanese.

3.4 Other Post Processing

In order to reduce unknown words in SMT, we applied RBMT to SMT results. For example, in ja-zh, we translated KATAKANA words, which remain in SMT results, into Chinese or English words, if the words were found in RBMT dictionaries. Also, Hangul words in SMT results of JPOko-ja were translated into Japanese words.

4 Experimental Results

This section shows experimental results of our translation systems.

Table 1 and 2 show the overall BLEU and RIBES scores for "scientific papers subtask" and "patents subtask", respectively. COMB means results of the system combination and Rerank means results of reranking using RNNLM (100-best for SMT and SPE, 200-best for COMB). In all tasks, SPE improves translation results of RBMT on the BLEU and RIBES. In tasks except JPOko-ja, SPE achieves performance equal to or better than phrase-based SMT.

Moreover, in most tasks, Rerank improves about 0.3-0.5 BLEU score, and COMB shows better performance than other systems. In JPOko-ja, SMT, SPE and COMB show very high performances which are close to 70 BLEU, and SMT with reranking achieves the highest BLEU and RIBES scores. In ja-en, en-ja, ja-zh and zh-ja, more than half of translations selected from SPE and the others selected from SMT. In particular SPE accounted for about 80% translations in ja-en, en-ja and zh-ja. On the other hand, more than half of translations selected from SMT in JPOzh-ja and JPOko-ja. Table 3 shows the translation examples that COMB achieves better results than SPE with reranking in sentence-level BLEU.

Finally, we compared between phrase-based model and hierarchical phrase-based model. Table 4 shows comparison in ja-zh task. In all systems including SPE, hierarchical phrase-based model improves about 0.4 BLEU. We applied hierarchical phrase-based model to ja-zh only, because significant improvements were not confirmed in other language pairs.

Table 3: Translation examples indicating that COMB achieves better results than SPE in sentece-level BLEU.

ja-en	SRC	揺動時に比べて，発電量は40倍である。
	REF	In comparison with the fluctuation, the electric power generation is the 40 twice.
	SPE	Compared with the time of rocking, production of electricity is 40 times.
	COMB	Compared with the time of fluctuations, the electric power generation is 40 times.
en-ja	SRC	SiO2 films showed excellent performance even at 430℃ or less, and the memory effect of Si dot MOS capacitor was confirmed.
	REF	SiO2膜は，430℃以下でも優れた性能を示し，SiドットMOSコンデンサのメモリ効果を確認した。
	SPE	SiO2膜は430℃でも優れた性能を示す以下であり，SiドットMOSキャパシタの記憶効果が確認された。
	COMB	SiO2膜は430℃でも優れた性能を示し，以下，SiドットMOSキャパシタの記憶効果を確認した。
ja-zh	SRC	この擾乱からの回復についても考察した。
	REF	对这种干扰的恢复也进行了考察。
	SPE	考察了从该干扰恢复。
	COMB	在这种干扰的恢复也进行了考察。
zh-ja	SRC	还对在完成来所登记之前的各个环节进行了介绍。
	REF	来所登録が完了するまでの流れ等も紹介した。
	SPE	登録の完了までの各段階について紹介した。
	COMB	登録が完了するまでの各段階について紹介した。
JPO zh-ja	SRC	在固体中加入 BHT，混合物在丙酮中溶解。
	REF	BHTを固体に加え、混合物をアセトンに溶解する。
	SPE	固体BHTを加え、この混合物は、アセトンに溶解した。
	COMB	固体BHTを加え、混合物をアセトンに溶解した。
JPO ko-ja	SRC	원재료 필름(1)에서의 비접합부의 적어도 일부를 덮도록 배치되어도 좋다.
	REF	原反フィルム1における非接合部の少なくとも一部を覆うように配置されてもよい 。
	SPE	原反フィルム1での非接合部の少なくとも一部を覆うように配置されてもよい。
	COMB	原反フィルム1における非接合部の少なくとも一部を覆うように配置されてもよい。

Table 4: A Comparison of Phrase-based Model.

System	hierarchical	ja-zh	
		BLEU	RIBES
SMT	No	28.46	0.809
	Yes	29.82	0.810
SPE	No	29.49	0.809
	Yes	29.89	0.809
COMB	No	29.60	0.810
	Yes	**30.07**	**0.817**

5 Official Results

This section shows official results of our translation systems.

We basically submitted two results, one is SPE[7] and the other is the system combination between SPE and SMT. Furthermore, top two systems on the BLEU scores were evaluated by the crowdsourcing. In the crowdsourcing evaluation, pair-wise evaluation against the baseline system (phrase-based SMT) was performed by 5 evaluators, and HUMAN score was calculated

[7] In JPOko-ja, because SMT showed higher BLEU score than SPE, we submitted SMT result.

Table 5: Overall official results for "scientific papers subtask". B, R and H mean BLEU, RIBES, HUMAN, respectively. HUMAN was evaluated by 5 evaluators using crowdsorcing.

System	ja-en			en-ja			ja-zh			zh-ja		
	B	R	H	B	R	H	B	R	H	B	R	H
SPE	22.89	0.719	**25.00**	32.06	0.771	40.25	30.17	0.813	2.50	35.85	0.825	-1.00
COMB	23.00	0.716	21.25	31.82	0.770	-	30.07	0.817	**17.00**	37.47	0.827	**18.00**

Table 6: Overall official results for "patents subtask".

System	JPOzh-ja			JPOko-ja		
	B	R	H	B	R	H
SMT	-	-	-	71.01	0.944	4.50
SPE	41.12	0.822	**24.25**	-	-	-
COMB	41.82	0.821	14.50	70.51	0.942	3.00

based on majority voting (Nakazawa et al., 2014).

In WAT2015 results (Nakazawa et al., 2015), we note that Toshiba systems were ranked as one of the top three systems in human evaluation in ja-en, ja-zh and JPOzh-ja. Especially, ja-zh achieved the highest score although the BLEU score is lower than other systems. On the other hand, as for JPOko-ja, we got a comparatively high BLEU score, but were disappointed by its low HUMAN score.

Table 5 and 6 are the overall official results for each task, respectively. In ja-zh and zh-ja, COMB shows higher HUMAN score than SPE. On the other hand, SPE or SMT is higher than COMB in ja-en, JPOzh-ja and JPOko-ja. These results indicate that the system combination improves human evaluation of Chinese translation in the scientific documents, at least. We guess that the system combination between equivalent systems achieves complementary translation to improve human evaluations. For example, BLEU scores of SPE and SMT are nearly equal in ja-zh and zh-ja (shown in Table 1).

6 Discussion

On receiving the crowdsourcing results, we analyzed differences between our system and Online A, which obtained the highest HUMAN score in JPOko-ja. Table 7 shows the comparison between our system (COMB) and Online A. Here, 'Baseline' column is the HUMAN score in the result of crowdsourcing (official results) and the other was evaluated by inner evaluators. The inner evaluation was conducted excluding expressional differences as described in detail below. Although Online A achieves a very high HUMAN score to the baseline system, superior results of COMB over Online A are shown in the pair-wise evaluation.

We hypothesize that the significant difference between the crowdsourcing and the inner evaluators occurs from the evaluation of the number expressions, such as "システム(100)" and "システム 100". In the training data of JPOko-ja, a lot of brackets of numbers in the source sentences disappear in the target sentences. Thus, brackets are dropped in SPE and SMT. As for well-translated target sentences such as JPOko-ja, it is possible that evaluators in the crowdsourcing judged faithful translation as better by focusing on existence of brackets.

Table 7: The relationship between automatic evaluations and human evaluations.

	BLEU	RIBES	HUMAN		
			Baseline	COMB	Online A
COMB	70.51	0.94	3.00	-	10.75
Online A	55.05	0.91	38.75	-10.75	-

7 Conclusion

The overview of Toshiba machine translation systems, which applied the statistical post editing and the system combination with RNNLM, is described in this paper.

SPE and reranking with RNNLM achieved higher BLEU than phrase-based SMT in most language pairs. Furthermore, the system combination between SPE and SMT improved BLEU score in Japanese-English pair and Japanese-Chinese pair. In the other hand, a straightforward correlation between automatic evaluation and human evaluation is not confirmed in our system. We need to establish the combination of multi-systems for practical use purpose, taking advantage of their characteristics and qualities.

Reference

Hirokazu Suzuki and Akira Kumano. 2005. Learning Translations from Monolingual Corpora. In *Proc. of MT Summit X.*Akira Kumano. 2013. Korean Translation System for Patent Documents. In *Japio YEAR BOOK 2013*, pages 298-301. (In Japanese)

Hiroyuki Tanaka, Satoshi Sonoh, Satoshi Kinoshita and Satoshi Kamatani. 2014. Improvement of Korean machine translation using statistical word selection. In *Proc. of the 3rd Symposium on Patent Information Processing*, pages 97-100. (In Japanese)

Hirokazu Suzuki. 2011. Automatic Post-Editing based on SMT and its selective application by Sentence-Level Automatic Quality Evaluation. In *Proc. of MT Summit XIII.*

Toshiaki Nakazawa, Hideya Mino, Isao Goto, Sadao Kurohashi and Eiichiro Sumita. 2014. Overview of the 1st Workshop on Asian Translation. In *Proc. of the 1st Workshop on Asian Translation (WAT2014).*

Satoshi Sonoh, Satoshi Kinoshita, Hiroyuki Tanaka and Satoshi Kamatani. 2014. Toshiba MT System Description for the WAT2014 Workshop. In *Proc. of the 1st Workshop on Asian Translation (WAT2014).*

Tomas Mikolov, Martin Karafiat, Lukas Burget, Jan Cernocky, and Sanjeev Khudanpur. 2010. Recurrent neural network based language model. In *Proc. of INTERSPEECH 2010* pages 1045–1048.

Tatsuya Izuha, Akira Kumano and Yuka Kuroda. 2008. Toshiba Rule-Based Translation System at NTCIR-7 PAT MT. In *Proc. of NTCIR-7 Workshop Meeting*, pages 430-434.

Michel Simard, Cyril Goutte and Pierre Isabell. 2007. Statistical Phrase-based Post-editing. In *Proc. of NAACL HLT 2007, ACL,* pages 508-515.

Philipp Kohen, Marcell Federuci, Brooke Cowan, Richard Zens, Chris Dyer, Ondrej Bojar Alexandra Constantin and Evan Herbst. 2007. Moses: Open Source Toolkit for Statistical Machine Translation. In *Proc. of the ACL,* pages 177-180.

Graham Neubig, Yosuke Nakata and Shinsuke Mori. 2011. Pointwise Prediction for Robust, Adaptable Japanese Morphological Analysis. In *Proc. of ACL-HLT.*

Kenneth Heafield, Ivan Pouzyrevsky, Jonathan H. Clark, and Philipp Koehn. 2013. Scalable modified Kneser-Ney language model estimation. In *Proc. of the ACL*, pages 690–696.

Toshiaki Nakazawa, Hideya Mino, Isao Goto, Graham Neubig, Sadao Kurohashi and Eiichiro Sumita. 2015. Overview of the 2nd Workshop on Asian Translation. In *Proc. of the 2nd Workshop on Asian Translation (WAT2015).*

KyotoEBMT System Description for the 2nd Workshop on Asian Translation

John Richardson[†] **Raj Dabre**[†] **Chenhui Chu**[‡]
Fabien Cromières[‡] **Toshiaki Nakazawa**[‡] **Sadao Kurohashi**[†]
[†]Graduate School of Informatics, Kyoto University, Kyoto 606-8501
[‡]Japan Science and Technology Agency, Kawaguchi-shi, Saitama 332-0012
{john, dabre}@nlp.ist.i.kyoto-u.ac.jp, {fabien, nakazawa, chu}@pa.jst.jp,
kuro@i.kyoto-u.ac.jp

Abstract

This paper introduces the KyotoEBMT example-based machine translation framework. Since last year's workshop we have replaced input trees with forests, improved alignment, added new features, and introduced bilingual neural network reranking. The major benefits of our system include online example retrieval and flexible reordering. We also use syntactic dependency analysis for both source and target languages in the hope of learning how to translate non-local structure. The system implementation (this paper refers to version 1.0) is available as open-source.

1 Introduction

This paper describes the KyotoEBMT system used in the 2nd Workshop on Asian Translation (Nakazawa et. al, 2015).

Our system is a fully-fledged Example-Based Machine Translation (EBMT) platform making use of both source-language and target-language dependency structure. This approach has been explored comparatively less in studies on syntax-based SMT/EBMT, which tend to focus on constituent trees rather than dependency trees, and on tree-to-string rather than tree-to-tree approaches. Furthermore, we employ separate dependency parsers for each language rather than projecting the dependencies from one language to another, as in (Quirk et. al, 2005).

The dependency structure information is used end-to-end: for improving the quality of the alignment of the translation examples, for constraining the translation rule extraction and for guiding the decoding. We believe that dependency structure, which considers more than just local context, is important in order to generate fluent and accurate translations of complex sentences across distant language pairs.

The experiments described in this paper focus on technical domain translation for Japanese-Chinese and Japanese-English, however our implementation is applicable to any domain and language pair for which there exist parallel sentences and dependency parsers.

A further unique characteristic of our system is that, again contrary to the majority of similar systems, it does not rely on precomputation of translation rules. Instead it matches each input sentence to the full database of translation examples before extracting translation rules online. This has the merit of maximizing the information available when creating and combining translation rules, while retaining the ability to produce excellent translations for input sentences similar to an existing translation example.

The system is mostly developed in C++ and is available as open source. The code and documentation are available from http://nlp.ist.i.kyoto-u.ac.jp/kyotoebmt/. Experiments are facilitated through the inclusion of an end-to-end experiment management system (EMS) which has been greatly improved in this version. The framework is simple to use and supports model training with multiple threads or across a cluster.

2 System Overview

Figure 1 shows the basic structure of the KyotoEBMT translation pipeline.

The training process begins with parsing and aligning parallel sentences from the training corpus. The alignments are then used to build an example database ('translation mem-

Proceedings of the 2nd Workshop on Asian Translation (WAT2015), pages 54-60,
Kyoto, Japan, 16th October 2015.

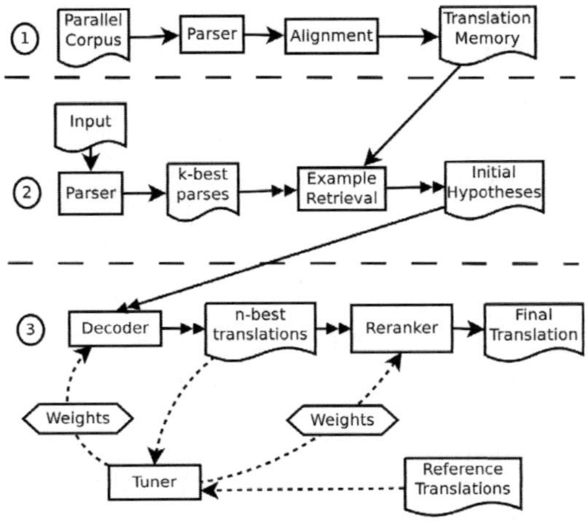

Figure 1: The translation pipeline can be roughly divided in 3 steps. Step 1 is the creation of the example database, trained from a parallel corpus. Step 2 is the parsing of an input sentence and the generation of sets of initial hypotheses. Step 3 consists in decoding and reranking. The tuning of the weights for decoding and reranking is done by a modified version of step 3.

ory') containing 'examples' or 'treelets' that form the hypotheses to be combined during decoding.

Translation is performed by first parsing an input sentence then searching for treelets matching entries in the example database. The retrieved treelets are combined by a lattice-based decoder that optimizes a log linear model score. Finally, we use a reranker to select the optimal translation from the n-best list provided by the decoder using additional non-local features (see section 3.4).

Figure 2 shows the process of combining examples matching the input tree to create an output sentence.

2.1 Example retrieval and translation hypothesis construction

An important characteristic of our system is that we do not extract and store translation rules in advance: the alignment of translation examples is performed offline. However, for a given input sentence i, the steps for finding examples partially matching i and extracting their translation hypotheses is an online process. This approach could be considered to be more faithful to the original EBMT approach advocated by Nagao (1984). It has already been proposed for phrase-based (Callison-Burch et al., 2005), hierarchical (Lopez, 2007), and syntax-based (Cromières and Kurohashi, 2011) systems. It does not however, seem to be very commonly integrated in syntax-based MT.

This approach has several benefits. The first is that we are not required to impose a limit on the size of translation hypotheses. Systems extracting rules in advance typically restrict the size and number of extracted rules for fear of becoming unmanageable. In particular, if an input sentence is the same or very similar to one of our translation examples, we will be able to retrieve a perfect translation. A second advantage is that we can make use of the full context of the example to assign features and scores to each translation hypothesis.

The main drawback of our approach is that it can be computationally more expensive to retrieve arbitrarily large matchings in the example database online than it is to match precomputed rules. We use the techniques described in Cromières and Kurohashi (2011) to perform this step as efficiently as possible.

Once we have found an example translation (s, t) for which s partially matches i, we proceed to extract a translation hypothesis from it. A translation hypothesis is defined as a generic translation rule for a part p of the input sentence that is represented as a target-language treelet, with non-terminals representing the insertion positions for the translations of other parts of the sentence. A translation hypothesis is created from a translation example as follows:

1. We project the part of s that is matched into the target side t using the alignment of s and t. This is trivial if each word of s and t is aligned, but this is not typically the case. Therefore our translation hypotheses will often have some target words/nodes marked as *optionals*: this means that we will decide if they should be added to the final translation only at the moment of combination.

2. We insert the non-terminals as child nodes of the projected subtree. This is

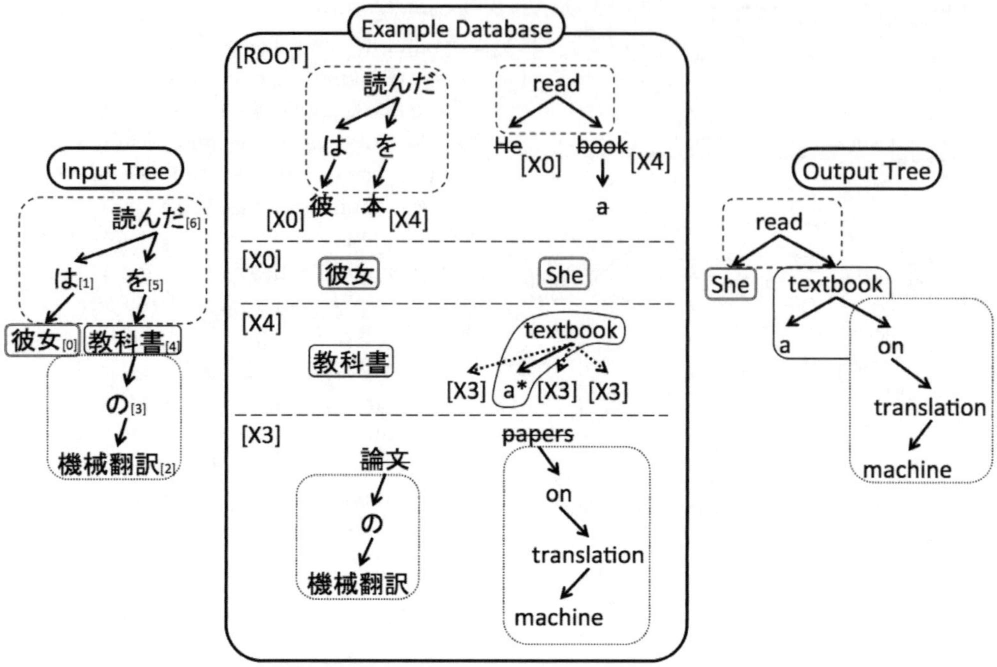

Figure 2: The process of translation. The source sentence is parsed and matching subtrees from the example database are retrieved. From the examples, we extract translation hypotheses than can contain optional target words and several position for each non-terminals. For example the translation hypothesis containing "textbook" has three possible position for the non-terminal X3 (as a left-child before "a", as a left-child after "a" or as a right-child). The translation hypotheses are then combined during decoding. Choice of optional words and final non-terminal positions is also done during decoding.

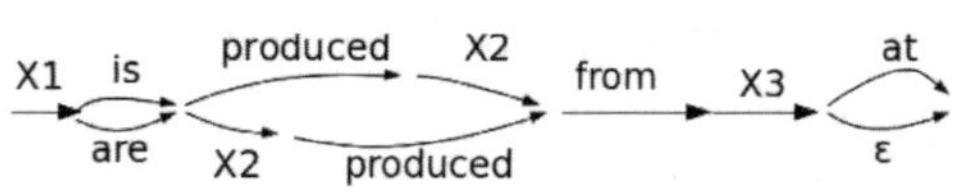

Figure 3: A translation hypothesis endoded as a lattice. This representation allows us to handle efficiently the ambiguities of our translation rules. Note that each path in this lattice corresponds to different choices of insertion position for X2, morphological forms of "be", and the optional insertion of "at".

simple if i, s and t have the same structure and are perfectly aligned, but again this is not typically the case. A consequence is that we will sometimes have *several possible insertion positions* for each non-terminal. The choice of insertion position is again made during combination.

2.2 Decoding

After having extracted translation hypotheses for as many parts of the input tree as possible, we need to decide how to select and combine them. Our approach here is similar to what has been proposed for Corpus-Based Machine Translation. We first choose a number of features and create a linear model scoring each possible combination of hypotheses (see Section 3.3). We then attempt to find the combination that maximizes this model score.

The combination of rules is constrained by the structure of the input dependency tree. If we only consider local features[1], then a simple bottom-up dynamic programming approach can efficiently find the optimal combination with linear $O(|\mathcal{H}|)$ complexity[2]. However, non-local features (such as language models)

[1] The score of a combination will be the sum of the local scores of each translation hypothesis.

[2] $\mathcal{H}$ = set of translation hypotheses

will force us to prune the search space. This pruning is done efficiently through a variation of cube-pruning (Chiang, 2007). We use KenLM[3] (Heafield, 2011) for computing the target language model score. Decoding is made more efficient by using some of the more advanced features of KenLM such as state-reduction ((Li and Khudanpur, 2008), (Heafield et al., 2011)) and rest-cost estimations(Heafield et al., 2012).

Compared with the original cube-pruning algorithm, our decoder is designed to handle an arbitrary number of non-terminals. In addition, as we have seen in Section 2.1, the translation hypotheses we initially extract from examples are ambiguous in term of which target word is going to be used and which will be the final position of each non-terminal. In order to handle such ambiguities, we use a lattice-based internal representation that can encode them efficiently (see Figure 3). This lattice representation also allows the decoder to make choices between various morphological variations of a word (e.g. be/is/are). We use the decoding algorithm described in (Cromières and Kurohashi, 2014).

3 Improvements from WAT2014

3.1 Alignment

Based on the findings of Neubig and Duh (2014), we experimented with supervised alignment using Nile (Riesa et al., 2011) as part of our translation framework. We found that using supervised alignments made a considerable improvement to translation quality. Since Nile supports only constituency parses, we also perform constituency parsing for source and target languages for generating bidirectional word alignments.

For the initial alignments for Nile, we use the alignments generated from the model described in last year's system description (Richardson et al., 2014), which makes use of our dependency parses in order to capture non-local reorderings.

3.2 Forest Input

We found that the quality of the source-side dependency parsing had an important impact on translation quality. Unfortunately, parsing errors are unavoidable. Chinese parsing is maybe especially challenging and our Chinese parser still produces a significant number of parsing errors. In order to mitigate this problem, last year we used a k-best list of input parses. We found this was somewhat successful but inefficient, and therefore have moved from a k-best list representation of multiple parses to a more compact and efficient forest representation.

In the future, we will consider also using forests for all the translation examples (and not just the input sentence).

3.3 Features

During decoding we use a linear model to score each possible combination of hypotheses. This linear model is based on a linear combination of both local features (local to each translation hypothesis) and non-local features (such as a 5-gram language model score of the final translation). Despite our already relatively large set of dense features, we found there were a number of cases where these features were not enough to differentiate between good and bad translation hypotheses.

This year we have added ten new features, now reaching a total of 52, a selection of which are shown below:

- Forest parse scores
- Number of content/function words aligned to content/function words
- Number of times a subtree is inserted in a position (left or right of parent) that is not the most common in the training data
- Number of examples sharing the same information used to create an initial hypothesis
- Similarity between source and input word embeddings (Mikolov et al., 2013)

The optimal weights for each feature are as before estimated using the implementation of k-best batch MIRA (Cherry and Foster, 2012) included in Moses.

[3]http://kheafield.com/code/kenlm/

3.4 Reranking

A final reranking step allows us to use more advanced features for selecting the best translations. We reranked the n-best output of our system using several additional language models: a standard 7-gram language model with Modified Kneser-Ney smoothing, a Recurrent Neural Network Language Model (RNNLM) (Mikolov et. al, 2010) and several variations of a Bilingual Recurrent Neural Network Language Model.

The RNNLM model was trained with hidden layer size 200, and 5000 sentences from the training fold were used as validation data.

For the bilingual language model, we used the Neural Machine Translation Model of (Bahdanau et. al, 2014) which has an open source implementation in the GroundHog/Theano framework[4]. For each language pair we trained two models, one for each translation direction. In addition, for Japanese and Chinese, we considered two types of segmentation: the segmentation produced by our morphological analyzer, and a character-level segmentation. We had therefore up to four models per language pair. Rescoring our translations with these models gave up to four additional features. It is interesting to note that although trying to directly translate our input sentences using these neural MT models typically resulted in a comparatively low BLEU score, they turned out to be useful for reranking in our system. This is probably due to the fact that, since they represent a very different approach to translation, the models tend to learn different aspects of the translation and make different mistakes to our system. Using a character-based segmentation further ensured the neural models learned a different kind of information. The models took two to four days each to train on a GPU. The settings we used were mostly the defaults of the implementations[5].

Reranking was conducted by first calculating the various language model scores for each translation in the n-best list. These features were added to those used in the first round of tuning, then one final iteration of tuning was run. The tuning algorithm and settings were the same as for standard tuning. This retuning step was added in order to find an optimal combination of the additional features with related features such as sentence length and the score given by the 5-gram language model used inside the decoder.

4 Experiments

We conducted translation experiments on the four language pairs in the scientific papers subtask: Japanese-English (JA–EN), English-Japanese (EN–JA), Japanese-Chinese (JA–ZH) and Chinese-Japanese (ZH–JA).

The proposed system used the following dependency parsers and show below their approximate parsing accuracies (micro-average), which were evaluated by hand on a random subset of sentences from the test data. The parsers were trained on domains different to those used in the experiments.

- English: NLParser[6] (92%) (Charniak and Johnson, 2005)
- Japanese: KNP (96%) (Kawahara and Kurohashi, 2006)
- Chinese: SKP (88%) (Shen et al., 2012)

For generating input for Nile we used the following constituency parsers:

- English: Berkeley Parser (Petrov et al., 2006)
- Japanese: Cyklark (Oda et al., 2015)
- Chinese: Berkeley Parser (Petrov et al., 2006)

Forests were created by packing the 200-best dependency parses for Japanese and English, and 50-best parses for Chinese.

4.1 Results

Table 1 shows the results of our proposed system (WAT15) and a comparison with the system from last year (WAT14) (Richardson

[4]https://github.com/lisa-groundhog/GroundHog

[5]More precisely, the hidden layer size was 1000. Training done with a minibatch size of 64 and the adadelta algorithm (rho = 0.95, eps = 1e-6). Vocabulary size was reduced to 20,000 for the word-segmented model. Backpropagation through time number of steps increased to up to 100 for the character-based models.

[6]Converted to dependency parses with in-house tool.

Language Pair	System	BLEU	RIBES	HUMAN
JA–EN	Baseline	18.45	64.51	n/a
	WAT15	21.31	70.65	16.50
	WAT15+Rerank	**22.89**	**72.46**	**32.50**
	WAT14	20.60	70.12	(21.50)
	WAT14+Rerank	21.07	69.90	(25.00)
EN–JA	Baseline	27.48	68.37	n/a
	WAT15	30.69	76.78	40.50
	WAT15+Rerank	**33.06**	**78.95**	**51.00**
	WAT14	29.76	75.21	(33.75)
	WAT14+Rerank	31.09	75.96	(38.00)
JA–ZH	Baseline	27.96	78.90	n/a
	WAT15	29.99	80.71	**16.00**
	WAT15+Rerank	**31.40**	**82.70**	12.50
	WAT14	27.21	79.13	(-0.75)
	WAT14+Rerank	27.67	78.83	(-8.75)
ZH–JA	Baseline	34.65	77.25	n/a
	WAT15	36.30	81.97	16.75
	WAT15+Rerank	**38.53**	**84.07**	**18.50**
	WAT14	33.57	80.10	(6.00)
	WAT14+Rerank	34.75	80.26	(7.50)

Table 1: Official evaluation results for BLEU/RIBES/HUMAN. *(NB: Human evaluation scores of WAT2014 and WAT2015 are not comparable.)*

et al., 2014) and official baseline (phrase-based SMT, for details see Nakazawa et al. (2015)). We give results for evaluation on the test set after tuning (WAT15, WAT14) and tuning plus reranking (WAT15+Rerank, WAT14+Rerank). Tuning was conducted over 10 iterations on the development set using an n-best list of length 500, and we used the 1000-best for reranking.

WAT15+Rerank was the strongest system in our comparison, outperforming the official baseline, non-reranked system (WAT15) and last year's systems in all metrics for all languages, with the minor exception of JA–ZH human evaluation for reranked vs. non-reranked.

5 Conclusion

In this paper we have described the latest version of the KyotoEBMT example-based translation system. Since last year we have improved alignment, introduced forest input, added new features and used bilingual neural network features in reranking.

In our preparation for this workshop we have focused mainly on improving Japanese–Chinese and Chinese–Japanese translation, particularly in terms of dealing with poor quality Chinese dependency parses. As future work we plan to perform more extensive error analysis on the other language pairs. We also found that despite using forest input there are still many issues caused by incorrect parsing and will consider in the future how best to overcome this.

References

Dzmitry Bahdanau, Kyunghyun Cho and Yoshua Bengio. 2014. Neural machine translation by jointly learning to align and translate. In *arXiv preprint arXiv:1409.0473.* .

Chris Callison-Burch, Colin Bannard, and Josh Schroeder. 2005. Scaling phrase-based statistical machine translation to larger corpora and longer phrases. In *Proceedings of the 43rd Annual Meeting on Association for Computational Linguistics*, pages 255–262. Association for Computational Linguistics, 2005.

Eugene Charniak and Mark Johnson. 2005. Coarse-to-Fine n-Best Parsing and MaxEnt Discriminative Reranking. In *Proceedings of the 43rd Annual Meeting of the Association for Computational Linguistics, ACL 2005.*

Colin Cherry and George Foster. 2012. Batch Tuning Strategies for Statistical Machine Translation. In *HLT-NAACL*, 2012.

David Chiang. 2007. Hierarchical phrase-based translation. In *Computational Linguistics.*

Fabien Cromières and Sadao Kurohashi. 2011. Efficient retrieval of tree translation examples for syntax-based machine translation. In *Proceedings of the 2011 Conference on Empirical Methods in Natural Language Processing.*

Fabien Cromières and Sadao Kurohashi. 2014. Translation Rules with Right-Hand Side Lattices. In *Proceedings of EMNLP 2014*

Isao Goto, Ka Po Chow, Bin Lu, Eiichiro Sumita and Benjamin Tsou. 2013. Overview of the Patent Machine Translation Task at the NTCIR-10 Workshop. In *Proceedings of the 10th NTCIR Workshop Meeting on Evaluation of Information Access Technologies (NTCIR-10).*

Kenneth Heafield. 2011. KenLM: faster and smaller language model queries. In *Proceedings of the EMNLP 2011 Sixth Workshop on Statistical Machine Translation*, 2011.

Kenneth Heafield, Hieu Hoang, Philipp Koehn, Tetsuo Kiso, and Marcello Federico. 2011. Left language model state for syntactic machine translation. In *Proceedings of the International Workshop on Spoken Language Translation*, 2011.

Kenneth Heafield, Philipp Koehn, and Alon Lavie. 2012. Language model rest costs and space-efficient storage. In *Proceedings of the Joint Conference on Empirical Methods in Natural Language Processing and Computational Natural Language Learning*, 2012.

Daisuke Kawahara and Sadao Kurohashi. 2006. A Fully-Lexicalized Probabilistic Model for Japanese Syntactic and Case Structure Analysis. In *Proceedings of the Human Language Technology Conference of the NAACL.*

Zhifei Li and Sanjeev Khudanpur. 2008. A scalable decoder for parsing-based machine translation with equivalent language model state maintenance. In *Proceedings of the Second Workshop on Syntax and Structure in Statistical Translation.* Association for Computational Linguistics, 2008.

Adam Lopez. 2007. Hierarchical phrase-based translation with suffix arrays. In *EMNLP-CoNLL*, 2007.

Tomas Mikolov, Martin Karafiat, Lukas Burget, Jan Cernocky and Sanjeev Khudanpur. 2010. Recurrent Neural Network Based Language Model. In *Proceedings of the 11th Annual Conference of the International Speech Communication Association*, 2010.

Tomas Mikolov, Kai Chen, Greg Corrado, and Jeffrey Dean. 2013. Efficient Estimation of Word Representations in Vector Space. In *Proceedings of Workshop at ICLR, 2013.*

Toshiaki Nakazawa, Hideya Mino, Isao Goto, Graham Neubig, Sadao Kurohashi and Eiichiro Sumita. 2015. Overview of the 2nd Workshop on Asian Translation. In *Proceedings of the 2nd Workshop on Asian Translation (WAT2015).*

Makoto Nagao. 1984. A framework of a mechanical translation between Japanese and English by analogy principle. In *A. Elithorn and R. Banerji. Artificial and Human Intelligence.*

Toshiaki Nakazawa and Sadao Kurohashi. 2012. Alignment by bilingual generation and monolingual derivation. In *Proceedings of COLING 2012.*

Graham Neubig and Kevin Duh. 2014. On the Elements of an Accurate Tree-to-String Machine Translation System. In *The 52nd Annual Meeting of the Association for Computational Linguistics (ACL).*

Yusuke Oda, Graham Neubig, Sakriani Sakti, Tomoki Toda, and Satoshi Nakamura. 2015. Ckylark: A More Robust PCFG-LA Parser. In *Proceedings of NAACL 2015: Demo Track.*

Slav Petrov, Leon Barrett, Romain Thibaux and Dan Klein. 2006. Learning Accurate, Compact, and Interpretable Tree Annotation. In *Proceedings of COLING-ACL 2006.*

Chris Quirk, Arul Menezes, and Colin Cherry. 2005. Dependency Treelet Translation: Syntactically Informed Phrasal SMT. In *Proceedings of the 43rd Annual Meeting on Association for Computational Linguistics.* Association for Computational Linguistics, 2005.

John Richardson, Fabien Cromières, Toshiaki Nakazawa, Sadao Kurohashi. 2014. KyotoEBMT System Description for the 1st Workshop on Asian Translation. In *Proceedings of the 1st Workshop on Asian Translation.*

Jason Riesa, Ann Irvine, and Daniel Marcu. 2011. Feature-Rich Language-Independent Syntax-Based Alignment for Statistical Machine Translation. In *Proceedings of EMNLP 2011.*

Mo Shen, Daisuke Kawahara and Sadao Kurohashi. 2012. A Reranking Approach for Dependency Parsing with Variable-sized Subtree Features. In *Proceedings of 26th Pacific Asia Conference on Language Information and Computing.*

Evaluating Neural Machine Translation in English-Japanese Task

Zhongyuan Zhu
Weblio Inc.
chugen.shu@weblio.co.jp

Abstract

In this paper, we evaluate Neural Machine Translation (NMT) models in English-Japanese translation task. Various network architectures with different recurrent units are tested. Additionally, we examine the effect of using pre-reordered data for the training. Our experiments show that even simple NMT models can produce better translations compared with all SMT baselines. For NMT models, recovering unknown words is another key to obtaining good translations. We describe a simple workaround to find missing translations with a back-off system. To our surprise, performing pre-reordering on the training data hurts the model performance. Finally, we provide a qualitative analysis demonstrates a specific error pattern in NMT translations which omits some information and thus fail to preserve the complete meaning.

1 Introduction

In the last two decades, Statistical Machine Translation (SMT) with log-linear models in the core has shown promising results in the field. However, as stated in (Duh and Kirchhoff, 2008), log-linear models may suffer from the underfitting problem and thus give poor performance. While for recurrent neural networks (RNNs), as demonstrated in (Mikolov et al., 2010), they brought significant improvement in Natural Language Processing tasks. In their research, RNNs are shown to be capable of giving more prediction power compared with conventional language models when large training data is given. Using these neural language models to rescore SMT outputs generally gives better translation results (Auli and Gao, 2014). Other approaches rescore with RNNs that predict the next word by taking the word in current step and $\mathcal{S}$ as inputs (Kalchbrenner and Blunsom, 2013; Cho, Merrienboer, et al., 2014). Here, $\mathcal{S}$ is a vector representation summarizes the whole input sentence.

Neural machine translation is a brand-new approach that samples translation results directly from RNNs. Most published models involve an encoder and a decoder in the network architecture (Sutskever, Vinyals, and Le, 2014), called Encoder-Decoder approach. Figure 1 gives a general overview of this approach. In Figure 1, the vector output $\mathcal{S}$ of the encoder RNN represents the whole input sentence. Hence, $\mathcal{S}$ contains all information required to produce the translation. In order to boost up the performance, (Sutskever, Vinyals, and Le, 2014) used stacked Long Short-Term Memory (LSTM) units for both encoder and decoder, their ensembled models outperformed phrase-based SMT baseline in English-French translation task.

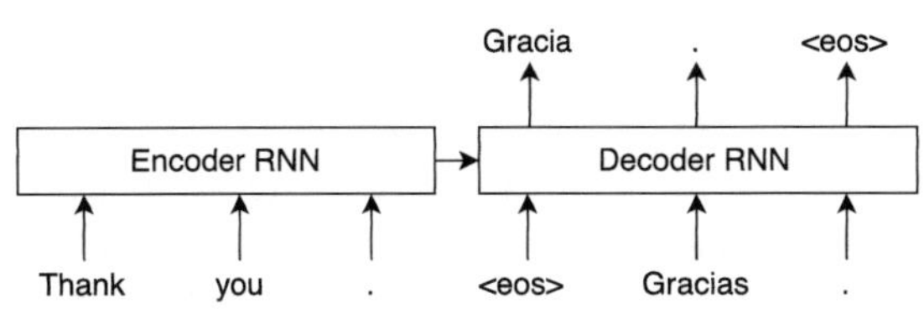

Figure 1: Basic neural network architecture in Encoder-Decoder approach

Recently, by scaling up neural network models and incorporating some techniques during the training, the performance of NMT models have already achieved the state-of-the-art in English-French translation task (Luong et al.,

Proceedings of the 2nd Workshop on Asian Translation (WAT2015), pages 61-68,
Kyoto, Japan, 16th October 2015.

2015) and English-German translation task (Jean et al., 2015).

In this paper, we describe our works on applying NMT to English-Japanese translation task. The main contributions of this work are detailed as follows:

- We examined the effect of using different network architecture and recurrent units for English-Japanese translation
- We empirically evaluated NMT models trained on pre-reordered data
- We demonstrate a simple solution to recover unknown words in the translation results with a back-off system
- We provide a qualitative analysis on the translation results of NMT models

2 Recurrent neural networks

Recurrent neural network is the solution for modeling temporal data with neural networks. The framework of widely used modern RNN is introduced by Elman (Elman, 1990), it is also known as Elman Network or Simple Recurrent Network. At each time step, RNN updates its internal state $\mathbf{h_t}$ based on a new input $\mathbf{x_t}$ and the previous state $\mathbf{h_{t-1}}$, produces an output $\mathbf{y_t}$. Generally, they are computed recursively by applying following operations:

$$\mathbf{h_t} = f(\mathbf{W_i x_t} + \mathbf{W_h h_{t-1}} + \mathbf{b_h}) \quad (1)$$

$$\mathbf{y_t} = f(\mathbf{W_o h_t} + \mathbf{b_o}) \quad (2)$$

Where f is an element-wise non-linearity, such as sigmoid or tanh. Figures 2 illustrates the computational graph of a RNN. Solid lines in the figure mark out the Affine transformations followed with a non-linear activation. Dashed lines indicate that the result of previous computation is just a parameter of next operation. The bias term $\mathbf{b_h}$ is omitted in the illustration.

RNN can be trained with Backpropagation Through Time (BPTT), which is a gradient-based technique that unfolds the network through time so as to compute the actual gradients of parameters in each time step.

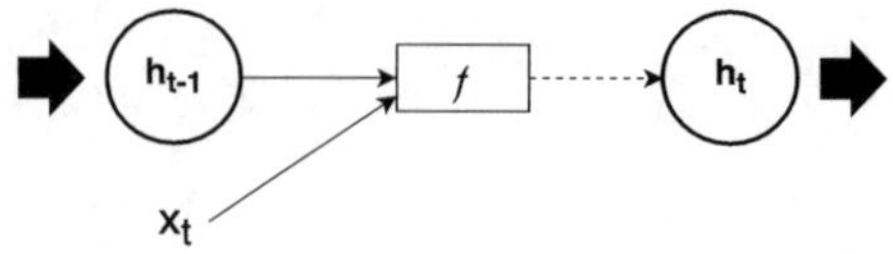

Figure 2: An illustration of the computational graph of a RNN

2.1 Long short-term memory

For RNN, as the internal state $\mathbf{h_t}$ is completely changed in each time step, BPTT algorithm dilutes error information after each step of computation. Hence, RNN suffers from the problem that it is difficult to capture long-term dependencies.

Long short-term memory units (Hochreiter and Schmidhuber, 1997) incorporate some gates to control the information flow. In addition to the hidden units in RNN, memory cells are used to store long-term information, which is updated linearly. Empirically, LSTM can preserve information for arbitrarily long periods of time.

Figure 3 gives an illustration of the computational graph of a basic LSTM unit. In which, input gate $\mathbf{i_t}$, forget gate $\mathbf{f_t}$ and output gate $\mathbf{o_t}$ are marked with rhombuses. "$\times$" and "$+$" are element-wise multiplication and element-wise addition respectively. The computational steps follows (Graves, 2013), 11 weight parameters are involved in this model, compared with only 2 weight parameters in RNN. We can see from Figure 3 that the memory cells $\mathbf{c_t}$ can keep unchanged when $\mathbf{f_t}$ outputs 1 and $\mathbf{i_t}$ outputs 0.

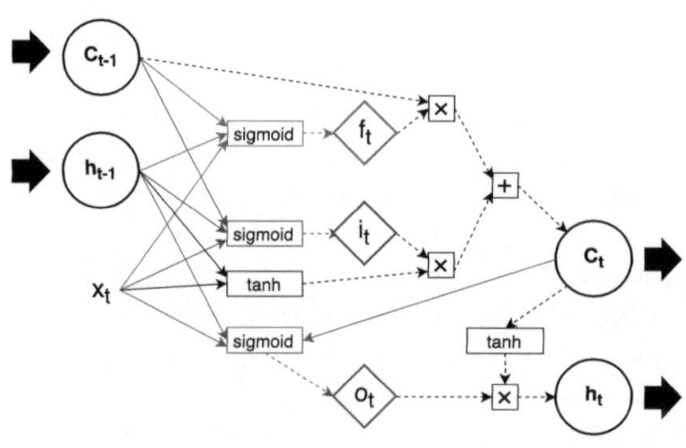

Figure 3: An illustration of a basic LSTM unit

2.2 Gated recurrent unit

Gated recurrent unit (GRU) is originally proposed in (Cho, Merrienboer, et al., 2014). Similarly to LSTM unit, GRU also has gating units to control the information flow. While LSTM unit has a separate memory cell, GRU unit only maintains one kind of internal states, thus reduces computational complexity. The computational graph of a GRU unit is demonstrated in Figure 4. As shown in the figure, 6 weight parameters are involved.

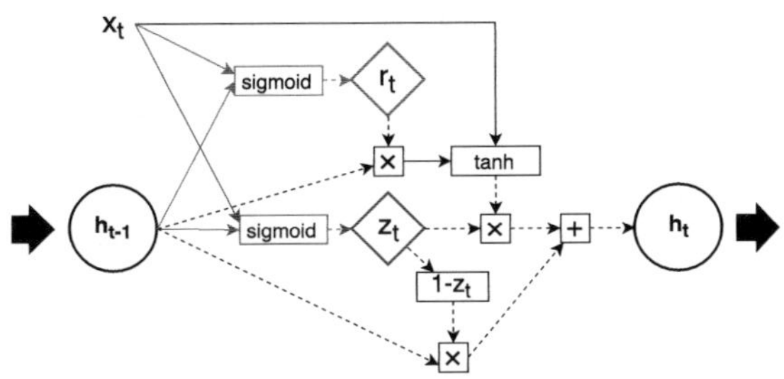

Figure 4: An illustration of a GRU unit

3 Network architectures of Neural Machine Translation

A basic architecture of NMT is called Encoder-Decoder approach (Sutskever, Vinyals, and Le, 2014), which encodes the input sequence into a vector representation, then unrolls it to generate the output sequence. Then softmax function is applied to the output layer in order to compute cross-entropy. Instead of using one-hot embeddings for the tokens in the vocabulary, trainable word embeddings are used.

As a pre-processing step, "<eos>" token is appended to the end of each sequence. When translating, the token with the highest probability in the output layer is sampled and input back to the neural network to get next output. This is done recursively until "<eos>" is observed. Figure 5 gives a detailed illustration of this architecture when using stacked multi-layer recurrent units.

3.1 Soft-attention models in NMT

As stated in (Cho, Merriënboer, et al., 2014), two critical drawbacks exist in the basic Encoder-Decoder approach: (1) the performance degrades when the input sentence gets longer, (2) the vocabulary size in the target

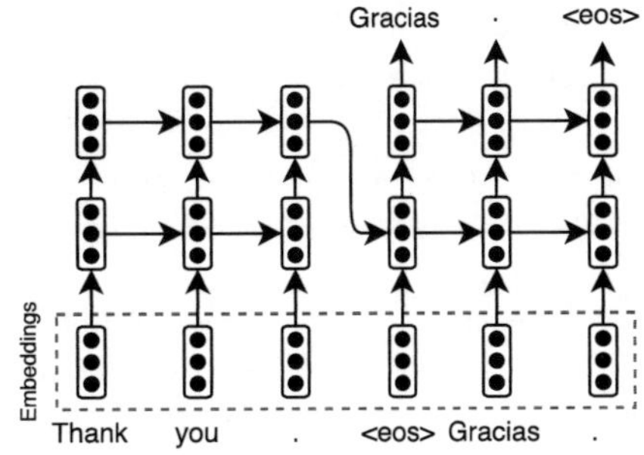

Figure 5: Illustration of a basic neural network architecture for NMT with stacked multi-layer recurrent units.

size is limited.

Attentional models are first proposed in the field of computer vision, which allows the recurrent network to focus on a small portion in the image at each step. The internal state is updated only depends on this glimpse. Soft-attention first evaluates the weights for all possible positions to attend, then make a weighted summarization of all hidden states in the encoder. The summarized vector is finally used to update the internal state of the decoder. Contrary to hard-attention mechanism which selects only one location at each step and thus has to be trained with reinforce learning techniques, soft-attention mechanism makes the computational graph differentiable and thus able to be trained with standard backpropagation.

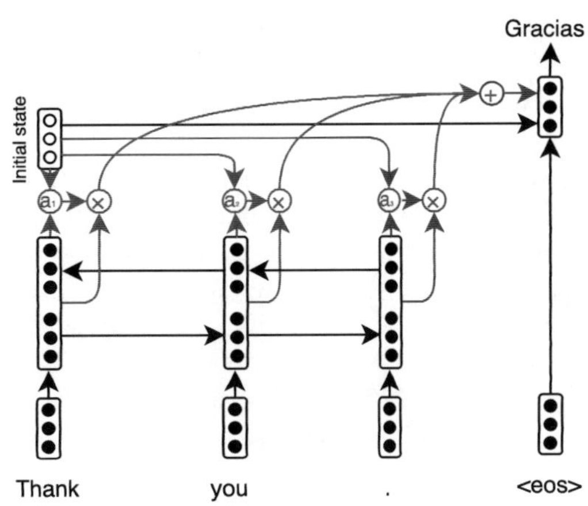

Figure 6: The recurrent network using soft-attention mechanism to predict next output.

The application of soft-attention mechanism in machine translation is firstly described in (Bahdanau, Cho, and Bengio, 2014), which is referred as "RNNsearch" in this paper. The computational graph of a soft-attention NMT model is illustrated in Figure 6. In which, the encoder is replaced by a bi-directional RNN, the hidden states of two RNNs is finally concatenated in each input position. At each time step of decoding, an alignment weight a_i is computed based on the previous state of the decoder and the concatenated hidden state of position i in the encoder. The alignment weights are finally normalized by softmax function. The weighted summarization of the hidden states in the encoder is then fed into the decoder. Hence, the internal state of the decoder is updated based on 3 inputs: the previous state, weighted summarization of the encoder and the target-side input token.

The empirical results in (Bahdanau, Cho, and Bengio, 2014) show that the performance of RNNsearch does not degrade severely like normal Encoder-Decoder approach.

4 Solutions of unknown words

A critical practical problem of NMT is the fixed vocabulary size in the output layer. As the output layer uses dense connections, enlarging it will significantly increase the computational complexity and thus slow down the training.

According to existing publications, two kinds of approaches are used to tackle this problem: model-specific and translation-specific approach. Well known model-specific approaches are noise-contrastive training (Mnih and Kavukcuoglu, 2013) and class-based models (Mikolov et al., 2010). In (Jean et al., 2015), another model-specific solution is proposed by using only a small set of target vocabulary at each update. By using a very large target vocabulary, they were able to outperform the state-of-the-art system in English-German translation task.

Solutions of Translation-specific approach usually take advantage of the alignment of tokens in both sides. For examples, the proposed method in (Luong et al., 2015) annotates the unknown target words with "$unkpos_i$" instead of "*unk*". Where the subscript i is the position of the aligned source word for the unknown target word. The alignments can be obtained by conventional aligners. The purpose of this processing step put some cues for recovering missing words into the output. By applying this approach, they were able to surpass the state-of-the-art SMT system in English-French translation task.

5 Experiments

5.1 Experiment setup

In our experiments, we are curious to see how NMT models work in English-Japanese translation and how well the existing approaches for unknown words fit into this setting. As Japanese language drastically differs from English in terms of word order and grammar structure. NMT models must capture the semantics of long-range dependencies in a sentence in order to translate it well.

We use Japanese-English Scientific Paper Abstract Corpus (ASPEC-JE) as training data and focus on evaluating the models for English-Japanese translation task. In order to make the training time-efficient, we pick 1.5M sentences according to similarity score then filter out long sentences with more than 40 words in either English or Japanese side. This processing step gives 1.1M sentences for training. We randomly separate out 1,280 sentences as valid data.

As almost zero pre-knowledge of NMT experiments in English-Japanese translation can be found in publications, our purpose is to conduct a thorough experiment so that we can evaluate and compare different model architectures and recurrent units. However, the limitation of computational resource and time disallows us to massively test various models, training schemes, and hyper-parameters.

In our experiments, we evaluated four kinds of models as follow:

- **LSTM Search**: Soft-attention model with LSTM recurrent units
- **pre-reordered LSTM Search**: Same as LSTM Search, but the model is trained on pre-reordered corpus
- **GRU Search**: Soft-attention model with GRU recurrent units

- **LSTM Encoder-Decoder**: Basic Encoder-Decoder model with 4 stacked LSTM layers

Most of the details of these models are common. The recurrent layers of all the models contain 1024 neurons each. The size of word embedding is 1000. We truncate the source-side and target-side vocabulary sizes to 80k and 40k respectively. For all models, we insert a dense layer contains 600 neurons immediately before the output layer. We basically use SGD with learning rate decay as optimization method, the batch size is 60 and initial learning rate is 1. The gradients are clipped to ensure L2 norm lower than 3. Although we sort the training data according to the input length, the order of batches is shuffled before training. For LSTM units, we set the bias of forget gate to 1 before training (Jozefowicz, Zaremba, and Sutskever, 2015). During the translation, we set beam size to 20, if no valid translation is obtained, then another trail with beam size of 1000 will be performed.

5.2 Evaluating models by perplexity

For our in-house experiments, the evaluation of our models mainly relies on the perplexity measured on valid data, as a strong correlation between perplexity and translation performance is observed in many existing publications (Luong et al., 2015). The changing perplexities of the models described in Section 5.1 are visualized in Figure 7.

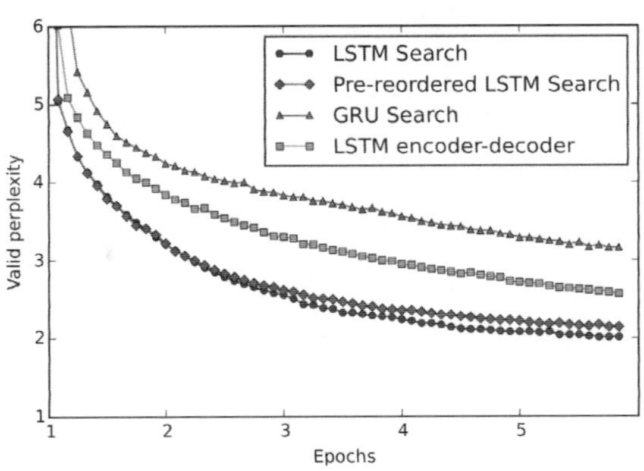

Figure 7: Visualization of the training for different models.

In Figure 7, we can see that soft-attention models with LSTM unit constantly outperforms the muti-layer Encoder-Decoder model. This matches our expectation as the alignment between English and Japanese is too complicated thus it is difficult for simple Encoder-Decoder models to capture it correctly. Another observation is that the performance of the soft-attention model with GRU unit is significantly lower than that with LSTM unit. As this is conflict with the results reported in other publications (Jozefowicz, Zaremba, and Sutskever, 2015), one possible explanation is that some implementation issues exist and further investigation is required.

One surprising observation is that using pre-reordered data to train soft-attention models does not benefit the perplexity, but degrades the performance by a small margin. We show that the same conclusion can be drawn by measuring translation performance directly in latter sections.

5.3 Replacing unknown words

Initially, we adapt the solution described in (Luong et al., 2015), which annotate the unknown words with "$unkpos_i$", where i is the position of aligned source word. We find this require source-side and target-side sentences roughly aligned. When testing on the soft-attention model with pre-reordered training data, we found this method can correctly point out the rough aligned position of a missing word. This allows us to recover the missing output words with a dictionary or SMT systems.

However, for the training data in natural order, the position of aligned words in two languages differs drastically. The solution described above can hardly be applied as it annotates the unknown words with relative positions.

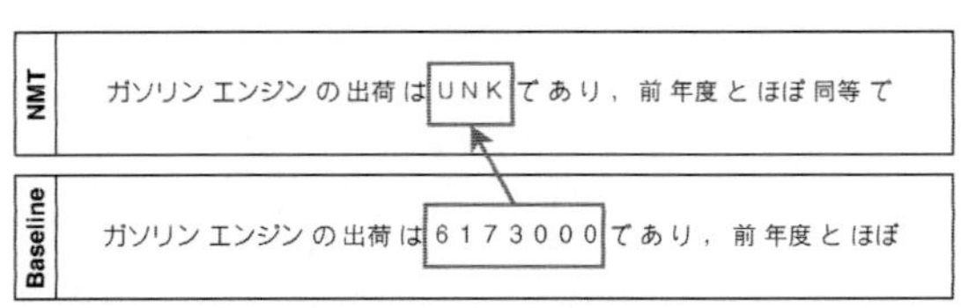

Figure 8: Illustration of replacing unknown words with a back-off system.

Here, we propose a simple workaround for

recovering the unknown words with a back-off system. We translate the input sentence using both a NMT system and a baseline SMT system. Assume the translation results are similar, then if we observe an unknown word in the result of the NMT system, then it is reasonable to infer that the rarest word in the baseline result which is missing in the NMT result should be this unknown translation. This is demonstrated in Figure 8, the rarest word in the baseline result is picked out to replace the unknown word in the NMT result. Practically, the assumption will not be true, the results of NMT systems and conventional SMT systems differ tremendously. Hence, some incorrect word replacements are introduced. This method can be generalized to recover multiple unknown words by selecting the rarest word in a near position.

5.4 Evaluating translation performance

In this section, we describe our submitted systems and report the evaluation results in the English-Japanese translation task of The 2nd Workshop on Asian Translation [1] (Nakazawa et al., 2015). We train these models with AdaDelta for 5 epochs. Then, we fine-tune the model with AdaGrad using an enlarged training data, that each sentence contains no more than 50 words. With this fine-tuning step, we are able to achieve perplexity of 1.76 in valid data.

The automatic evaluation results are shown in Table 1. Three SMT baselines are picked for comparison. In the middle of the table, we list two single soft-attention NMT models with LSTM unit. The results show that training models on pre-reordered corpus leads to degrading of translation performance, where the pre-reordering step is done using the model described in (Zhu, 2014).

Our submitted systems are basically an ensemble of two LSTM Search models trained on natural-order data, as shown in the bottom of Table 1. After we replaced unknown words with the technique described in 5.3, we gained 0.8 BLEU on test data. This is our first submitted system, marked with "S1".

We also found it is useful to perform a sys-

[1]Our team ID is "WEBLIO MT"

Table 1: Automatic evaluation results in WAT2015

Model	BLEU	RIBES
PB basline	29.80	0.691
HPB baseline	32.56	0.746
T2S baseline	33.44	0.758
Single LSTM Search	32.19	0.797
Pre-reordered LSTM Search	30.97	0.779
Ensemble of 2 LSTM Search	33.38	0.800
+ UNK replacing (S1)	34.19	0.802
+ System combination	35.97	0.807
+ 3 pre-reordered ensembles (S2)	36.21	0.809

tem combination based on perplexity scores. We evaluate the perplexity for all outputs produced by a baseline system and the NMT model. These two sets of perplexity score are normalized by mean and standard deviation respectively. Then for each NMT result, we rescore it with the difference of perplexity against the baseline system. Intuitively, if the NMT result is better than the baseline result, the new score shall be a positive number. In our experiment, we pick the system described in (Zhu, 2014) as baseline system. We pick top-1000 results from NMT and the rest from the baseline system, this gives us a gain of 1.8 in BLEU.

Table 2: Human evaluation results for submitted system in WAT2015

Model	HUMAN
T2S baseline	30.000
Submitted system 1 (S1)	43.500
Submitted system 2 (S2)	53.750

Finally, we added 3 pre-reordered LSTM Search models to the ensemble, results in a 5-model ensemble. During the translation, these three models receive pre-reordered input, another two LSTM Search models receive input in natural order. We gain 0.24 BLEU with this setting, and this is the second submitted system, marked with "S2". Human evaluation results of our submitted systems are shown in Table 2. As we already know that pre-reordering does not help improving translation performance, a natural choice is to train more normal LSTM Search models and put into the ensemble. We failed to do it because of insufficient time.

5.5 Qualitative analysis

To find some insights in the translation results of NMT systems, we performed qualitative analysis on a proportion of held-out development data. During the inspection, we found many errors share the same pattern. It turns out that NMT model tends to make a perfect translation by omitting some information during the translation. In this case, the output tends to be a valid sentence, but the meaning is partially lost. One example of this phenomenon is shown in the following snippet:

```
Input: this paper discusses some systematic
    uncertainties including casimir force ,
    false force due to electric force , and
    various factors for irregular
    uncertainties due to patch field and
    detector noise .
NMT result: ここ で は , Ｃａｓｉｍｉｒ 力 を
    考慮 し た いく つ か の 系統 的 不 確実 性
    に つ い て 論 じ た 。
Reference: Ｃａｓｉｍｉｒ 力 や 電気 力 に よ
    る 偽 の 力 , パッチ 場 や 検出 器 雑音 に
    よ る 不 規則 な 不確か さ の 種々 の 要因
    を 含め , 幾 つ か の 系統 的 不確か さ
    を 論 じ た 。
```

6 Conclusion

In this paper, we performed a systematic evaluation of various kinds for NMT models in the setting of English-Japanese translation. Based on the empirical evaluation results, we found soft-attention NMT models can already make good translation results in English-Japanese translation task. Their performance surpasses all SMT baselines by a substantial margin according to RIBES scores. We also found that NMT models can work well without extra data processing steps such as pre-reordering. Finally, we described a simple workaround to recover unknown words with a back-off system.

However, a sophisticated solution for dealing with unknown words is still an open question in the English-Japanese setting. As some patterns of mistakes can be observed from the translation results, there exists some space for further improvements.

References

Auli, Michael and Jianfeng Gao (2014). "Decoder integration and expected bleu training for recurrent neural network language models". In: *Proceedings of the 52nd Annual Meeting of the Association for Computational Linguistics (ACL' 14)*, pp. 136–142.

Bahdanau, Dzmitry, Kyunghyun Cho, and Yoshua Bengio (2014). "Neural machine translation by jointly learning to align and translate". In: *arXiv preprint arXiv:1409.0473*.

Cho, Kyunghyun, Bart van Merrienboer, et al. (2014). "Learning Phrase Representations using RNN Encoder–Decoder for Statistical Machine Translation". In: *Proceedings of the 2014 Conference on Empirical Methods in Natural Language Processing (EMNLP)*. Doha, Qatar: Association for Computational Linguistics, pp. 1724–1734.

Cho, Kyunghyun, Bart van Merriënboer, et al. (2014). "On the Properties of Neural Machine Translation: Encoder–Decoder Approaches". In: *Syntax, Semantics and Structure in Statistical Translation*, p. 103.

Duh, Kevin and Katrin Kirchhoff (2008). "Beyond log-linear models: boosted minimum error rate training for N-best Re-ranking". In: *Proceedings of the 46th Annual Meeting of the Association for Computational Linguistics on Human Language Technologies: Short Papers*. Association for Computational Linguistics, pp. 37–40.

Elman, Jeffrey L (1990). "Finding structure in time". In: *Cognitive science* 14.2, pp. 179–211.

Graves, Alex (2013). "Generating sequences with recurrent neural networks". In: *arXiv preprint arXiv:1308.0850*.

Hochreiter, Sepp and Jürgen Schmidhuber (1997). "Long short-term memory". In: *Neural computation* 9.8, pp. 1735–1780.

Jean, Sébastien et al. (2015). "On Using Very Large Target Vocabulary for Neural Machine Translation". In: *Proceedings of the 53rd Annual Meeting of the Association for Computational Linguistics and the 7th International Joint Conference on Natural Language Processing (Volume 1: Long Pa-*

pers). Beijing, China: Association for Computational Linguistics, pp. 1–10.

Jozefowicz, Rafal, Wojciech Zaremba, and Ilya Sutskever (2015). "An Empirical Exploration of Recurrent Network Architectures". In: *Proceedings of the 32nd International Conference on Machine Learning (ICML-15)*, pp. 2342–2350.

Kalchbrenner, Nal and Phil Blunsom (2013). "Recurrent Continuous Translation Models". In: *Proceedings of the 2013 Conference on Empirical Methods in Natural Language Processing*. Seattle, Washington, USA: Association for Computational Linguistics, pp. 1700–1709.

Luong, Thang et al. (2015). "Addressing the Rare Word Problem in Neural Machine Translation". In: *Proceedings of the 53rd Annual Meeting of the Association for Computational Linguistics and the 7th International Joint Conference on Natural Language Processing (Volume 1: Long Papers)*. Beijing, China: Association for Computational Linguistics, pp. 11–19.

Mikolov, Tomas et al. (2010). "Recurrent neural network based language model." In: *INTERSPEECH 2010, 11th Annual Conference of the International Speech Communication Association, Makuhari, Chiba, Japan, September 26-30, 2010*, pp. 1045–1048.

Mnih, Andriy and Koray Kavukcuoglu (2013). "Learning word embeddings efficiently with noise-contrastive estimation". In: *Advances in Neural Information Processing Systems 26*. Ed. by C.J.C. Burges et al. Curran Associates, Inc., pp. 2265–2273.

Nakazawa, Toshiaki et al. (2015). "Overview of the 2nd Workshop on Asian Translation". In: *Proceedings of the 2nd Workshop on Asian Translation (WAT2015)*.

Sutskever, Ilya, Oriol Vinyals, and Quoc VV Le (2014). "Sequence to sequence learning with neural networks". In: *Advances in neural information processing systems*, pp. 3104–3112.

Zhu, Zhongyuan (2014). "Weblio Prereordering Statistical Machine Translation System". In: *Proceedings of the 1st Workshop on Asian Translation (WAT2014)*.

NAVER Machine Translation System for WAT 2015

Hyoung-Gyu Lee[1], Jaesong Lee[1], Jun-Seok Kim[1] and Chang-Ki Lee[2]
[1]NAVER LABS, NAVER Corp., Seongnam-si, Gyeonggi-do, South Korea
[2]Kangwon National University, Chuncheon-si, Gangwon-do, South Korea
{hg.lee, jaesong.lee, jun.seok}@navercorp.com
leeck@kangwon.ac.kr

Abstract

In this paper, we describe NAVER machine translation system for English to Japanese and Korean to Japanese tasks at WAT 2015. We combine the traditional SMT and neural MT in both tasks.

1 Introduction

This paper explains the NAVER machine translation system for the 2nd Workshop on Asian Translation (WAT 2015) (Nakazawa et al., 2015). We participate in two tasks; English to Japanese (En-Ja) and Korean to Japanese (Ko-Ja).

Our system is a combined system of traditional statistical machine translation (SMT) and neural machine translation (NMT). We adopt the tree-to-string syntax-based model as En-Ja SMT baseline, while we adopt the phrase-based model as Ko-Ja. We propose improved SMT systems for each task and an NMT model based on the architecture using recurrent neural network (RNN) (Cho et al., 2014; Sutskever et al., 2014).

We give detailed explanations of each SMT system in section 2 and section 3. We describe our NMT model in section 4.

2 English to Japanese

2.1 Training data

We used 1 million sentence pairs that are contained in `train-1.txt` of ASPEC-JE corpus for training the translation rule tables and NMT models. We also used 3 million Japanese sentences that are contained in `train-1.txt`, `train-2.txt`, `train-3.txt` of ASPEC-JE corpus for training the 5-gram language model. We also used 1,790 sentence pairs of `dev.txt` for tuning the weights of each feature of SMT linear model and as validation data of neural network. We filtered out the sentences that have 100 or more tokens from training data.

2.2 Language Analyzer

We used Moses tokenizer and Berkeley constituency parser[1] for tokenizing and parsing an English sentence. We used our own Japanese tokenizer and part-of-speech tagger for tokenizing and tagging a Japanese sentence. After running the tokenizer and the tagger, we make a token from concatenation of a word and its part-of-speech.

2.3 Tree-to-string Syntax-based SMT

To determining the baseline model, we first performed comparative experiments with the phrase-based, hierarchical phrase-based and syntax-based models. As a result, we chose the tree-to-string syntax-based model.

The SMT models that consider source syntax such as tree-to-string and forest-to-string brought out better performance than the phrase-based and hierarchical phrase-based models in the WAT 2014 En-Ja task.

The tree-to-string model was proposed by Huang (2006) and Liu (2006). It utilizes the constituency tree of source language to extract translation rules and decode a target sentence. The translation rules are extracted from a source-parsed and word-aligned corpus in the training step. We use synchronous context free grammar (SCFG) rules.

In addition, we used a rule augmentation method which is known as syntax-augmented machine translation (Zollmann and Venugopal, 2006). Because the tree-to-string SMT makes some constraints on extracting rules by considering syntactic tree structures, it usually extracts fewer rules than hierarchical phrase-based SMT (HPBSMT) (Chiang, 2005). Thus it is required to augment tree-to-string translation rules. The rule augmentation method allows the training system to extract more rules by modifying parse trees. Given a parse tree, we produce additional nodes

[1] `https://github.com/slavpetrov/berkeleyparser`

Proceedings of the 2nd Workshop on Asian Translation (WAT2015), pages 69-73,
Kyoto, Japan, 16th October 2015.

by combining any pairs of neighboring nodes, not only children nodes, e.g. NP+VP. We limit the maximum span of each rule to 40 tokens in the rule extraction process. The tree-to-string decoder use a chart parsing algorithm with cube pruning proposed by Chiang (2005).

Our En-Ja SMT system was developed by using the open source SMT engines; Moses and Giza++. Its other specifications are as follows:

- Grow-diag-final-and word alignment heuristic
- Good-Turing discounting for smoothing probabilities
- Minimum Error Rate Training (MERT) for tuning feature weights
- Cube-pruning-pop-limit = 3000

2.4 Handling Out-of-Vocabulary

In order to handle out-of-vocabulary (OOV) words, we use two techniques; hyphen word split and spell error correction. The former is to split a word with hyphen (-) to two separate tokens before running the language analyzer. The latter is to automatically detect and correct spell errors in an input sentence. We give a detailed description of spell error correction in section 2.4.1.

2.4.1 English Spell Correction

It is not easy to translate a word including errata, because the erroneous word has only a slim chance of occurrence in the training data. We discovered a lot of spell errors among OOV words that appear in English scientific text. We introduce English spell correction for reducing OOV words in input sentences. We developed our spell corrector by using Aspell[2].

For detecting a spell error, we skip words that have only capitals, numbers or symbols, because they are likely to be abbreviations or mathematic expressions. Then we regard words detected by Aspell as spell error words.

For correcting spell error, we use only top-3 suggestion words from Aspell. We find that a large gap between an original word and its suggestion word makes wrong correction. To avoid excessive correction, we introduce a gap thresholding technique, that ignores the suggestion word that has 3 or longer edit distance and selects one that has the shortest edit distance between an original word and its suggestion word.

3 Korean to Japanese

3.1 Training data

We used 1 million sentence pairs that are contained in JPO corpus for training phrase tables and NMT models. We also used Japanese part of the corpus for training the 5-gram language model. We also used 2,000 sentence pairs of `dev.txt` for tuning the weights of each feature of SMT linear model and as validation data of neural network. We did not filter out any sentences.

3.2 Language Analyzer

We used MeCab-ko[3] for tokenizing a Korean sentence. We used Juman[4] for tokenizing a Japanese sentence. We did not perform part-of-speech tagging for both languages.

3.3 Phrase-based SMT

As in the En-Ja task, we first performed comparative experiments with the phrase-based and hierarchical phrase-based models, and then adopt the phrase-based model as our baseline model.

For the Ko-Ja task, we develop two phrase-based systems; word-level and character-level. We use word-level tokenization for the word-based system. We found that setting the distortion limit to zero yields better translation in aspect of both BLEU and human evaluation. We use the 5-gram language model. We use character-level tokenization for character-based system. We use the 10-gram language model and set the maximum phrase length to 10 in the phrase pair extraction process.

We found that the character-level system does not suffer from tokenization error and out-of-vocabulary issue. The JPO corpus contains many technical terms and loanwords like chemical compound names, which are more inaccurately tokenized and allow a lot of out-of-vocabulary tokens to be generated. Since Korean and Japanese share similar transliteration rules for loanwords, the character-level system can learn translation of unseen technical words. It generally produces better translations than a table-based transliteration.

[2] `http://aspell.net/`

[3] `https://bitbucket.org/eunjeon/mecab-ko/`

[4] `http://nlp.ist.i.kyoto-u.ac.jp/EN/index.php?JUMAN`

Moreover, we tested jamo-level tokenization[5] for Korean text, however, the preliminary test did not produce effective results.

We also investigated a parentheses imbalance problem. We solved the problem by filtering out parentheses-imbalanced translations from the n-best results. We found that the post-processing step can improve the BLEU score with low order language models, but cannot do with high order language models. We do not use the step for final submission.

To boosting the performance, we combine the word-level phrase-based model (Word PB) and the character-level phrase-based model (Char PB). If there are one or more OOV words in an input sentence, our translator choose the Char PB model, otherwise, the Word PB model.

Our Ko-Ja SMT system was developed by using the open source SMT engines; Moses and Giza++. Its other specifications are as follows:

- Grow-diag-final-and word alignment heuristic
- Good-Turing discounting for smoothing probabilities
- Minimum Error Rate Training (MERT) for tuning feature weights

4 Neural Machine Translation

Neural machine translation (NMT) is a new approach to machine translation that has shown promising results compared to the existing approaches such as phrase-based statistical machine translation (Cho et al., 2014; Sutskever et al., 2014; Bahdanau et al., 2015). An NMT system is a single neural network that reads a source sentence and generates its translation. Using the bilingual corpus, the whole neural network is jointly trained to maximize the conditional probability of a correct translation given a source sentence. NMT has several advantages over the existing statistical machine translation systems such as the phrase-based system. First, NMT uses minimal domain knowledge. Second, the NMT system is jointly trained to maximize the translation performance, unlike the existing phrase-based system which consists of many separately trained features. Third, the NMT system removes the need to store explicit phrase tables and language models. Lastly, the decoder of an NMT system is easy to implement. Despite these advantages and promising results, NMT has a limitation in handling a larger target vocabulary, as the complexity of training and decoding increases proportionally to the number of target words.

In this paper, we propose a new approach to avoid the large target vocabulary problem by preprocessing the target word sequences, encoding them as a longer character sequence drawn from a small character vocabulary. The proposed approach removes the need to replace rare words with the unknown word symbol. Our approach is simpler than other methods recently proposed to address the same issue (Luong et al., 2015; Jean et al., 2015).

4.1 Model

In this paper, we use our in-house software of NMT that uses an attention mechanism, as recently proposed by Bahdanau et al. (2015). The encoder of NMT is a bi-directional recurrent neural network such that

$$h_t = [\overleftarrow{h}_t; \overrightarrow{h}_t] \quad (1)$$

$$\overleftarrow{h}_t = f_{GRU}(W_{s\_we}x_t, \overleftarrow{h}_{t+1}) \quad (2)$$

$$\overrightarrow{h}_t = f_{GRU}(W_{s\_we}x_t, \overrightarrow{h}_{t-1}) \quad (3)$$

where h_t is a hidden state of the encoder, x_t is a one-hot encoded vector indicating one of the words in the source vocabulary, W_{s_we} is a weight matrix for the word embedding of the source language, and f_{GRU} is a gated recurrent unit (GRU) (Cho et al., 2014).

At each time, the decoder of NMT computes the context vector c_t as a convex combination of the hidden states $(h_1,\ldots,h_T)$ with the alignment weights $\alpha_1,\ldots,\alpha_T$:

$$c^t = \sum_{i=1}^{T} \alpha_{ti} h_i \quad (4)$$

$$\alpha_{ti} = \frac{\exp(e_{tj})}{\sum_{j=1}^{T} \exp(e_{tj})} \quad (5)$$

$$e_{ti} = f_{FFNN}(z_{t-1}, h_i, y_{t-1}) \quad (6)$$

where f_{FFNN} is a feedforward neural network with a single hidden layer, z_{t-1} is a previous hidden state of the decoder, and y_{t-1} is a previous generated target word (one-hot encoded vector).

[5] Jamo is Korean alphabet letters which represent consonants and vowels. A Korean character can be usually separated to three jamoes; choseong, jungseong and jongseong.

A new hidden state z_t of the decoder which uses GRU is computed based on z_{t-1}, y_{t-1}, and c_t:

$$z_t = f_{GRU}(y_{t-1}, z_{t-1}, c_t) \quad (7)$$

The probability of the next target word y_t is then computed by

$$\begin{aligned} p(y_t|y_{<t}, x) = y_t^T f_{softmax}\{W_{z'y}z'_t \\ + W_{zy}z_t + W_{cy}c_t \\ + W_{yy}(W_{t\_we}y_{t-1}) + b_y\} \end{aligned} \quad (8)$$

$$z'_t = f_{ReLU}(W_{zz'}z_t) \quad (9)$$

where $f_{softmax}$ is a softmax function, f_{ReLU} is a rectified linear unit (ReLU), W_{t_we} is a weight matrix for the word embedding of the target language, and b_y is a target word bias.

4.2 Settings

We constructed the source word vocabulary with the most common words in the source language corpora. For the target character vocabulary, we used a BI (begin/inside) representation (e.g., 結/B, 果/I), because it gave better accuracy in preliminary experiment. The sizes of the source vocabularies for English and Korean were 245K and 60K, respectively, for the En-Ja and Ko-Ja tasks. The sizes of the target character vocabularies for Japanese were 6K and 5K, respectively, for the En-Ja and Ko-Ja tasks. We chose the dimensionality of the source word embedding and the target character embedding to be 200, and chose the size of the recurrent units to be 1,000. Each model was optimized using stochastic gradient descent (SGD). We did not use dropout. Training was early-stopped to maximize the performance on the development set measured by BLEU.

5 Experimental Results

All scores of this section are reported in experiments on the official test data; `test.txt` of the ASPEC-JE corpus.

5.1 En-Ja SMT

Table 1 shows the evaluation results of our En-Ja traditional SMT system. The first row in the table indicates the baseline of the tree-to-string systax-based model. The second row shows the system that reflects the tree modification described in section 2.3. The augmentation method drastically increased both the number of rules and the BLEU score. Our OOV handling methods described in section 2.4 also caused a positive effect as shown in the last row of the table.

SYS	BLEU	#Rules
Tree-to-string SB	31.34	250M
+ Rule augmentation	32.48	1950M
+ Parameter modification	32.63	1950M
+ OOV handling	32.76	1950M

Table 1: En-Ja SMT.

SYS	BLEU	#Rules
Word PB	70.36	57M
Char PB	70.31	55M
Word PB + Char PB	70.91	57M & 55M

Table 2: Ko-Ja SMT.

The decoding time of the rule-augmented tree-to-string SMT is about 1.3 seconds per a sentence in our 12-core machine. Even though it is not a terrible problem, we are required to improve the decoding speed by pruning the rule table or using the incremental decoding method (Huang and Mi, 2010).

5.2 Ko-Ja SMT

Table 2 shows the evaluation results of our Ko-Ja traditional SMT system. We obtained the best result in the combination of two phrase-based SMT systems.

5.3 NMT

Table 3 shows effects of our NMT model. "Human" indicates the pairwise crowdsourcing evaluation scores provided by WAT 2015 organizers. In the table, "T2S/PBMT only" is the final T2S/PBMT systems shown in section 5.1 and section 5.2. "NMT only" is the system using only RNN encoder-decoder without any traditional SMT methods. The last row is the combined system that reranks T2S/PBMT n-best translations by NMT. Our T2S/PBMT system outputs 100,000-best translations in En-Ja and 10,000-best translations in Ko-Ja. The final output is 1-best translation selected by considering only NMT score.

NMT outperforms the traditional SMT in En-Ja, while it does not in Ko-Ja. This result means that NMT produces a strong effect in the language pair with long linguistic distance. Moreover, the reranking system achieved a great synergy of T2S/PBMT and NMT in both task, even

SYS	En-Ja		Ko-Ja	
	BLEU	**Human**	**BLEU**	**Human**
T2S/PBMT only	32.76	N/A	70.91	6.75
NMT only	33.14	48.50	65.72	N/A
T2S/PBMT + NMT reranking	34.60	53.25	71.38	14.75

Table 3: Effect of NMT.

if "NMT only" is not effective in Ko-Ja. From the human evaluation, we can be clear that our NMT model produces successful results.

6 Conclusion

This paper described NAVER machine translation system for En-Ja and Ko-Ja tasks at WAT 2015. We developed both the traditional SMT and NMT systems and integrated NMT into the traditional SMT in both tasks by reranking n-best translations of the traditional SMT. Our evaluation results showed that a combination of the NMT and traditional SMT systems outperformed two independent systems.

For the future work, we try to improve the space and time efficiency of both the tree-to-string SMT and the NMT model. We also plan to develop and evaluate the NMT system in other language pairs.

Acknowledgments

We would like to thank Kevin Cho, who has visited for the summer internship program in NAVER LABS, for his contribution for development of the English spell corrector.

References

Dzmitry Bahdanau, Kyunghyun Cho, and Yoshua Bengio. 2015. Neural machine translation by jointly learning to align and translate. In *Proceedings of the 3rd International Conference on Learning Representations (ICLR)*.

David Chiang. 2005. A hierarchical phrase-based model for statistical machine translation. In *Proceedings of the 43rd Annual Meeting of the Association for Computational Linguistics (ACL)*.

Kyunghyun Cho, Bart van Merrienboer, Caglar Gulcehre, Dzmitry Bahdanau, Fethi Bougares, Holger Schwenk, and Yoshua Bengio. 2014. Learning phrase representations using rnn encoder–decoder for statistical machine translation. In *Proceedings of the 2014 Conference on Empirical Methods in Natural Language Processing (EMNLP)*, pages 1724–1734, Doha, Qatar, October.

Liang Huang and Haitao Mi. 2010. Efficient incremental decoding for tree-to-string translation. In *Proceedings of the 2010 Conference on Empirical Methods in Natural Language Processing (EMNLP)*.

Liang Huang, Kevin Knight, and Aravind Joshi. 2006. Statistical syntax-directed translation with extended domain of locality. In *Proceedings of the 7th biennial conference of the Association for Machine Translation in the Americas (AMTA)*.

Sébastien Jean, Kyunghyun Cho, Roland Memisevic, and Yoshua Bengio. 2015. On using very large target vocabulary for neural machine translation. In *Proceedings of the 53rd Annual Meeting of the Association for Computational Linguistics and the 7th International Joint Conference of the Asian Federation of Natural Language Processing (ACL-IJCNLP)*.

Yang Liu, Qun Liu, and Shouxun Lin. 2006. Tree-to-string alignment template for statistical machine translation. In *Proceedings of the joint conference of the International Committee on Computational Linguistics and the Association for Computational Linguistics (Coling-ACL)*.

Minh-Thang Luong, Ilya Sutskever, Quoc V. Le, Oriol Vinyals, and Wojciech Zaremba. 2015. Addressing the rare word problem in neural machine translation. In *Proceedings of the 53rd Annual Meeting of the Association for Computational Linguistics and the 7th International Joint Conference of the Asian Federation of Natural Language Processing (ACL-IJCNLP)*.

Toshiaki Nakazawa, Hideya Mino, Isao Goto, Graham Neubig, Sadao Kurohashi, and Eiichiro Sumita. 2015. Overview of the 2nd workshop on asian translation. In *Proceedings of the 2nd Workshop on Asian Translation (WAT2015)*, Kyoto, Japan, October.

Ilya Sutskever, Oriol Vinyals, and Quoc V. Le. 2014. Sequence to sequence learning with neural networks. In *Proceedings of the Twenty-eighth Annual Conference on Neural Information Processing Systems (NIPS)*.

Andreas Zollmann and Ashish Venugopal. 2006. Syntax augmented machine translation via chart parsing. In *Proceedings of the Workshop on Statistical Machine Translation (WMT)*.

An Awkward Disparity between BLEU / RIBES Scores and Human Judgements in Machine Translation

Liling Tan
Universität des Saarland
Campus, Saarbrücken, Germany
liling.tan@uni-saarland.de

Jon Dehdari, Josef van Genabith
Deutsches Forschungszentrum für Künstliche Intelligenz / Saarbrücken, Germany
{first.last_name}@dfki.de

Abstract

Automatic evaluation of machine translation (MT) quality is essential in developing high quality MT systems. Despite previous criticisms, BLEU remains the most popular machine translation metric. Previous studies on the schism between BLEU and manual evaluation highlighted the poor correlation between MT systems with low BLEU scores and high manual evaluation scores. Alternatively, the RIBES metric—which is more sensitive to reordering—has shown to have better correlations with human judgements, but in our experiments it also fails to correlate with human judgements. In this paper we demonstrate, via our submission to the Workshop on Asian Translation 2015 (WAT 2015), a patent translation system with very high BLEU and RIBES scores and very poor human judgement scores.

1 Introduction

Automatic Machine Translation (MT) evaluation metrics have been criticized for a variety of reasons (Babych and Hartley, 2004; Callison-Burch et al., 2006). However, the relatively consistent correlation of higher BLEU scores (Papineni et al., 2002) and better human judgements in major machine translation shared tasks has led to the conventional wisdom that translations with significantly higher BLEU scores generally suggests a better translation than its lower scoring counterparts (Bojar et al., 2014; Bojar et al., 2015; Nakazawa et al., 2014; Cettolo et al., 2014).

Callison-Burch et al. (2006) has anecdotally presented possible failures of BLEU by showing examples of translations with the same BLEU score but of different translation quality. Through meta-evaluation[1] of BLEU scores and human judgements scores of the 2005 NIST MT Evaluation exercise, they have also showed high correlations of R^2 = 0.87 (for adequacy) and R^2 = 0.74 (for fluency) when an outlier rule-based machine translation system with poor BLEU score and high human score is excluded; when included the correlations drops to 0.14 for adequacy and 0.74 for fluency.

Despite showing the poor correlation between BLEU and human scores, Callison-Burch et al. (2006) had only empirically meta-evaluated a scenario where low BLEU score does not necessary result in a poor human judgement score. In this paper, we demonstrate a real-world example of machine translation that yielded high automatic evaluation scores but failed to obtain a good score on manual evaluation in an MT shared task submission.

2 BLEU

Papineni et al. (2002) originally define BLEU n-gram precision p_n by summing the n-gram matches for every hypothesis sentence S in the test corpus C:

$$p_n = \frac{\sum_{S \in C} \sum_{ngram \in S} Count_{matched}(ngram)}{\sum_{S \in C} \sum_{ngram \in S} Count(ngram)} \tag{1}$$

BLEU is a precision based metric; to emulate recall, the brevity penalty (BP) is introduced to compensate for the possibility of high precision translation that are too short. The BP is calculated as:

[1]Meta-evaluation refers to the measurement of the Pearson correlation R^2 between an automatic evaluation metrics and human judgment scores. More recently, meta-evaluation involves the calculation using other correlation measures such as the Spearman's rank correlation ρ (Callison-Burch et al., 2007) or the Kendall's Tau τ (Stanojević et al., 2015; Graham et al., 2015)

Proceedings of the 2nd Workshop on Asian Translation (WAT2015), pages 74-81,
Kyoto, Japan, 16th October 2015.

$$BP = \begin{cases} 1 & \text{if} \quad c > r \\ e^{1-r/c} & \text{if} \quad c \leq r \end{cases} \tag{2}$$

where c and r respectively refers to the length of the hypothesis translations and the reference translations. The resulting system BLEU score is calculated as follows:

$$\text{BLEU} = \text{BP} \times \exp(\sum_{n=1}^{N} w_n \log p_n) \tag{3}$$

where n refers to the orders of n-gram considered for p_n and w_n refers to the weights assigned for the n-gram precisions; in practice, the weights are uniformly distributed.

A BLEU score can range from 0 to 1 and the closer to 1 indicates that a hypothesis translation is closer to the reference translation[2].

Traditionally, BLEU scores has showed high correlation with human judgements and is still used as the *de facto* standard automatic evaluation metric for major machine translation shared tasks. And BLEU continues to show high correlations primarily for n-gram-based machine translation systems (Bojar et al., 2015; Nakazawa et al., 2014).

However, the fallacy of BLEU-human correlations can be easily highlighted with the following example:

Source:
ㅇ ㅓ흐 자 안ㅡ븜 위흐 하9 휘 ㅐㅊ, ㄱㄴ ㅏ 0.005%
ㅇ 시 ㅏ음화ㅎ 그 언 ㅅㅒ 자힘 ㅓ다

Hypothesis:
このような作用を発揮するためには、夫々０．００５％以上含有することが好ましい。

Baseline:
このような作用を発揮するためには、それぞれ０．００５％以上含有することが好ましい。

Reference:
このような作用を発揮させるためには、夫々０．００５％以上含有させることが好ましい。

[2]Alternatively, researchers would choose to inflate the BLEU score to a range between 0 to 100 to improve readability of the scores without the decimal prefix.

Source/Reference English Gloss:
"So as to achieve the reaction, it is preferable that it contains more 0.005% of each [chemical]"

The unigram, bigram, trigrams and fourgrams (p_1, p_2, p_3, p_4) precision of the hypothesis translation are 90.0, 78.9, 66.7 and 52.9 respectively. The p_n score for the hypothesis sentence precision score for the reference is 70.75. When considering the brevity penalty of 0.905, the overall BLEU is 64.03. Comparatively, the n-gram precisions for the baseline translations are p_1=84.2, p_2=66.7, p_3=47.1 and p_4=25.0 and the overall BLEU is 43.29 with a BP of 0.854. In this respect, one would consider the baseline translation inferior to the hypothesis with a >10 BLEU difference. However, there is only a subtle difference between the hypothesis and the baseline translation (それぞれvs 夫々).

This is an actual example from the 2nd Workshop on Asian Translation (WAT 2015) MT shared task evaluation, and five crowd-sourced evaluators consider the baseline translation a better translation. For this particular example, the human evaluators preferred the natural translation from Korean ㄱ ㅏ *gaggag* to Japanese それぞれ *sorezore* instead of the patent document usage of 夫々 *sorezore*, both それぞれ and 夫々 can be loosely translated as '*respectively*' or '*(for) each*' in English.

The big difference in BLEU for a single lexical difference in translation is due to the geometric averaged scores for the individual n-gram precisions. It assumes the independence of n-gram precisions and accentuates the precision disparity by involving the single lexical difference in all possible n-grams that capture the particular position in the sentence. This is clearly indicated by the growing precision difference in the higher order n-grams.

2.1 RIBES

Another failure of BLEU is the lack of explicit consideration for reordering. Callison-Burch et al. (2006) highlighted that since BLEU only takes reordering into account by rewarding the higher n-gram orders, freely permuted unigrams and bigrams matches are able to sustain a high BLEU score with little penalty caused by tri/fourgram mismatches. To overcome reordering, the RIBES score was introduced by adding a rank correlation coefficient[3] prior to unigram matches without the need for higher order *n*-gram matches (Isozaki et al., 2010).

Let us consider another example:

Source:
T용융(DSC) = 89.9℃; T결정화(DSC) = 72℃(5℃/분으로 DSC로 측정)。

Hypothesis:
Ｔｍｅｌｔ（ＤＳＣ）＝７２℃（５℃／分でＤＳＣ測定（ＤＳＣ）＝89．９結晶化度（Ｔ）。

Baseline:
Ｔ溶融（ＤＳＣ）＝８９．９℃；Ｔ結晶化（ＤＳＣ）＝７２℃（５℃／分でＤＳＣで測定）。

Reference:
Ｔｍｅｌｔ（ＤＳＣ）＝８９．９℃；Ｔｃｒｙｓｔ（ＤＳＣ）＝７２℃（５℃／分でＤＳＣを用いて測定）。

Source/Reference English Gloss:
Tmelt (DSC) = 8 9. 9 °C; Tcryst (DSC) = 7 °C (measured using DSC at 5 °C / min)

The example above shows the marginal effectiveness of RIBES when penalizing wrongly ordered phrases in the hypothesis. The baseline translation accurately translates the meaning of the sentence with a minor partial translation of the technical variables (i.e. *Tmelt* -> Ｔ溶融 and T결정화 -> Ｔ結晶化. However, the hypothesis translation made serious adequacy errors when inverting the values of the technical variables but the hypothesis translation was minimally penalized in RIBES and also BLEU.

The RIBES score for the hypothesis and baseline translations are 94.04 and 86.33 respectively whereas their BLEU scores are 53.3 and 58.8. In the WAT 2015 evaluation, five evaluators unanimously voted in favor for the baseline translation. Although the RIBES score presents a wider difference between the hypothesis and baseline translation than BLEU, it is insufficient to account for the arrant error that the hypothesis translation made.

[3]normalized Kendall τ of all *n*-gram pairs between the hypothesis and reference translations

2.2 Other Shades of BLEU / RIBES

It is worth noting that there are other automatic MT evaluation metrics that depend on the same precision-based score with primary differences in how the $Count_{match}(ngram)$ is measured; Giménez and Màrquez (2007) described other linguistics features that one could match in place of surface *n*-grams, such as lexicalized syntactic parse features, semantic entities and roles annotations, etc. As such, the modified BLEU-like metrics can present other aspects of syntactic fluency and semantic adequacy complementary to the string-based BLEU.

A different approach to improve upon the BLEU scores is to allow paraphrases or gappy variants and replace the proportion of $Count_{match}(ngram)$ / Count(ngram) by a lexical similarity measure. Banerjee and Lavie (2005) introduced the METEOR metric that allows hypotheses' *n*-grams to match paraphrases and stems instead of just the surface strings. Lin and Och (2004) presented the ROUGE-S metrics that uses skip-grams matches. More recently, pre-trained regression models based on semantic textual similarity and neural network-based similarity measures trained on skip-grams are applied to replace the *n*-gram matching (Vela and Tan, 2015; Gupta et al., 2015).

While enriching the surface *n*-gram matching allows the automatic evaluation metric to handle variant translations, it does not resolves the "prominent crudeness" of BLEU (Callison-Burch, 2006) involving (i) the omission of content-bearing materials not being penalized, and (ii) the inability to calculate recall despite the brevity penalty.

3 Experimental Setup

We describe our system submission[4] to the WAT 2015 shared task (Nakazawa et al., 2015) for Korean to Japanese patent translation.[5].

The Japan Patent Office (JPO) Patent Corpus is the official resource provided for the shared task. The training dataset is made up of 1 million sentences (250k each from the chemistry, electricity, mechanical engineering and physics do-

[4]Our Team ID in WAT 2015 is `Sense`

[5]Although, we have also participated in the English-Japanese-Chinese scientific text translation subtask using the ASPEC corpus, our results have been presented in Tan and Bond (2014) and Tan et al. (2015)

Parameters	Organizers	Ours
Input document length	40	80
Korean tokenizer	MeCab	KoNLPy
Japanese tokenizer	Juman	MeCab
LM n-gram order	5	5
Distortion limit	0	20
Quantized & binarized LM	no	yes
`devtest.txt` in LM	no	yes
Binarized phrase tables	no	yes
MERT runs	1	2

Table 1: Differences between Organizer's and our Phrase-based SMT system

mains). Two development datasets[6] and one test set each comprises 2000 sentences with 500 sentences from each of the training domains. The Korean and Japanese texts were tokenized using KoNLPy (Park and Cho, 2014) and MeCab (Kudo et al., 2004) respectively.

We used the phrase-based SMT implemented in the Moses toolkit (Koehn et al., 2003; Koehn et al., 2007) with the following vanilla Moses experimental settings:

- `MGIZA++` implementation of IBM word alignment model 4 with grow-diagonal-final-and heuristics for word alignment and phrase-extraction (Och and Ney, 2003; Koehn et al., 2003; Gao and Vogel, 2008)(Koehn et al., 2003; Och and Ney, 2003; Gao and Vogel, 2008)
- Bi-directional lexicalized reordering model that considers monotone, swap and discontinuous orientations (Koehn, 2005; Galley and Manning, 2008)
- To minimize the computing load on the translation model, we compressed the phrase-table and lexical reordering model (Junczys-Dowmunt, 2012)
- Language modeling is trained using KenLM using 5-grams, with modified Kneser-Ney smoothing (Heafield, 2011; Kneser and Ney, 1995; Chen and Goodman, 1998). The language model is quantized to reduce filesize and improve querying speed (Heafield et al., 2013; Whittaker and Raj, 2001).
- Minimum Error Rate Training (MERT) (Och, 2003) to tune the decoding parameters.

[6] `dev.txt` and `devtest.txt`

3.1 Human Evaluation

The human judgment scores for the WAT evaluations were acquired using the Lancers crowdsourcing platform (WAT, 2014). Human evaluators were randomly assigned documents from the test set. They were shown the source document, the hypothesis translation and a baseline translation generated by the baseline phrase-based MT system.

3.1.1 Baseline System

Human evaluations were conducted as pairwise comparisons between translations from our system and the WAT organizers' phrase-based statistical MT baseline system. Table 1 highlights the parameter differences between the organizers and our phrase-based SMT system.

3.1.2 Pairwise Comparison

The human judgment scores for the WAT evaluations were acquired using the Lancers crowdsourcing platform. Human evaluators were randomly assigned documents from the test set. They were shown the source document, the hypothesis translation and a baseline translation generated by the phrase-based MT system. Five evaluators were asked to judge each document.

The crowdsourced evaluators were non-experts, thus their judgements were not necessary precise, especially for patent translations. The evaluators were asked to judge whether the hypothesis or the baseline translation was better, or they were tied. The translation that was judged better constituted a *win* and the other a *loss*. For each, the majority vote between the five evaluators for the hypothesis decided whether the hypothesis *won*, *lost* or *tied* the baseline. The final human judgment score,

HUMAN, is calculated as follows:

$$\text{HUMAN} = 100 \times \frac{W - L}{W + L + T} \quad (4)$$

By definition, the *HUMAN* score ranges from -100 to $+100$, where higher is better.

4 Results

Moses' default parameter tuning method, MERT, is non-deterministic, and hence it is advisable to tune the phrase-based model more than once (Clark et al. 2011). We repeated the tuning step and submitted the system translations that achieved the higher BLEU score for manual evaluation.

As a sanity check we also replicated the organizers' baseline system and submitted it for manual evaluation. We expect this system to score close to zero. We submitted a total of three sets of output to the WAT 2015 shared task, two of which underwent manual evaluation.

Systems	RIBES	BLEU	HUMAN
Organizers' PBMT baseline	94.13	69.22	0.0
Our replica baseline	94.29	70.23	**+3.50**
Ours (MERT 1)	95.03	84.26	-
Ours (MERT 2)	**95.15**	**85.23**	-17.75

Table 2: BLEU and HUMAN scores for WAT 2015

Table 2 presents the BLEU scores achieved by our phrase-based MT system in contrast to the organizers' baseline phrase-based system. The difference in BLEU between the organizers' system and ours may be due to our inclusion of the second development set in building our language model and the inclusion of more training data by allowing a maximum of 80 tokens per document as compared to 40 (see Table 1).

Another major difference is the high distortion limit we have set as compared to the organizers' monotonic system, it is possible that the high distortion limit compensates for the long distance word alignments that might have been penalized by the phrasal and reordering probabilities which results in the higher RIBES and BLEU score.[7]

However, the puzzling fact is that our system being 15 BLEU points better than the organizers' baseline begets a terribly low human judgement score. We discuss this next.

5 Segment Level Meta-Evaluation

We perform a segment level meta-evaluation by calculating the BLEU and RIBES score difference for each hypothesis-baseline translation. Figures 1 and 2 show the correlations of the BLEU and RIBES score difference against the positive and negative human judgements score for every sentence.

Figure 1 presents the considerable incongruity between our system's high BLEU improvements (>+60 BLEU) being rated marginally better than the baseline translation, indicated by the orange and blue bubbles on the top right corner. There were even translations from our system with >+40 BLEU improvements that tied with the organizer's baseline translations, indicated by the grey bubbles at around the +40 BLEU and +5 RIBES region. Except for the a portion of segments that scored worse than the baseline system (lower right part of the graph where BLEU and RIBES falls below 0), the overall trend in Figure 1 presents the conventional wisdom that the BLEU improvements from our systems reflects positive human judgement scores.

However, Figure 2 presents the awkward disparity where many segments with BLEU improvements were rated strongly as poorer translations when compared against the baseline. Also, many segments with high BLEU improvements were tied with the baseline translations, indicated by the grey bubbles across the positive BLEU scores.

As shown in the examples in Section 2, a number of prominent factors contribute to these disparity in high BLEU / RIBES improvements and low HUMAN judgement scores:

- Minor lexical differences causing a huge difference in n-gram precision
- Crowd-sourced *vs.* expert preferences on terminology, especially for patents

[7] In our submission `Byte2String` refers to the encoding problem we encountered when tokenizing the Korean text with MeCab causing our system to read Korean byte-code instead of Unicode. But the decoder could still output Unicode since our Japanese data was successfully tokenized using MeCab, we submitted this output under the submission name `Byte2String`; the `Byte2String` submission is not reported in this paper. Later we rectified the encoding problem by using KoNLPy and re-ran the alignment, phrase extraction, MERT and decoding, hence the submission name, `Unicode2String`, i.e. the system reported in Table 2.

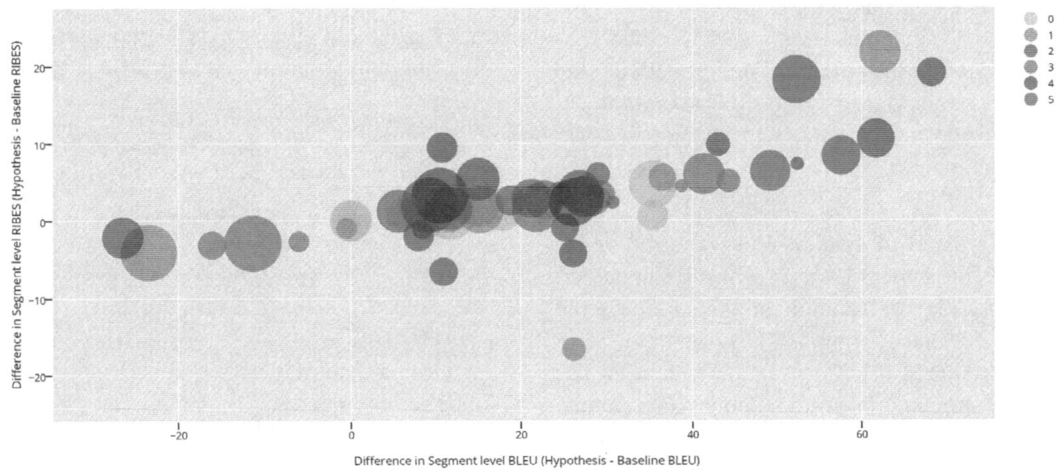

Figure 1: Correlation between BLEU, RIBES differences and *Positive* HUMAN Judgements (HUMAN Scores of 0, +1, +2, +3, +4 and +5 represented by the colored bubbles: *grey, orange, blue, green, red and purple*; larger area means more segments with the respective HUMAN Scores)

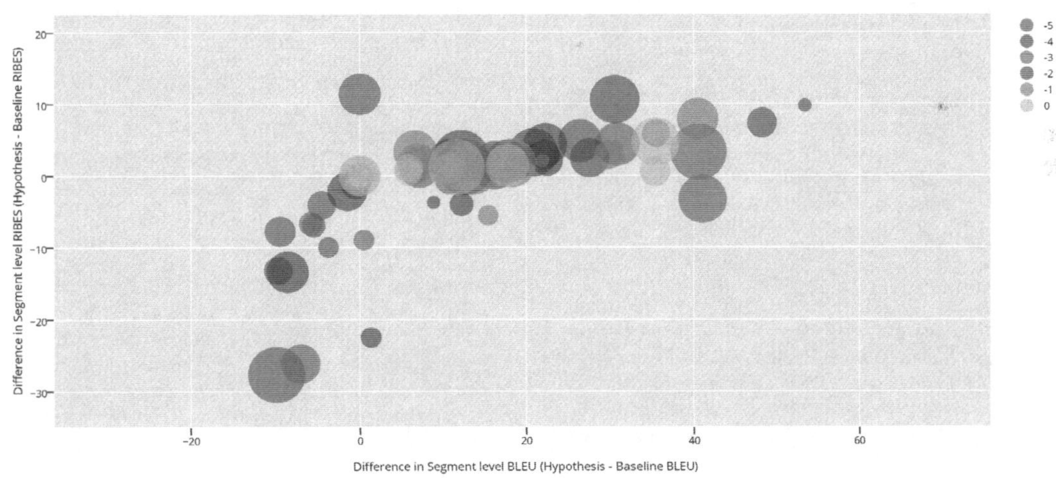

Figure 2: Correlation between BLEU, RIBES differences and *Negative* HUMAN Judgements (HUMAN Scores of 0, -1, -2, -3, -4 and -5 represented by the colored bubbles: *grey, orange, blue, green, red and purple*; larger area means more segments with the respective HUMAN Scores)

- Minor MT evaluation metric differences not reflecting major translation inadequacy

Each of these failures contributes to an increased amount of disparity between the automatic translation metric improvements and human judgement scores.

6 Conclusion

In this paper we have demonstrated a real-world case where high BLEU and RIBES scores do not correlate with better human judgement. Using our system's submission for the WAT 2015 patent shared task, we presented several factors that might contribute to the poor correlation, and also performed a segment level meta-evaluation to identify segments where our system's high BLEU / RIBES improvements were deemed substantially worse than the baseline translations. We hope our results and analysis will lead to improvements in automatic translation evaluation metrics.

Acknowledgements

We thank the Workshop on Asian Translation organizers for sharing the results of the manual annotations, the organization of the task and the helpful feedbacks to improve this paper.

The research leading to these results has received funding from the People Programme (Marie Curie Actions) of the European Union's Seventh Framework Programme FP7/2007-2013/ under REA grant agreement no. 317471.

References

Bogdan Babych and Anthony Hartley. 2004. Extending the BLEU MT evaluation method with frequency weightings. In *Proceedings of the 42nd Annual Meeting on Association for Computational Linguistics*, page 621.

Satanjeev Banerjee and Alon Lavie. 2005. METEOR: An automatic metric for MT evaluation with improved correlation with human judgments. In *Proceedings of the ACL Workshop on Intrinsic and Extrinsic Evaluation Measures for Machine Translation and/or Summarization*, volume 29, pages 65–72.

Ondřej Bojar, Christian Buck, Christian Federmann, Barry Haddow, Philipp Koehn, Johannes Leveling, Christof Monz, Pavel Pecina, Matt Post, Herve Saint-Amand, et al. 2014. Findings of the 2014 workshop on statistical machine translation. In *Proceedings of the Ninth Workshop on Statistical Machine Translation*, pages 12–58.

Ondřej Bojar, Rajen Chatterjee, Christian Federmann, Barry Haddow, Matthias Huck, Chris Hokamp, Philipp Koehn, Varvara Logacheva, Christof Monz, Matteo Negri, Matt Post, Carolina Scarton, Lucia Specia, and Marco Turchi. 2015. Findings of the 2015 workshop on statistical machine translation. In *Proceedings of the Tenth Workshop on Statistical Machine Translation*, pages 1–46, Lisbon, Portugal.

Chris Callison-Burch, Miles Osborne, and Philipp Koehn. 2006. Re-evaluation the role of Bleu in machine translation research. In *EACL*, volume 6, pages 249–256.

Chris Callison-Burch, Cameron Fordyce, Philipp Koehn, Christof Monz, and Josh Schroeder. 2007. (meta-) evaluation of machine translation. In *Proceedings of the Second Workshop on Statistical Machine Translation*, pages 136–158.

Mauro Cettolo, Jan Niehues, Sebastian Stüker, Luisa Bentivogli, and Marcello Federico. 2014. Report on the 11th IWSLT evaluation campaign, IWSLT 2014. In *Proceedings of the eleventh International Workshop on Spoken Language Translation (IWSLT), Lake Tahoe, CA*, pages 2–17.

Stanley Chen and Joshua T. Goodman. 1998. An empirical study of smoothing techniques for language modeling. Technical Report 10-98, Harvard University.

Michel Galley and Christopher D Manning. 2008. A simple and effective hierarchical phrase reordering model. In *Proceedings of the Conference on Empirical Methods in Natural Language Processing*, pages 848–856.

Qin Gao and Stephan Vogel. 2008. Parallel implementations of word alignment tool. In *Software Engineering, Testing, and Quality Assurance for Natural Language Processing*, pages 49–57.

Jesús Giménez and Lluís Màrquez. 2007. Linguistic features for automatic evaluation of heterogenous MT systems. In *Proceedings of the Second Workshop on Statistical Machine Translation*, pages 256–264, Stroudsburg, PA, USA.

Yvette Graham, Timothy Baldwin, and Nitika Mathur. 2015. Accurate evaluation of segment-level machine translation metrics. In *Proceedings of the 2015 Conference of the North American Chapter of the Association for Computational Linguistics: Human Language Technologies*, pages 1183–1191, Denver, Colorado.

Rohit Gupta, Constantin Orasan, and Josef van Genabith. 2015. ReVal: A simple and effective machine translation evaluation metric based on recurrent neural networks. In *Proceedings of the 2015 Conference on Empirical Methods in Natural Language Processing*, pages 1066–1072, Lisbon, Portugal.

Kenneth Heafield, Ivan Pouzyrevsky, Jonathan H. Clark, and Philipp Koehn. 2013. Scalable modified Kneser-Ney language model estimation. In *Proceedings of the 51st Annual Meeting of the Association for Computational Linguistics (Volume 2: Short Papers)*, pages 690–696, Sofia, Bulgaria.

Kenneth Heafield. 2011. KenLM: Faster and smaller language model queries. In *Proceedings of the EMNLP 2011 Sixth Workshop on Statistical Machine Translation*, pages 187–197, Edinburgh, Scotland, United Kingdom.

Hideki Isozaki, Tsutomu Hirao, Kevin Duh, Katsuhito Sudoh, and Hajime Tsukada. 2010. Automatic evaluation of translation quality for distant language pairs. In *Proceedings of the 2010 Conference on*

Empirical Methods in Natural Language Processing, pages 944–952.

Marcin Junczys-Dowmunt. 2012. Phrasal rank-encoding: Exploiting phrase redundancy and translational relations for phrase table compression. *The Prague Bulletin of Mathematical Linguistics*, 98:63–74.

Reinhard Kneser and Hermann Ney. 1995. Improved backing-off for m-gram language modeling. In *Acoustics, Speech, and Signal Processing, 1995. ICASSP-95., 1995 International Conference on*, volume 1, pages 181–184.

Philipp Koehn, Franz Josef Och, and Daniel Marcu. 2003. Statistical phrase-based translation. In *Proceedings of the 2003 Conference of the North American Chapter of the Association for Computational Linguistics on Human Language Technology-Volume 1*, pages 48–54.

Philipp Koehn, Hieu Hoang, Alexandra Birch, Chris Callison-Burch, Marcello Federico, Nicola Bertoldi, Brooke Cowan, Wade Shen, Christine Moran, Richard Zens, et al. 2007. Moses: Open source toolkit for statistical machine translation. In *Proceedings of the 45th annual meeting of the ACL on interactive poster and demonstration sessions*, pages 177–180.

Philipp Koehn. 2005. Europarl: A parallel corpus for statistical machine translation. In *Proceedings of MT Summit, vol. 5, pp. 79-86.*

Taku Kudo, Kaoru Yamamoto, and Yuji Matsumoto. 2004. Applying conditional random fields to Japanese morphological analysis. In *Proceedings of the Conference on Empirical Methods in Natural Language Processing*, pages 230–237.

Chin-Yew Lin and Franz Josef Och. 2004. Automatic evaluation of machine translation quality using longest common subsequence and skip-bigram statistics. In *Proceedings of the 42nd Annual Meeting on Association for Computational Linguistics*, Stroudsburg, PA, USA.

Toshiaki Nakazawa, Hideya Mino, Isao Goto, Sadao Kurohashi, and Eiichiro Sumita. 2014. Overview of the first workshop on Asian translation. In *Proceedings of the First Workshop on Asian Translation (WAT2014)*, Tokyo, Japan.

Toshiaki Nakazawa, Hideya Mino, Isao Goto, Graham Neubig, Sadao Kurohashi, and Eiichiro Sumita. 2015. Overview of the 2nd workshop on Asian translation. In *Proceedings of the 2nd Workshop on Asian Translation (WAT2015)*, Kyoto, Japan.

Franz Josef Och and Hermann Ney. 2003. A systematic comparison of various statistical alignment models. *Computational linguistics*, 29(1):19–51.

Franz Josef Och. 2003. Minimum error rate training in statistical machine translation. In *Proceedings of the 41st Annual Meeting on Association for Computational Linguistics-Volume 1*, pages 160–167.

Kishore Papineni, Salim Roukos, Todd Ward, and Wei-Jing Zhu. 2002. BLEU: a method for automatic evaluation of machine translation. In *Proceedings of the 40th annual meeting on association for computational linguistics*, pages 311–318.

Eunjeong L. Park and Sungzoon Cho. 2014. KoNLPy: Korean natural language processing in Python. In *Proceedings of the 26th Annual Conference on Human and Cognitive Language Technology*, Chuncheon, Korea.

Miloš Stanojević, Amir Kamran, Philipp Koehn, and Ondřej Bojar. 2015. Results of the WMT15 metrics shared task. In *Proceedings of the Tenth Workshop on Statistical Machine Translation*, pages 256–273, Lisbon, Portugal.

Liling Tan and Francis Bond. 2014. Manipulating input data in machine translation. In *Proceedings of the 1st Workshop on Asian Translation (WAT2014).*

Liling Tan, Josef van Genabith, and Francis Bond. 2015. Passive and pervasive use of bilingual dictionary in statistical machine translation. In *Proceedings of the Fourth Workshop on Hybrid Approaches to Translation (HyTra)*, pages 30–34, Beijing.

Mihaela Vela and Liling Tan. 2015. Predicting machine translation adequacy with document embeddings. In *Proceedings of the Tenth Workshop on Statistical Machine Translation*, pages 402–410, Lisbon, Portugal.

Edward W.D. Whittaker and Bhiksha Raj. 2001. Quantization-based language model compression. In *Proceedings of INTERSPEECH*, pages 33–36.

A Dependency-to-String Model for Chinese-Japanese SMT System

Hua Shan **Yujie Zhang** **Lu Bai** **Te Luo**
School of Computer and Information technology, Beijing Jiaotong University
{13120422, yjzhang, 13120379, 14120472}@bjtu.edu.cn

Abstract

This paper describes the Beijing Jiaotong University Chinese-Japanese machine translation system which participated in the 2st Workshop on Asian Translation (WAT2015). We exploit the syntactic and semantic knowledge encoded in dependency tree to build a dependency-to-string translation model for Chinese-Japanese statistical machine translation (SMT). Our system achieves a BLEU of 34.87 and a RIBES of 79.25 on the Chinese-Japanese translation task in the official evaluation.

1 Introduction

Motivated by representing the grammatical function of the constituents of a sentence or phrase, dependency grammar holds both syntactic and semantic knowledge. How to building translation model by exploiting the syntactic and semantic knowledge encoded in dependency tree has been now one of the most popular research topics in the recent years.

In dependency tree based models, researchers propose some tree decomposition methods or grammars to build translation model. These models can be classified into string-to-tree model, tree-to-tree model and tree-to-string model. Our system participated in WAT2015 (Nakazawa et al., 2015) adopts tree-to-string model. Particularly, we use the dependency-to-string translation method proposed by (Xie et al., 2011) in Chinese-Japanese translation task. This method proposes a novel tree decompose tion, which takes head-dependents relation (HDR) fragments as elementary structures of rule extraction. An HDR is a tree fragment composed of a head and all its dependents. In this method, the translation rules are expressed with the source side as generalized HDR fragments and the target sides as strings. The model takes substitution as the only operation and can specify reordering information directly into translation rules, thus requires no additional heuristics or reordering models as the previous works. And the model is more concise.

Section 2 describes dependency-to-string translation model in detail. Section 3 reports on our experiment results on a Chinese- SMT system. Section 4 concludes this paper.

2 Dependency-to-String Translation Model

In this paper, we describes the translation model in four aspects, dependency-to-string grammar, translation rule acquisition, the model and the decoding.

2.1 Dependency-to-String Grammar

A dependency structure for a sentence is a directed acyclic graph with words as nodes and modification relations as edges, each edge directing from a head to a dependent. Figure 1 (a) shows an example dependency structure of a Chinese sentence.

2010年 FIFA 世界杯 在 南非 成功 举行

Proceedings of the 2nd Workshop on Asian Translation (WAT2015), pages 82-86,
Kyoto, Japan, 16th October 2015.

2010 FIFA World Cup in South Africa successfully hold

Here are some properties of a HDR fragment :

1) head determines the syntactic category of HDR, and can often replace HDR;
2) head determines the semantic category of HDR; dependent gives semantic specification.

According to the above properties, we can represent the corresponding HDR fragment with head. The translation rules of dependency-to-string model can be classified into two categories:

-HDR rules, which represent the source side as generalized HDR fragments and the target sides as strings and act as both translation rules and reordering rules.

-H rules, which represent the source side as a word and the target side as words or strings and are used for translating words.

Figure 1 shows examples of the two translation rules. (b), (c) and (d) are three examples of HDR rules, and (d) is an example of H rules. In the figure, the nodes modified by "*" are head of HDR fragment. By the way, the three HDR rules describes translation ways of the same sentence pattern (that is, constituted by "noun phrase + preposition phrase + adverb + verb") and different contexts. Thereinto, rule (b) appoints its context completely, rule (c) restrains its context partially and rule (d) has no restraint for its context.

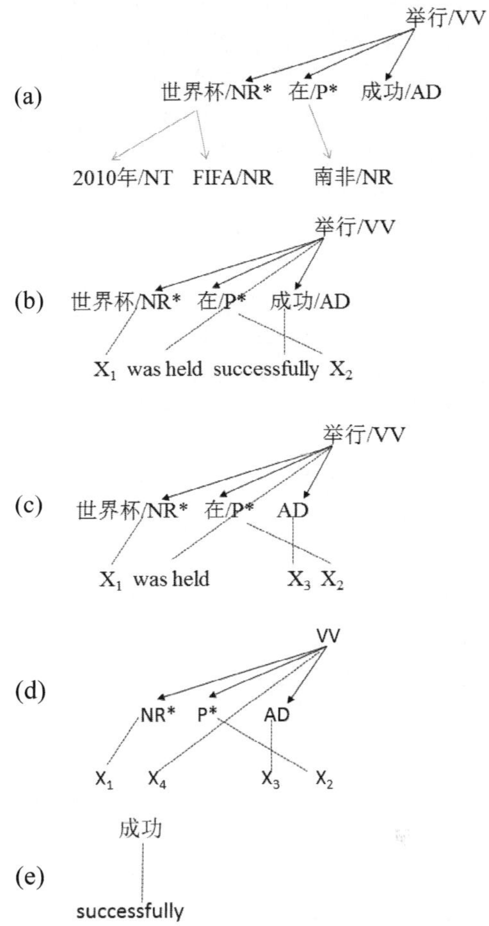

Figure 1: Examples of dependency structure (a), HDR rules (b), (c) , (d)and H rules (e).

2.2 Rule Acquisition

The rule acquisition of dependency-to-string model begins with a parallel corpus with word-aligned results, the source dependency structures and the target side sentence. We accomplish the rule automatic acquisition through the following three steps:

1) Tree annotation: annotate the necessary information on each node of dependency trees for translation rule acquisition.
2) Acceptable HDR fragments identification: identify HDR fragments from the annotated trees for HDR rules generation.
3) HDR rules generation: generate a series of HDR rules according to the identified acceptable HDR fragments.

The following describes each of these in detail.

2.2.1 Tree Annotation and Acceptable HDR Fragments Identification

The tree annotation can be accomplished by a single postorder transversal of dependency tree *T*. For each node *n* of *T*, we annotated with head span *hsp(n)* and dependency span *dsp(n)* (Xie et al., 2011). During the recursive walk, we calculate *hsp(n)* according to alignment relation for each node *n* accessed. The *dsp(n)* can be obtained according to *hsp(n)* and dependency span of all dependents of *n*. After tree annotation, we can identify HDR fragments for HDR rules generation, according to head span and dependency span of each node.

2.2.2 HDR Rules and H Rules Generation

According to the identified acceptable HDR fragments, a series of lexicalized and unlexicalized HDR rules will be generated. This paper will not describe in detail about it and you can refer to (Xie et al., 2011).

H rules acquisition can be implemented as a sub procedure of HDR rules acquisition. Specifically, in the recursive walk of dependency tree, a H rule is generated according to alignment information for each node accessed.

2.3 Translation Model

Given the dependency-to-string grammar, for a given source language dependency tree *T*, it may generate more than one derivations *D* that convert a source dependency tree *T* into a target string e, thus producing varieties of candidate translations. To compare the candidate translations, we adopt a general log-linear model (Och and Ney, 2002) to define D as:

$$P(D) \propto \prod \phi_i (D)^{\lambda i} \qquad (1)$$

where ϕ_i (D) is feature function defined on derivation *D* and λ_i are the feature weights.

Our paper used seven features as follows:

1) translation probabilities: $P(t|s)$ and $P(s|t)$;
2) lexical translation probabilities: $P_{lex}(t|s)$ and $P_{lex}(s|t)$;
3) rule penalty: $exp(-1)$;
4) target word penalty: $exp(|e|)$;
5) language model : $P_{lm}(e)$;

2.4 Decoding

Our decoder is based on bottom up chart parsing algorithm that convert the input dependency structure into a target string. It finds the best derivation among all possible derivations *D*. Given a source dependency structure *T*, the decoder traverses each internal node *n* of *T* in post-order. And we process it as follows.

1) If *n* is a leaf node, it checks the rule set for matched translation rules H and uses the rules to generate candidate translation;
2) If *n* is a internal node, it enumerates all instances of the related sentence, clauses or phrases of the HDR fragment rooted at *n*, and checks the translation rule set for matched translation rules. If there is no matched rules, we construct a pseudo translation rule according to the word order of the HDR fragment in the source side;
3) Make use of Cube Pruning algorithm (Chiang, 2007; Huang and Chiang, 2007) to generate the candidate translation for the node *n*.

To balance the decoder's performance and speed, we use four constraints as follows:

1) Beam-threshold: we get the score threshold from the best score in the current stack multiplied by a fixed ratio. The candidate translations with a score worse than the score threshold will be discarded;
2) beam-limit: the maximum number of candidate translations in the beam;
3) rule-threshold: we get the rule score threshold from the best score multiplied by a fixed ratio in the rule table queue. The rules with a score worse than rule score threshold will be dis-

carded;

4) rule-limit: the maximum number of rules in the rule table queue.

For our experiments, we set the beam-threshold = 10^{-2}, beam-limit = 100, rule-threshold = 10^{-2} and rule-limit = 100.

3 Experiments

3.1 Data preparation

We use ASPEC[1] Chinese-Japanese paper excerpt corpus. The training data contains 672,315 sentence pairs, the development data contains 2090 sentence pairs, and the test data contains 2107 sentence pairs.

We employ the Stanford Word Segmenter[2] for Chinese word segmentation, with the standard of CTB. And we use JUMAN[3] for Japanese word segmentation.

After word segmentation, we use the Stanford Parser [4] for Chinese dependency parsing. The parser can create dependency tree for a Chinese sentence and provide the part-of-speech (POS) for each node and the dependency relation type for each edge. Meanwhile, the sentences with special symbols and the sentences whose dependency results contain cross phenomenon will be filtered out. As a result, about 590,000 sentence pairs were obtained for training data.

We apply SRI Language Modeling Toolkit[5] to train a 4-gram language model on the Japanese corpus preprocessed.

We obtain the word alignments by running GIZA++[6] on the corpus in both directions and applying "grow-diag-and" refinement.

We make use of MERT to tune the feature weights in order to maximize the system's BLEU[7] score on the development set.

System	Rule #	BLEU	RIBES
Baseline	35M	34.25	78.94
Dep2str	8.8M	34.87	79.25

Table 1 The comparison results of the two systems

Then, we use dependency-to-string model described in Section 2 to build a Chinese-Japanese translation system. And use the BLUE score and RIBES score for evaluation.

3.2 Experiments and Evaluation Results

The Chinese-Japanese translation system (Dep2str) consists of three modules:

1) Rule extraction module: extract rules using the Chinese dependency tree, the Japanese sentence and alignment information of the training corpus.

2) Decoding module: decode the Chinese sentences for the n-best Japanese translations according to the model parameters that have been set.

3) Training module: train the translation model using minimum error rate to get the best parameters on the development data.

We then decode the test data using the system.

Table 1 shows the number of the extracted translation rules and the translation performance on the test data. Furthermore, we implemented a MOSES PBSMT system (Koehn et al., 2002) as the baseline for a comparison. In our experiments the value of the distortion limit of the baseline system is the default. The number of translation rules and translation performance of the baseline system are also showed in the table.

In terms of the number of translation rules, the number of the extracted translation rules in the baseline system is over 3 times more than that of dep2str system. We think that the lack of restrictions on syntactic structure resulted in this. In terms of translation performance, the BLEU score and RIBES score on the test data

1 http://orchid.kuee.kyoto-u.ac.jp/ASPEC/
2 http://nlp.stanford.edu/software/segmenter.shtml
3 http://nlp.ist.i.kyoto-u.ac.jp/EN/index.php?JUMAN
4 http://nlp.stanford.edu/software/lex-parser.shtml
5 http://www.speech.sri.com/projects/srilm/
6 http://www.statmt.org/moses/giza/GIZA++.html
7 ftp://jaguar.ncsl.nist.gov/mt/resources/mteval-v11b.pl

achieved by dep2str system are higher than the baseline system by 0.62 and 0.31 respectively. These evaluation results illustrate that the translation system based on the dependency-to-string model is effective on the Chinese-Japanese translation task.

4 Conclusions

This paper describes the Beijing Jiaotong University Chinese-Japanese machine translation system participated in WAT2015. The system employs a dependency-to-string model, which takes the HDR fragments as elementary structures for the rule extraction and directly specifies the ordering information in translation rules, making the decoding algorithm simplified. The experiment results on the ASPEC data showed that the BLEU score and the RIBES score are increased by 0.62 and 0.31 respectively, compared with the phrase-based system.

At present, the accuracy of the Chinese dependency parsing is not very high, and our system's performance is affected by the accuracy. Meanwhile, we filtered out the sentences which could not be parsed by the dependency parser. This caused a decrease in the amount of training data by about 100 thousand sentence pairs. We think that the system's performance will be improved with Chinese dependency parsing with high accuracy.

References

Jun Xie, Haitao Mi, and Qun Liu. A novel dependency-to-string model for statistical machine translation. In Proceedings of the 201 1 Conference On Empirical Methods in Natumf Language Processing, pages 216—226, Edinburgh, Scotland, UK·, July 2011·Association for Computational Linguistics.

Nakazawa, Toshiaki and Mino, Hideya and Goto, Isao and Neubig, Graham and Kurohashi, Sadao and Sumita, Eiichiro. 2015. Overview of the 2nd Workshop on Asian Translation. In proceedings of the 2nd Workshop on Asian Translation(WAT2015), October 2015, Kyoto, Japan.

Franz Josef Och and Hermann Ney. 2002. Discriminative training and maximum entropy models for statistical machine translation. In Proceedings of 40th Annual Meeting of the Association for Computational Linguistics, pages 295–302, Philadelphia, Pennsylvania, USA, July.

Philipp Koehn, Hieu Hoang, Alexandra Birch, Chris Callison-Burch, Marcello Federico, Nicola Bertoldi, Brooke Cowan, Wade Shen, Christine Moran,Richard Zens, Chris Dyer, Ondrej Bojar, AlexandraConstantin, and Evan Herbst. 2007. Moses: Open source toolkit for statistical machine translation. In Proceedings of the 45th Annual Meeting of the Association for Computational Linguistics Companion Volume Proceedings of the Demo and Poster Sessions, pages 177-180.

David Chiang. 2005. A hierarchical phrase-based model for statistical machine translation. In Proceedings of 225 ACL 2005, pages 263–270.

Liang Huang and David Chiang. 2007. Forest rescoring: Faster decoding with integrated language models. In Proceedings of ACL 2007, pages 144–151, Prague, Czech Republic, June.

Hideki Isozaki, Tsutomu Hirao, Kevin Duh, Kat suhito Sudoh, and Hajime Tsukada. 2010. Automatic evaluation of translation quality for distant language pairs. In Proceedings of the 2010 Conference on Empirical Methods in Natural Language Processing, pages 944-952.

Sampling-based Alignment and Hierarchical Sub-sentential Alignment in Chinese–Japanese Translation of Patents

Wei Yang, Zhongwen Zhao, Baosong Yang and Yves Lepage
Graduate School of Information, Production and Systems, Waseda University
{kevinyoogi@akane., zzw890827@fuji., yangbaosong@fuji.}waseda.jp
yves.lepage@waseda.jp

Abstract

This paper describes Chinese–Japanese translation systems based on different alignment methods using the JPO corpus and our submission (ID: WASUIPS) to the subtask of the 2015 Workshop on Asian Translation. One of the alignment methods used is bilingual hierarchical sub-sentential alignment combined with sampling-based multilingual alignment. We also accelerated this method and in this paper, we evaluate the translation results and time spent on several machine translation tasks. The training time is much faster than the standard baseline pipeline (GIZA++/Moses) and MGIZA/Moses.

1 Introduction

Phrase-based Statistical Machine Translation (PB-SMT) as a data-oriented approach to machine translation has been widely used for over 10 years. The Moses (Koehn et al., 2007) open source statistical machine translation toolkit was developed by the Statistical Machine Translation Group at the University of Edinburgh. During the three processes (training, tuning and decoding) for building a phrase-based translation system using Moses, training is the most important step as it creates the core knowledge used in machine translation. Word or phrase alignment in the training step allows to obtain translation relationships among the words or phrases in a sentence-aligned bi-corpus. Word or phrase alignment affects the quality of translation. It is also one of the most time-consuming processing step.

The *probabilistic* approach attempts at determining the best set of alignment links between source and target words or phrases in parallel sentences. IBM models (Brown et al., 1993) and HMM alignment models (Vogel et al., 1996), which are typical implementation of the EM algorithm (Dempster et al., 1977), are the most widely used representatives in this category. GIZA++ (Och and Ney, 2003) implemented IBM Models, it aligns words based on statistical models. It is a global optimization process simultaneously considers all possible associations in the entire corpus and estimates the parameters of the parallel corpus. Several improvements were made: MGIZA (Gao and Vogel, 2008) is a parallel implementation of IBM models. However, the parallelization may lead to slightly different final alignment results, thus preventing reproduction of results to a certain extent.

The *associative* approaches, introduced in (Gale and Church, 1991), do not rely on an alignment model, but on independence statistical measures. The Dice coefficient, mutual information (Gale and Church, 1991), and likelihood ratio (Dunning, 1993) are representative cases of this approach. The associative approaches use a local maximization process in which each sentence is processed independently. Sampling-based multilingual alignment (*Anymalign*) (Lardilleux et al., 2013) and hierarchical sub-sentential alignment (*Cutnalign*) (Lardilleux et al., 2012) are two associative approaches.

Anymalign[1] is an open source multilingual associative aligner (Lardilleux and Lepage, 2009; Lardilleux et al., 2013). This method samples large numbers of sub-corpora randomly to obtain source and target word or phrase occurrence distributions. The more often two words or phrases have the same occurrence distribution over particular sub-corpora, the higher the association between them.

We can run Anymalign by setting with -t (running time) option and stop it at any time, and the option -i allows to to extract longer phrases

[1] https://anymalign.limsi.fr

Proceedings of the 2nd Workshop on Asian Translation (WAT2015), pages 87-94,
Kyoto, Japan, 16th October 2015.

by enforcing n-grams to be considered as tokens. For pre-segmented texts, option -i allows to group words into phrases more easily.

Cutnalign is a bilingual hierarchical sub-sentential alignment method (Lardilleux et al., 2012). It is based on a recursive binary segmentation process of the alignment matrix between a source sentence and its corresponding target sentence. We make use of this method in combination with Anymalign.

In the experiments, reported in this paper, we extend the work to decrease time costs in the training step. We obtained comparable results in only one fifth of the training time required by the GIZA++/Moses baseline pipeline.

2 Chinese and Japanese data used

The data used in our systems are the Chinese–Japanese JPO Patent Corpus (JPC)[2] provided by WAT 2015 for the patents subtask (Nakazawa et al., 2015). It contains 1 million Chinese–Japanese parallel sentences in four domains in the training data. These are Chemistry, Electricity, Mechanical engineering, and Physics. We used sentences of 40 words or less than 40 words as our training data for the translation models, but use all of the Japanese sentences in the parallel corpus for training the language models. We used all of the development data for tuning. For Chinese and Japanese segmentation we used the Stanford Segmenter (version: 2014-01-04 with Chinese Penn Treebank (CTB) model)[3] and Juman (version 7.0)[4]. Table 1 shows some statistics on the data we used in our systems (after tokenization, lowercase and clean).

3 Bilingual hierarchical sub-sentential alignment method

Cutnalign as a bilingual hierarchical sub-sentential alignment method based on a recursive binary segmentation process of the alignment matrix between a source sentence and its translation. It is a three-step approach:

- measure the strength of the translation link between any source and target pair of words;
- compute the optimal joint clustering of a bipartite graph to search the best alignment;
- segment and align a pair of sentences.

[2]http://lotus.kuee.kyoto-u.ac.jp/WAT/patent/index.html

[3]http://nlp.stanford.edu/software/segmenter.shtml

[4]http://nlp.ist.i.kyoto-u.ac.jp/index.php?JUMAN

	Baseline	Chinese	Japanese
train	sentences	820,184	820,184
	words	15,655,674	20,279,246
	mean ± std.dev.	19.39 ± 6.71	25.08 ± 7.75
tune	sentences	4,000	4,000
	words	114,363	143,853
	mean ± std.dev.	28.71 ± 18.34	36.12 ± 21.73
test	sentences	2,000	2,000
	words	55,582	70,117
	mean ± std.dev.	27.83 ±16.73	35.09 ± 20.16

Table 1: Statistics of our baseline training data of JPC.

When building alignment matrices, the strength between two words is evaluated using the following formula (Lardilleux et al., 2012).

$$w(s,t) = p(s|t) \times p(t|s) \quad (1)$$

($p(s|t)$ and $p(t|s)$) are translation probabilities estimated by Anymalign. An example of alignment matrix is shown in Table 2.

The optimal joint clustering of a bipartite graph is computed recursively using the following formula for searching the best alignment between words in the source and target languages (Zha et al., 2001; Lardilleux et al., 2012).

$$cut(X,Y) = W(X,\overline{Y}) + W(\overline{X},Y) \quad (2)$$

$X, \overline{X}, Y, \overline{Y}$ denote the segmentation of the sentences. Here the block we start with is the entire matrix. Splitting horizontally and vertically into two parts gives four sub-blocks.

$$W(X,Y) = \sum_{s \in X, t \in Y} w(s,t) \quad (3)$$

$W(X,Y)$ is the sum of all translation strengths between all source and target words inside a sub-block (X,Y).

The point where to is found on the x and y which minimize $Ncut$ (Lardilleux et al., 2012):

$$Ncut(X,Y) = \frac{cut(X,Y)}{cut(X,Y) + 2 \times W(X,Y)} + \frac{cut(\overline{X},\overline{Y})}{cut(\overline{X},\overline{Y}) + 2 \times W(\overline{X},\overline{Y})} \quad (4)$$

Table 3 shows several segmentations out of all the possible segmentation in two blocks by computing the sub-sentential alignment between a Chinese and a Japanese sentences. For each word pair (x, y), we compute $Ncut(x, y)$. In this case, we start at word pair (根据, それら), the search space is the rectangle area [(根据, それら), (。, 。)]. In Table 3, only 7 out of all the possible segmentations in two blocks are shown. The number of possible segmentation is: the length of the Japanese sentence minus one, multiplied by the length of the Chinese sentence minus one, multiplied by two, as there are two possible direction for segmenting. After computing all $Ncut(x, y)$, we compare and find the minimal $Ncut(x, y)$. Table 4 shows the flow of recursive segmentation and alignment.

In the our experiments, we introduced two types of improvements (Yang and Lepage, 2015) compared to the original implementation. The first one, introduces multi-processing in both the sampling-based alignment method and hierarchical sub-sentential alignment method so as to trivially accelerate the overall alignment process. We also re-implement the core of *Cutnalign* in C. The second one, approximations in the computation of $Ncut$ accelerate some decisions. Also a method to reduce the search space in hierarchical sub-sentential alignment has been introduced, so that important speed-ups are obtained. We refer the reader to (Yang and Lepage, 2015) for a detailed description of these improvements.

4 Experiments based on different alignment methods

4.1 Experiment settings

Here, we basically perform experiments with GIZA++ or MGIZA. The phrase tables are extracted from the alignments obtained using the grow-diag-final-and heuristic (Ayan and Dorr, 2006) integrated in the Moses toolkit. Our sampling-based alignment method and hierarchical sub-sentential alignment method are also evaluated within a PB-SMT system built by using the Moses toolkit, the Ken Language Modeling toolkit (Heafield, 2011) and a lexicalized reordering model (Koehn et al., 2005). We built systems from Chinese to Japanese. Each experiment was run using the same data sets (see Section 2). Translations were evaluated using BLEU (Papineni et al., 2002) and RIBES (Isozaki et al., 2010).

We used *Anymalign* (i=2, two words can be considered as one token) and *Cutnalign* to build phrase tables. As a timeout (-t) should be given, we set two different timeouts (5400 sec. and 1200 sec.). We also use different *Cutnalign* versions where core components are implemented in C or Python. We passed word-to-word associations output by Anymalign (i=2) to *Cutnalign* which produces sub-sentential alignments, which are in turn passed to the grow-dial-final-and heuristic of the Moses toolkit to build phrase tables.

4.2 Results

Evaluation results using different alignment methods based on the same data sets are given in Tables 5 and 7. The system built based on GIZA++/Moses pipeline as a baseline system is given in Table 5. We also show the evaluation results obtained by the WAT 2015 automatic evaluation[5] in Table 6 and 8. The results in Table 7 and 8 show that there are no significant differences among the evaluation results based on different versions of Moses, different *Anymalign* timeouts or different versions of *Cutnalign*. However, the training times changed considerably depending on the timeouts for Anymalign. The fastest training time is obtained with Moses version 2.1.1, a timeout of 1200 sec. for *Anymalign* and the C version of *Cutnalign*: 57 minutes, i.e., about one fifth of the time used by GIZA++ or MGIZA (Table 5 and 6). We also checked the confidence intervals between using GIZA++ and our method (the fastest one): 37.24 ± 0.86 and 35.72 ± 0.90. The probability of actually getting them (p-value) is 0.

5 Conclusion

In this paper, we have shown that it is possible to accelerate development of SMT systems following the work by Lardilleux et al. (2012) and Yang and Lepage (2015) on bilingual hierarchical sub-sentential alignment. We performed several machine translation experiments using different alignment methods and obtained a significant reduction of processing training time. Setting different timeouts for Anymalign did not change the translation quality. In other word, we get a relative steady translation quality even when less time is allotted to word-to-word association computation.

[5]http://orchid.kuee.kyoto-u.ac.jp/WAT/

Here, the fastest training time was only 57 minutes, one fifth compared with the use of GIZA++ or MGIZA.

Acknowledgments

The paper is part of the outcome of research performed under a Waseda University Grant for Special Research Project (Project number: 2015A-063).

References

Necip Fazil Ayan and Bonnie J Dorr. 2006. Going beyond AER: An extensive analysis of word alignments and their impact on MT. In *Proceedings of the 21st International Conference on Computational Linguistics and the 44th annual meeting of the Association for Computational Linguistics*, pages 9–16. Association for Computational Linguistics.

Peter F Brown, Vincent J Della Pietra, Stephen A Della Pietra, and Robert L Mercer. 1993. The mathematics of statistical machine translation: Parameter estimation. *Computational linguistics*, 19(2):263–311.

Arthur P Dempster, Nan M Laird, and Donald B Rubin. 1977. Maximum likelihood from incomplete data via the EM algorithm. *Journal of the royal statistical society. Series B (methodological)*, pages 1–38.

Ted Dunning. 1993. Accurate methods for the statistics of surprise and coincidence. *Computational linguistics*, 19(1):61–74.

William A Gale and Kenneth Ward Church. 1991. Identifying word correspondences in parallel texts. In *HLT*, volume 91, pages 152–157. Citeseer.

Qin Gao and Stephan Vogel. 2008. Parallel implementations of word alignment tool. In *Software Engineering, Testing, and Quality Assurance for Natural Language Processing*, pages 49–57. Association for Computational Linguistics.

Kenneth Heafield. 2011. KenLM: Faster and smaller language model queries. In *In Proc. of the Sixth Workshop on Statistical Machine Translation*.

Hideki Isozaki, Tsutomu Hirao, Kevin Duh, Katsuhito Sudoh, and Hajime Tsukada. 2010. Automatic evaluation of translation quality for distant language pairs. In *Proceedings of the 2010 Conference on Empirical Methods in Natural Language Processing*, pages 944–952. Association for Computational Linguistics.

Philipp Koehn, Amittai Axelrod, Alexandra Birch, Chris Callison-Burch, Miles Osborne, David Talbot, and Michael White. 2005. Edinburgh system description for the 2005 IWSLT speech translation evaluation. In *IWSLT*, pages 68–75.

Philipp Koehn, Hieu Hoang, Alexandra Birch, Chris Callison-Burch, Marcello Federico, Nicola Bertoldi, Brooke Cowan, Wade Shen, Christine Moran, Richard Zens, et al. 2007. Moses: Open source toolkit for statistical machine translation. In *Proceedings of the 45th annual meeting of the ACL on interactive poster and demonstration sessions*, pages 177–180. Association for Computational Linguistics.

Adrien Lardilleux and Yves Lepage. 2009. Sampling-based multilingual alignment. In *Recent Advances in Natural Language Processing*, pages 214–218.

Adrien Lardilleux, François Yvon, and Yves Lepage. 2012. Hierarchical sub-sentential alignment with anymalign, May.

Adrien Lardilleux, François Yvon, and Yves Lepage. 2013. Generalizing sampling-based multilingual alignment. *Machine Translation*, 27(1):1–23.

Toshiaki Nakazawa, Hideya Mino, Isao Goto, Graham Neubig, Sadao Kurohashi, and Eiichiro Sumita. 2015. Overview of the 2nd workshop on asian translation. In *Proceedings of the 2nd Workshop on Asian Translation (WAT2015)*, Kyoto, Japan, October.

Franz Josef Och and Hermann Ney. 2003. A systematic comparison of various statistical alignment models. *Computational linguistics*, 29(1):19–51.

Kishore Papineni, Salim Roukos, Todd Ward, and Wei-Jing Zhu. 2002. BLEU: A method for automatic evaluation of machine translation. In *Proceedings of the 40th Annual Meeting on Association for Computational Linguistics*, ACL '02, pages 311–318, Stroudsburg, PA, USA. Association for Computational Linguistics.

Stephan Vogel, Hermann Ney, and Christoph Tillmann. 1996. HMM-based word alignment in statistical translation. In *Proceedings of the 16th conference on Computational linguistics-Volume 2*, pages 836–841. Association for Computational Linguistics.

Baosong Yang and Yves Lepage. 2015. Leveraging the advantages of associative methods for faster training of smt systems. *Master thesis, Graduate School of Information, Production and Systems Waseda Univeristy*.

Hongyuan Zha, Xiaofeng He, Chris Ding, Horst Simon, and Ming Gu. 2001. Bipartite graph partitioning and data clustering. In *Proceedings of the tenth international conference on Information and knowledge management*, pages 25–32. ACM.

	それら	の	値	に	基づい	て	upgma	法	によって	クラ	スター	分析	を	行っ	た	。
根据	ε	ε	ε	0.27	0.46	0.01	ε	ε	0.002	ε	ε	ε	ε	ε	ε	0.02
这些	0.38	ε	ε	0.02	ε	ε	ε	0.001	ε	ε	ε	ε	ε	ε	ε	0.01
值	0.012	0.27	0.44	ε	ε	ε	ε	ε	ε	ε	ε	ε	ε	ε	ε	0.03
，	0.002	0.01	0.01	0.13	0.12	0.21	0.10	0.002	0.001	0.002	0.001	0.01	0.01	0.01	ε	0.01
通过	ε	ε	0.01	ε	ε	0.06	ε	ε	0.52	ε	ε	ε	ε	0.02	ε	0.01
upgma	ε	ε	ε	ε	ε	ε	0.75	ε	ε	ε	ε	ε	ε	ε	ε	0.02
法	ε	ε	ε	ε	ε	ε	ε	0.013	0.013	ε	ε	ε	ε	ε	ε	0.01
进行	ε	ε	ε	ε	ε	ε	ε	ε	ε	ε	ε	0.01	0.23	0.34	0.21	0.01
聚类	ε	ε	ε	ε	ε	ε	ε	ε	ε	0.045	0.045	ε	ε	ε	ε	0.02
分析	ε	ε	ε	ε	ε	ε	ε	ε	ε	ε	ε	0.5	ε	ε	ε	0.01
。	0.01	0.02	0.01	0.02	0.01	0.01	0.02	0.01	0.02	0.01	0.002	0.01	0.02	0.01	0.01	0.7

Table 2: An example of an alignment matrix which contains the translation strength for each word pair (Chinese–Japanese). The scores are obtained using Anymalign's output. Computing by w.

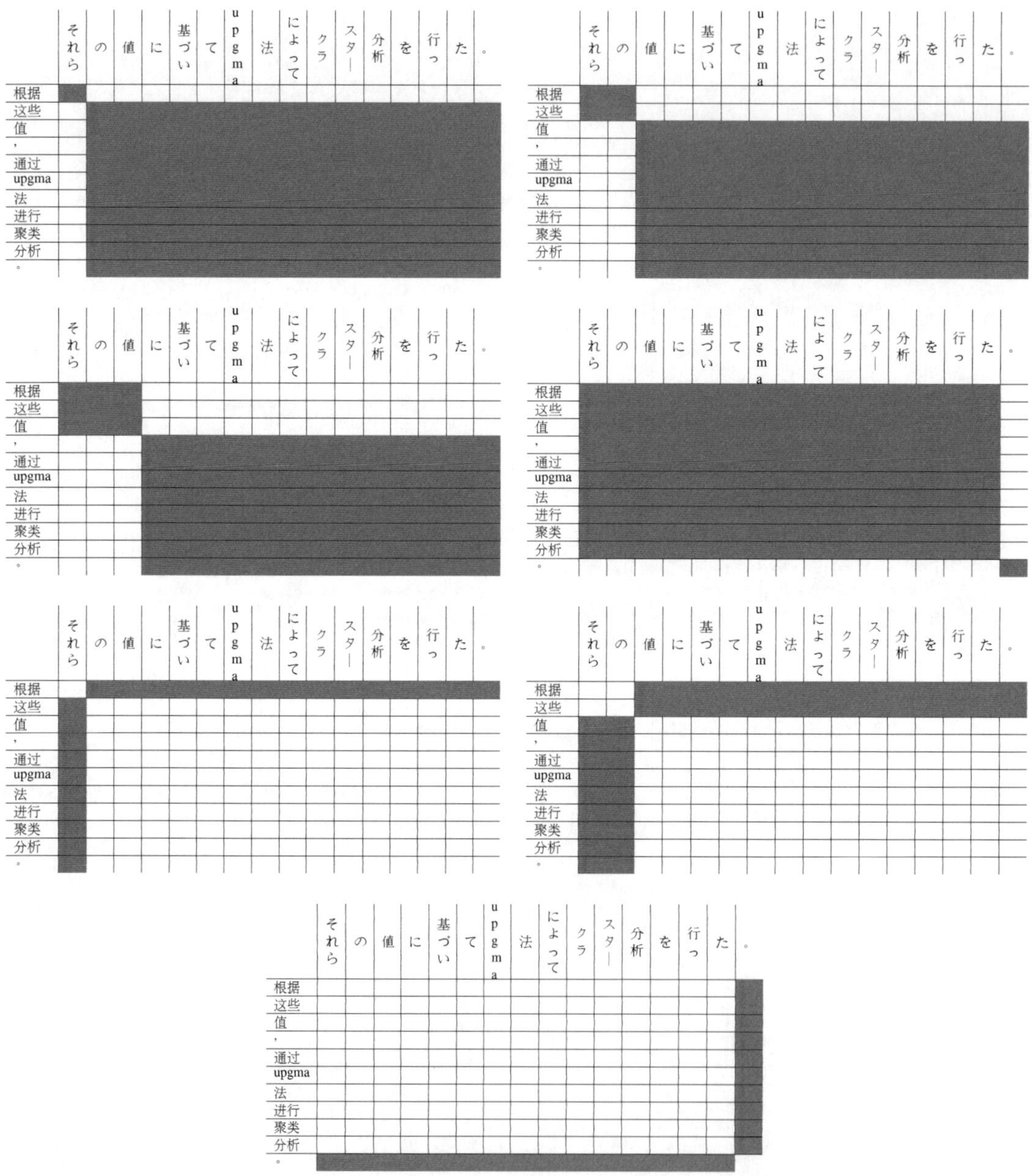

Table 3: 7 out of all the possible segmentation in two blocks are shown.

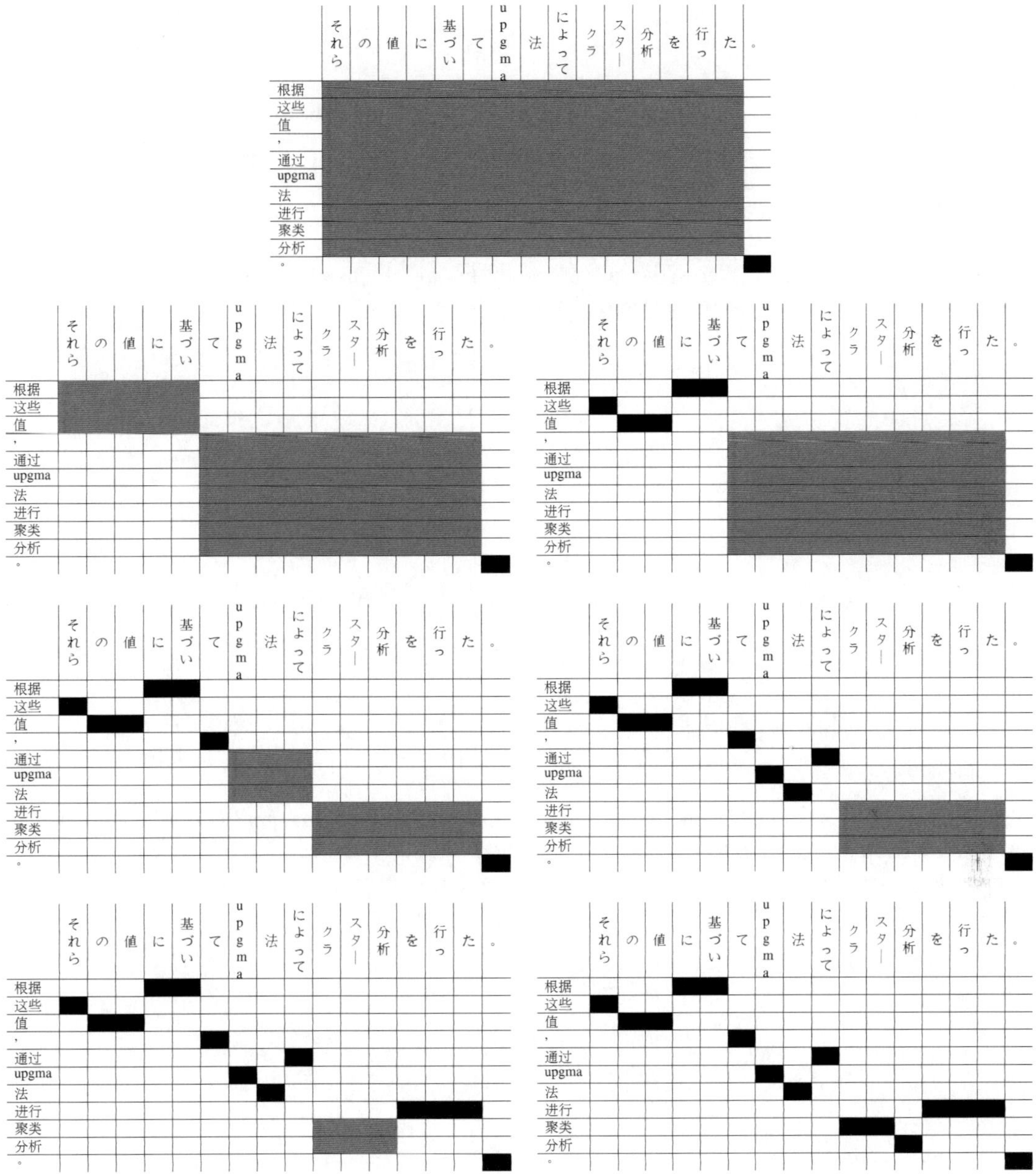

Table 4: Steps in recursive segmentation and alignment result using sampling-based alignment and hierarchical sub-sentential alignment method.

s→t	Moses	Aligner	BLEU	RIBES	Training time
zh→ja	2.1.1	MGIZA	37.70	0.783000	5:34:28
	2.1.1	GIZA++	37.46	0.778914	4:43:56

Table 5: Evaluation results by using different aligner (GIZA++ and MGIZA) based on the data of JPC given in Table 1.

s→t	Moses	Aligner	BLEU			RIBES			Training time
			Jum	Kyt	Mec	Jum	Kyt	Mec	
zh→ja	2.1.1	MGIZA	34.40	35.59	34.52	0.774606	0.771082	0.773494	5:34:28
	2.1.1	GIZA++	34.28	35.32	34.46	0.770829	0.767483	0.769517	4:43:56

Table 6: Evaluation results (Web server automatic evaluation) by using different aligner (GIZA++ and MGIZA) based on the data of JPC given in Table 1.

Language	Moses	Aligner		BLEU	Training time
		Anymalign + Cutnalign			
		Timeout (s)	i		
zh-ja	3.0	1200	2 (c)	36.11	1:2:8
zh-ja	3.0	5400	2 (c)	36.07	2:9:29
zh-ja	2.1.1	1200	2 (c)	35.95	0:57:1
zh-ja	2.1.1	1200	2 (python)	35.93	1:1:16

Table 7: Evaluation results by using the alignment method of combining sampling-based alignment and bilingual hierarchical sub-sentential alignment methods based on the data of JPC given in Table 1. In decreasing order of BLEU cores. Here, 2 (c) shows option -i of *Anymalign* is 2, and *Cutnlaign* version where core component is implemented in C.

Language	Moses	Aligner		BLEU			RIBES			Training time
		Anymalign + Cutnalign								
		Timeout (s)	i	Jum	Kyt	Mec	Jum	Kyt	Mec	
zh-ja	3.0	1200	2 (c)	33.00	33.96	33.09	0.777100	0.774241	0.776778	1:2:8
zh-ja	3.0	5400	2 (c)	32.98	33.97	33.04	0.775729	0.774008	0.774800	2:9:29
zh-ja	2.1.1	1200	2 (c)	33.24	33.70	32.95	0.771271	0.769397	0.770645	0:57:1
zh-ja	2.1.1	1200	2 (python)	33.01	33.89	33.03	0.771949	0.769415	0.770682	1:1:16

Table 8: Evaluation results (Web server automatic evaluation) by using the alignment method of combining sampling-based alignment and bilingual hierarchical sub-sentential alignment methods based on the data of JPC given in Table 1. In decreasing order of BLEU cores.

Chinese-to-Japanese Patent Machine Translation based on Syntactic Pre-ordering for WAT 2015

Katsuhito Sudoh **Masaaki Nagata**
NTT Communication Science Laboratories, Japan
sudoh.katsuhito@lab.ntt.co.jp

Abstract

This paper presents our Chinese-to-Japanese patent machine translation system for WAT 2015 (Group ID: ntt) that uses syntactic pre-ordering over Chinese dependency structures. A head word and its modifier words are reordered by hand-written rules or a learning-to-rank model. Our system outperforms baseline phrase-based machine translations and competes with baseline tree-to-string machine translations.

1 Introduction

Patent documents, which well-structured written documents that describe the technical details of inventions, are expected to have almost no semantic ambiguities caused by indirect or rhetorical expressions. Due to this aspect, patent documents are good candidates for literal translation, which most machine translation (MT) approaches aim to do.

One technical challenge for patent machine translation is the complex syntactic structure of patent documents, which typically have long sentences that complicate MT reordering, especially for the word order in distant languages. Chinese and Japanese have similar word order in noun modifiers but different subject-verb-object order, requiring long distance reordering in translation. In this year's WAT evaluation campaign (Nakazawa et al., 2015), we tackle long distance reordering by syntactic pre-ordering based on Chinese dependency structures (Sudoh et al., 2014) in a Chinese-to-Japanese patent translation task.

Our system basically consists of three components: Chinese syntactic analysis (word segmentation, part-of-speech (POS) tagging, and dependency parsing) adapted to patent documents; dependency-based syntactic pre-ordering with hand-written rules or a learning-to-rank model; and a standard phrase-based statistical MT. This paper describes our system's details and discusses our evaluation results.

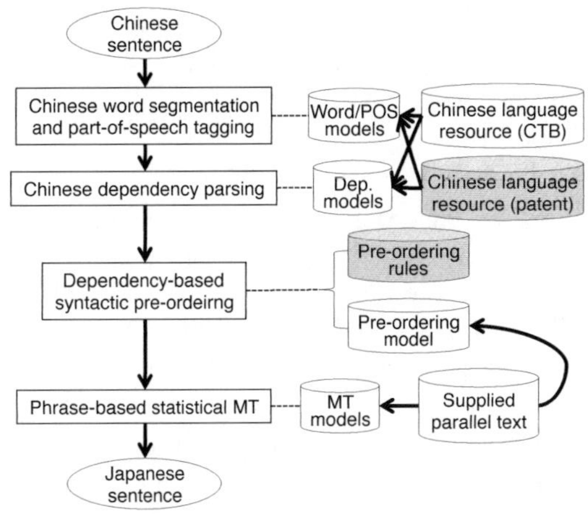

Figure 1: Brief workflow of our Chinese-to-Japanese MT system. Gray resources are in-house ones.

2 System Overview

Figure 1 shows a brief workflow of our Chinese-to-Japanese MT system. Its basic architecture is standard with syntactic pre-ordering. Input sentences are first applied to word segmentation and POS tagging, parsed into dependency trees, reordered using pre-ordering rules or a pre-ordering model, and finally translated into Japanese by a phrase-based statistical MT.

3 Chinese Syntactic Analysis: Word Segmentation, Part-of-Speech Tagging, and Dependency Parsing

Word segmentation and POS tagging are solved jointly (Suzuki et al., 2012) for better Chinese word segmentation based on the POS tag sequences. The dependency parser produces *un-*

Proceedings of the 2nd Workshop on Asian Translation (WAT2015), pages 95–98,
Kyoto, Japan, 16th October 2015.

typed dependency trees. The Chinese analysis models were trained using in-house Chinese treebanks in the patent domain (about 35,000 sentences) as well as the standard Penn Chinese Treebank dataset (Sudoh et al., 2014). The training also utilized unlabeled Chinese patent documents (about 100 G bytes) for semi-supervised training (Suzuki et al., 2009; Sudoh et al., 2014).

4 Syntactic Pre-ordering

We compared two different syntactic pre-ordering approaches, rule-based and data-driven, in this evaluation campaign.

4.1 Rule-based Pre-ordering

Rule-based pre-ordering is an intuitive approach that generates target language word order based on linguistic knowledge and analysis. For example, in an English-to-Japanese patent MT, a very simple pre-ordering rule called Head Finalization (Isozaki et al., 2012) gives very successful results.

Our pre-ordering rules are based on Head Final Chinese (Han et al., 2012) developed for Chinese HPSG trees. We modified the HPSG-oriented rules for dependency structure, but their basic actions are almost the same. One expected advantage of rule-based pre-ordering is that its stability is independent on bilingual corpora, while model-based approaches basically depend on bilingual corpora to determine *which reordering is the best.*

4.2 Data-driven Pre-ordering by Learning-to-Rank

Data-driven pre-ordering obtains the most probable reordering of a source language sentence that is *monotone* with the target language counterpart. It learns rules or models using reordering oracles over word-aligned bilingual corpora.

We used a learning-to-rank approach with Ranking SVMs (Yang et al., 2012), which reorders the head word and its modifier words in a dependency tree based on their *ranks*. The features resemble those by Yang et al. (2012); we did not use label-related ones because our dependency trees do not have labels. The reordering oracles were determined to maximize Kendall's τ over automatic word alignment in a similar manner to Hoshino et al. (2015). The only difference is the tree structure; Hoshino et al. (2015) used binary trees and just considered monotone or reverse for two child nodes of each tree node. But we use dependency trees and have to consider all the possible permutation over one head word and one or more modifier words.

5 Evaluation

5.1 Setup

We trained a word n-gram language model and two different phrase-based translation models by the above different pre-ordering approaches. We used all of the supplied Chinese-Japanese bilingual training corpora of one million sentence pairs (except for long sentences over 64 words) for the MT models: phrase tables, lexicalized reordering tables, and word 5-gram language models using standard Moses and KenLM training parameters. We applied modified Kneser-Ney phrase table smoothing with an additional phrase scoring option: `--KneserNey`. The model weights were optimized by standard Minimum Error Rate Training (MERT), but we compared five independent MERT runs and chose the best weights for the development test set. The distortion limits were also chosen from 0, 3, 6, and 9 by comparing the results of the MERT runs. We chose 9 both for the rule-based and data-driven pre-ordering.

The pre-ordering model for the data-driven method was trained by the word alignment used for the phrase table by a Ranking SVM implementation with Liblinear[1]. Its soft margin parameter `C` was chosen by the ranking accuracy on the development set.

5.2 Official Results

Table 1 shows the official evaluation results by the organizers in Pairwise Cloudsourcing Evaluation scores (Human), RIBES, and BLEU. Our rule-based system showed slightly better performance in RIBES and BLEU than the tree-to-string baseline, but the difference may not be significant. The performances of our systems were lower than the tree-to-string baseline in the Human evaluation. With respect to the difference in the pre-ordering approaches, the rule-based system outperformed the data-driven one.

5.3 Discussion

One critical concern is the difference between tree-to-string baseline and our pre-ordering systems. Syntactic pre-ordering based on child ranking/classification is a simple approximation of a

[1]http://www.csie.ntu.edu.tw/~cjlin/libsvmtools/

Table 1: Official evaluation results in Pairwise Cloudsourcing Evaluation scores (Human), RIBES, and BLEU. RIBES and BLEU are based on MeCab Japanese word segmentation. Scores in **bold** are the best ones.

System	Human	RIBES	BLEU
Organizer PBMT	n/a	0.781	0.382
Organizer T2S	**20.75**	0.814	0.394
Ours rule-based	16.25	**0.822**	**0.406**
Ours data-driven	8.00	0.812	0.399

standard tree-to-string MT[2]. The tree-to-string MT can compare different reordering hypotheses; our pre-ordering just chooses one-best pre-ordering.

A comparison between the results by rule-based and data-driven pre-ordering systems suggests our pre-ordering rules work robustly. Even though we expected model-based pre-ordering to capture the complex reordering phenomena in the dependency structure, it gave worse results than the rule-based one. One possible reason is the noisy automatic word alignment in the bilingual corpora; using better word alignment (manual annotation or supervised word alignment) is promising to learn a consistent pre-ordering model (Hoshino et al., 2015).

5.4 Issues for Context-aware Machine Translation

We did not include any context-aware constraints or features in our system, because it translated every sentence independently. We just tried using domain-dependent translation models based on the given category information (chemistry, electricity, mechanical engineering, and physics), but they did not work effectively in our pilot test.

6 Conclusion

This paper presented our pre-ordering-based system for Chinese-to-Japanese patent MT for the WAT 2015 evaluation campaign. Our results showed that pre-ordering had similar MT performance to the tree-to-string baseline, but it was slightly worse in the human evaluation. Future work will investigate sophisticated pre-ordering methodology such as pre-ordering lattices or forest-based pre-ordering and better word alignment for data-driven pre-ordering.

[2]Theoretically this is not true, since phrase-based MT can use phrases that have non-syntactic spans. The effect of these phenomena has not reported yet in the field of pre-ordering; they introduce more ambiguities in phrasal translations, but the ambiguities may work both positively and negatively. The use of non-syntactic spans was proposed as an extention in tree-to-string MT (Zollmann and Venugopal, 2006; Zhang et al., 2011).

Acknowledgments

We thank Dr. Jun Suzuki for his great help on the Chinese dependency parsing. The basis of our pre-ordering rules was developed in cooperation with Dr. Dan Han, whom we thank. Finally, we greatly appreciate the workshop organizers for this valuable evaluation campaign.

References

Dan Han, Katsuhito Sudoh, Xianchao Wu, Kevin Duh, Hajime Tsukada, and Masaaki Nagata. 2012. Head Finalization Reordering for Chinese-to-Japanese Machine Translation. In *Proceedings of the Sixth Workshop on Syntax, Semantics and Structure in Statistical Translation*, pages 57–66.

Sho Hoshino, Yusuke Miyao, Katsuhito Sudoh, Katsuhiko Hayashi, and Masaaki Nagata. 2015. Discriminative Preordering Meets Kendall's τ Maximization. In *Proceedings of the 53rd Annual Meeting of the Association for Computational Linguistics and the 7th International Joint Conference on Natural Language Processing (Volume 2: Short Papers)*, pages 139–144.

Hideki Isozaki, Katsuhito Sudoh, Hajime Tsukada, and Kevin Duh. 2012. HPSG-Based Preprocessing for English-to-Japanese Translation. *ACM Transactions on Asian Language Information Processing*, 11(3).

Toshiaki Nakazawa, Hideya Mino, Isao Goto, Graham Neubig, Sadao Kurohashi, and Eiichiro Sumita. 2015. Overview of the 2nd Workshop on Asian Translation. In *Proceedings of the 2nd Workshop on Asian Translation (WAT2015)*, Kyoto, Japan, October.

Katsuhito Sudoh, Jun Suzuki, Yasuhiro Akiba, Hajime Tsukada, and Masaaki Nagata. 2014. A English/Chinese/Korean-to-Japanese Statistical Machine Translation System for Patent Documents. In *Proceedings of the 20th Annual Meeting of the Association for Natural Language Processing*, pages 606–609. (in Japanese; 須藤,鈴木,秋葉,塚田,永田: 英中韓から日本語への特許文向け統計翻訳システム).

Jun Suzuki, Hideki Isozaki, Xavier Carreras, and Michael Collins. 2009. An Empirical Study of Semi-supervised Structured Conditional Models for Dependency Parsing. In *Proceedings of the 2009 Conference on Empirical Methods in Natural Language Processing*, pages 551–560.

Jun Suzuki, Kevin Duh, and Masaaki Nagata. 2012. Joint Natural Language Analysis using Augmented Lagrangian. In *Proceedings of the 18th Annual Meeting of the Association for Natural Language Processing*, pages 1284–1287. (in Japanese; 鈴木,Duh,永田: 拡張ラグランジュ緩和を用いた同時自然言語解析法).

Nan Yang, Mu Li, Dongdong Zhang, and Nenghai Yu. 2012. A Ranking-based Approach to Word Reordering for Statistical Machine Translation. In *Proceedings of the 50th Annual Meeting of the Association for Computational Linguistics (Volume 1: Long Papers)*, pages 912–920.

Hao Zhang, Licheng Fang, Peng Xu, and Xiaoyun Wu. 2011. Binarized forest to string translation. In *Proceedings of the 49th Annual Meeting of the Association for Computational Linguistics: Human Language Technologies*, pages 835–845.

Andreas Zollmann and Ashish Venugopal. 2006. Syntax augmented machine translation via chart parsing. In *Proceedings on the Workshop on Statistical Machine Translation*, pages 138–141.

Source Phrase Segmentation and Translation for Japanese-English Translation Using Dependency Structure

Junki Matsuo
Graduate School of System Design, Tokyo Metropolitan University, Japan
matsuo-junki@ed.tmu.ac.jp

Kenichi Ohwada
Graduate School of System Design, Tokyo Metropolitan University, Japan
ohwada-kenichi@ed.tmu.ac.jp

Mamaru Komachi
Graduate School of System Design, Tokyo Metropolitan University, Japan
komachi@tmu.ac.jp

Abstract

There are various approaches to statistical machine translation (SMT). In particular, phrase-based SMT (PBSMT) is used as a de facto standard for many language pairs because it works robustly across languages and it is easy to implement. However, the results of PBSMT can include ungrammatical sentences, since it typically does not take syntactic structure into account. To overcome this problem, we propose a linguistically motivated approach based on segmenting a source phrase using a dependency structure and translating each phrase with PBSMT. This paper presents the results of our method on Japanese-English translation and discusses potential improvements.

1 Introduction

It is difficult for statistical machine translation (SMT) to perform translation between languages such as Japanese and English, which have a systematic difference in their word orders: typically, Japanese is a subject-object-verb (SOV) language, whereas English is a subject-object-verb (SVO) language.

Although PBSMT is used as a de facto standard for many language pairs because it works robustly across languages and it is easy to implement; it typically does not take syntactic structure into account. It is difficult to recognize syntactic information for phrase-based SMT therefore it cannot handle long-distance reordering that frequently occurs in these language pairs.

To incorporate syntactic information into the PBSMT framework, we attempt to identify the SOV of the source language (Japanese) and then correctly produce the SVO of the target language (English). Concretely, we devise a dependency-based method that extracts a sentence's frame (hereafter "basic frame"), consisting of the predicate and its direct children (hereafter "anchor words"), and its dependent phrases consisting of the anchor words and their all descendants. After extracting these words and phrases, our method translates them separately and then combines their translation.

We conducted an experiment with the proposed method on a Japanese-to-English task at the Second Workshop on Asian Translation (Nakazawa et al., 2015). Although the results of our method are not positive, we discuss potential improvements.

The rest of this paper is organized as follows. In the next section, we discuss related work. In Section 3, the details of our method are explained. Then, we describe our experiments and analyze the results.

2 Related Work

A substantial, systematic difference in word orders creates difficulty for SMT, especially, PBSMT, which is not based on syntactic phrases. Good translation can be achieved in such situations by segmenting the input sentences into portion for simpler and adequate scale inputs.

For translating a long and complex sentence composed of several clauses in English into Japanese translation, Sudoh et al. (2010) proposed segmenting the sentence into clauses that include non-terminals as placeholders corresponding to embedded clauses using an HPSG parser, translating the clauses, and then replacing the non-terminals with the corresponding clause's translations. By representing an embedded clause with

Proceedings of the 2nd Workshop on Asian Translation (WAT2015), pages 99-104,
Kyoto, Japan, 16th October 2015.

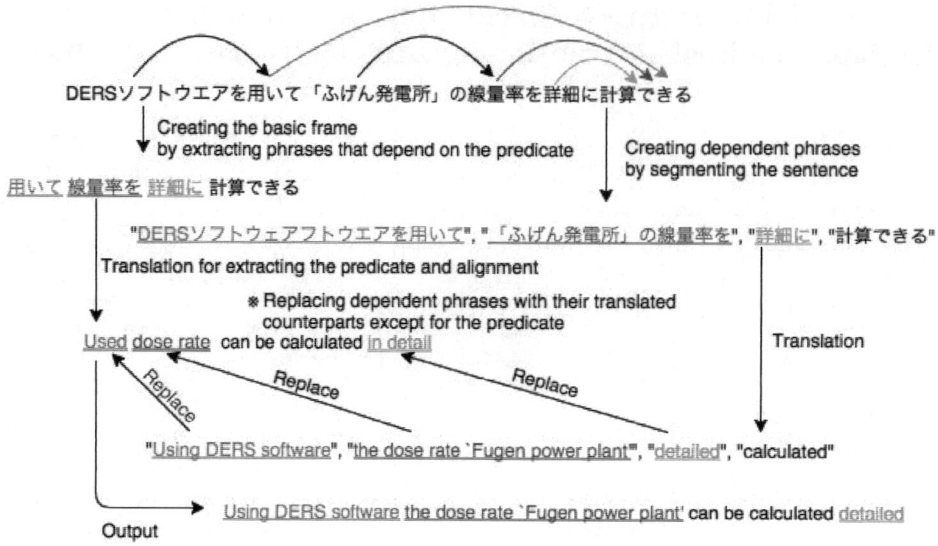

Figure 1 : Illustrative example of our method.

a non-terminal as a placeholder, they reduced the problem of reordering a complex sentence to a simple problem of word-level reordering. For each clause translation, non-terminals are treated as words and the clause including them is translated using the model trained on a clause-level aligned corpus that they developed. Their method uses a high-quality HPSG parser to segment an English sentence, but such a rich parser is not publicly available for Japanese. Thus, we opt to use dependency analysis to segment Japanese sentences. In addition, they segmented a sentence into clauses, whereas we segment a sentence into linguistically-motivated phrases, and in contrast to their approach, we do not arrange the corpus to be suitable for segmentation unit.

There are other segmentation methods in machine translation. Roh et al. (2001) proposed a method that recognizes the range of sub-sentences such as a relative and a conjunctive clause using sentence pattern information to overcome the problem of a syntactic ambiguity in a long sentence. Doi et al. (2003) split an input sentence into some smaller units to deal with long sentences in speech translation. Their method does not split sentences in a pre-processing phase or a parsing phase. It uses partial translation results and some criteria that judge the results to determine the best split positions. Other than that, Lee et al. (2012) proposed training a phrase segmentation model using a PBSMT decoder. The model is incorporated into the log-linear model of PBSMT, and the phrase segmenter based on the decoder annotates the source language phrase boundaries. The annotated data are used to train a new phrase segmentation model, which is then reused by the decoder. This process is performed iteratively, improving the phrase segmentation model.

Our approach also involves pre-ordering, one of the means of coping with the reordering problem. It reorders the word order of a source language sentence in the pre-processing phase to bring the sequence of words closer to the word order of the target language. Previous work addressing pre-ordering in SOV/SVO language pairs such as Japanese and English includes Isozaki et al. (2010), Komachi et al. (2006), Katz-Brown and Collins (2008), Xu et al. (2009), and Hoshino et al. (2013). These methods use some source language information to reorder the words of source language words with manual rules: morphological analysis (Katz-Brown and Collins, 2008), dependency analysis (Katz-Brown and Collins, 2008), and predicate argument structure analysis (Komachi et al., 2006; Hoshino et al., 2013). Our method also uses dependency analysis for preprocessing, but reordering is not performed. We use a dependency parser only to extract the basic frame and dependent phrases.

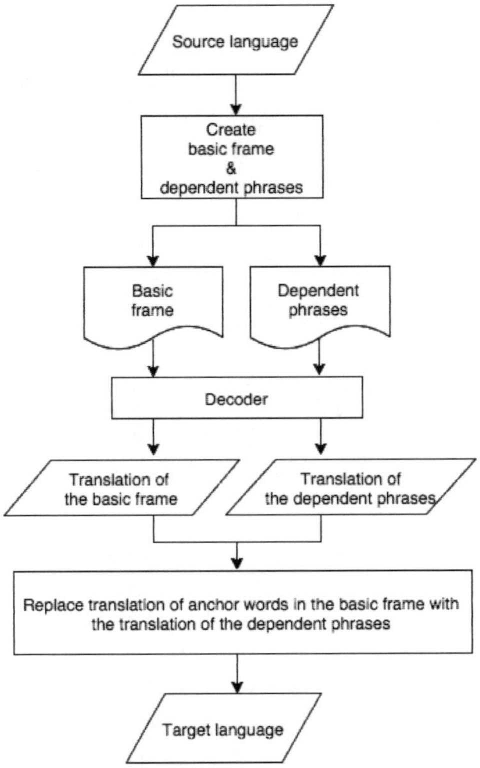

Figure 2: Flowchart of our method.

3 Source Phrase Segmentation and Translation Using Dependency Structure

Because of its ignorance of syntax, PBSMT may output ungrammatical sentences. Thus, we propose a source-phrase segmentation and translation approach to compensate for the lack of linguistically motivated information in the source language. We propose two methods. First method is "segmentation and translation", and second method is "segmentation and translation without preposition". "Segmentation and translation" is the method described in Subsection 3.1, and "segmentation and translation without preposition" is described in Subsection 3.2. In Subsection 3.3, we describe an additional rule for our method (for a sentence that includes a substantive verb).

Figures 1 and 2 show an example and outline of our method, respectively. Although our method is similar to that of Sudoh et al. (2010)'s work, we segment a sentence into its basic frame consisting of a predicate, anchor words and the dependent phrases that are the phrases consisting the subtrees rooted at the anchor words (Figure 3) by

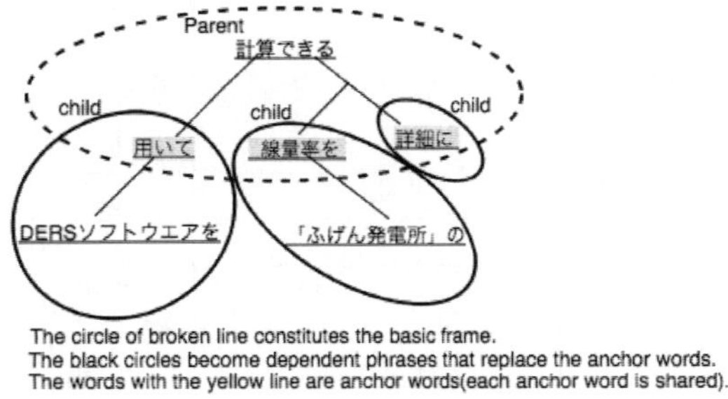

Figure 3 : Image of a basic frame, anchor words, and dependent phrases.

segmenting a sentence. The basic frame and dependent phrases are translated using a decoder. In the translation of a basic frame, each clause except for the predicate is subject to replacement. We replace the anchor words in the basic frame with the translations of the corresponding dependent phrases.

3.1 Segmentation and Translation

First, a basic frame is created by extracting the predicate and its direct children. Then, dependent phrases are created by segmenting the phrases that depend on the predicate. Second, the translation of the basic frame and those of the dependent phrases are obtained.

Finally, the output is created by replacing the translations of anchor words in the basic frame with those of the corresponding dependent phrases except for the translation of the predicate in the basic frame.

3.2 Segmentation and Translation without Preposition

We propose another but similar method that does not replace the preposition in the translation of the basic frame with one in the translation of dependent phrases. Because the translation of dependent phrases in our first method uses the language and translation models optimized for a sentence, our first method might not be able to use a model optimized for translating phrases.

For example, the adverbial phrase "詳細に (in detail)" in Figure 1 must be translated as an adverbial phrase "in detail". Our first method translates the phrase into "detailed", because the baseline decoder assumes a sentence as input. The baseline decoder correctly translates the phrase into "in detail" since it recognizes the verb "計算できる (can be calculated)" next to the phrase. In order

	energy	fluctuation	is	shown	.
エネルギー	■				
揺らぎ		■			
を			■		
示した				■	
。					■

Table 1: Alignment example to which the rule applies. The English word "is" is aligned to "を" included in the bunsetsu-chunk "揺らぎを". Hence, without the rule, "is" is replaced by the translation of "揺らぎを" and deleted.

	BLEU	RIBES
no-seg&trans	18.32	0.641456
seg&trans	15.85	0.628897
seg&trans (w/o prep)	15.72	0.628463

Table 2: BLEU and RIBES of the baseline and our methods.

error types	frequency
Dependency parsing	3
Translation of a basic frame	18
Translation of dependent phrases	46
Total (Each error may overlap)	57

Table 3: Types of errors in the first 100 sentences of the test-set.

not to replace the correct prepositions, our second method preserves the preposition coming from the basic frame.

3.3 Additional Rule for Predicate Alignment

We observe that there is a problem in aligning a Japanese predicate to an English counterpart. Here, if a word governed by VP in an English sentence is not aligned to one of the words included in the corresponding predicate bunsetsu-chunk of the Japanese sentence, the word of the English side will be deleted by our replacement.

For example, when translating "エネルギー揺らぎを示した (energy fluctuation is shown)" in Table 1, the predicate of Japanese sentence "示した" is not aligned to the English words "is shown" but to the word "shown". In this case, the English word "is" is not aligned to the word in the Japanese predicate bunsetsu-chunk "示した"; hence, the word will be deleted by the dependent phrases.

To avoid this unwanted occurrence, we add a rule to take effect that if there is a substantive verb in the translation of a basic frame, the replacement will not be applied to the substantive verb, since this accident occurs only for the substantive verb in our observation. As a result of this rule, "is shown" remains in the resulting sentence.

Our method uses this rule for both "segmentation and translation" and "segmentation and translation without preposition".

4 Experiments

4.1 Experimental Settings

We use three million parallel sentences from the Asian Scientific Paper Excerpt Corpus. We use JUMAN (version 7.0) for segmentation, and GIZA++ (version 1.0.7) for alignment. We use Moses (version 2.1.1)'s default configurations: monotone, swap, and discontinuous. The language and translation models of Moses are trained with the ASPEC. In translating the basic frame and dependent phrases, we use the same language and translation models. MERT is performed on the full dev-set. We follow the split of dev-set and test-set provided by the organizer of the workshop.

To preprocess the input sentences, basic frames and dependent phrases are extracted by a dependency parser CaboCha (version 0.68). [1]

We use Moses as a baseline. Moses's settings are the same as the above settings. Our method is evaluated using Bilingual Evaluation Understudy (BLEU) and Rank-based Intuitive Bilingual Evaluation Score (RIBES).

4.2 Experimental Results

Table 2 reports our official evaluation results for the WAT 2015 and an additional experiment after the official evaluation campaign. Both BLEU and RIBES deviated from the baseline.

5 Discussion

In Figure 1, we present an example for which our first method fails but our second method succeeds to translate. Our first method creates "DERS ソフトウェアを用いて", "「ふげん発電所」の線量率を", "詳細に", and

[1] We do not use CaboCha for segmentation but only to create dependency phrases.

"計算できる" as the dependent phrases. These dependent phrases are translated into "using DERS software", "the dose rate 'Fugen power plant'", "detailed", and "calculated", respectively. Our first method combines them with a translation of the basic frame to create output "using DERS software the dose rate 'Fugen power plant' can be calculated detailed", but this is ungrammatical.

This problem is caused by lack of contextual information in the the dependent phrases. For instance, the reason why the translation of the dependent phrase "詳細に" lacks any preposition is that the proper preposition corresponding to the particle "に" cannot be identified only by the information obtained from the input "詳細に". Our second method can solve this problem. It does not replace the preposition following the predicate to preserve the plausible preposition that seems to be translated properly in the translation of the basic frame.

However, the BLEU and RIBES scores of our second method are lower than those of our first method. Especially, the BLEU scores of our methods differ more than the RIBES scores. We will discuss the reason below.

We count the number of the pairs of input and reference that have different voices from the sample data, which comprises 100 sentences that we selected as the top 100 sentences from the test-set. Thirty-five percent of the translation outputs differ in their voice from the corresponding reference, and we suppose that this is the cause of the degradation in BLEU. For example, suppose a reference is in the active voice and the output of our methods is in the passive voice. Since BLEU penalizes incorrect translation based on n-gram precision, mis-ordering affect BLEU more than RIBIES.

In addition, the proposed methods have problems in the translation and language models. Since dependent phrases are typically noun phrases, the baseline decoder trained on parallel sentences might not produce appropriate translations. Moses tends to translate a noun phrase into a sentence if the dependent phrase contains a verb in a relative clause construction. For example, the dependent phrases "水の運動 (the water movement) の基本である (a basis of) 水素結合ネットワークの変化を (the change of hydrogen bond network)" were translated into "the change of hydrogen bond network is a basis of the water movement". From this perspective, we need to perform translation with different models for a basic frame and for dependent phrases.

In order to perform error analysis, we evaluate our methods quantitatively. Table 3 shows the number of errors in using a dependency parser (CaboCha in Table 3), translating a basic frame and dependent phrases (Translation of a basic frame and Translation of dependent phrases in Table 3). The errors resulting from CaboCha are very few; there are only three instances out of 100.

The most prominent errors originate in phrase translation. We can solve the problem by creating optimized language and translation models for noun phrases. Because the language and translation models must create a noun phrase when dependent phrase is noun phrase, they must be optimized for noun phrases.

The next most frequent errors are translations of basic frames. We count this type of error when the translation of a basic frame is not a sentence. In contrast to the case of dependent phrases, the translation of a basic frame must output a sentence with a predicate. Alternatively, we can re-rank the output to remove ungrammatical translations of a basic frame.

6 Conclusion

This paper proposed segmentation and translation methods for Japanese to English translation and presented its evaluation. We discussed the sample data consisting of the top 100 sentences that we had selected from the test-set. As a result, we found that the output has three problems: dependency parsing, translation of a basic frame, and translation of dependent phrases. In the future, we plan to optimize the language and the translation models suitable for phrase translation.

References

Takao Doi and Eiichiro Sumita. 2003. Input Sentence Splitting and Translating. In *Proceedings of the HLT-the North American Chapter of the Association for Computational Linguistics 2003 Workshop on Building and using parallel texts: data driven machine translation and beyond-Volume 3*, pages 104–110.

Sho Hoshino, Yusuke Miyao Katsuhito Sudoh, and Masaaki Nagata. 2013. Two-Stage Pre-ordering for Japanese-to-English Statistical Machine Translation. In *Proceedings of The 6th International Joint*

Conference on Natural Language Processing 2013, pages 1062–1066.

Hideki Isozaki, Katsuhito Sudoh, Hajime Tsukada, and Kevin Duh. 2010. Head Finalization: A Simple Reordering Rule for SOV Languages. In *Proceedings of the Joint 5th Workshop on Statistical Machine Translation and MetricsMATR*, pages 244–251.

Jason Katz-Brown and Michael Collins. 2008. Syntactic Reordering in Preprocessing for Japanese→English Translation: MIT System Discriptioin for NTCIR-7 Patent Translation Task. In *Proceedings of the NII Testbeds and Community for Information access Research-7 Workshop Meeting*, pages 409–414.

Mamoru Komachi, Yuji Matsumoto, and Masaaki Nagata. 2006. Phrase Reordering for Statistical Machine Translation Based on Predicate-Argument Structure. In *Proceedings of the International Workshop on Spoken Language Translation*, pages 77–82.

Hyoung-Gyu Lee and Hae-Chang Rim. 2012. Decoder-based Discriminative Training of Phrase Segmentation for Statistical Machine Translation. In *Proceedings of International Conference on Computational Linguistics*, pages 611–620.

Toshiaki Nakazawa, Hideya Mino, Isao Goto, Graham Neubig, Sadao Kurohashi, and Eiichiro Sumita. 2015. Overview of the 2nd Workshop on Asian Translation. In *Proceedings of the 2nd Workshop on Asian Translation (WAT2015)*.

Yoon-Hyung Roh, Young-Ae Seo, Ki-Young Lee, and ung Kwon Choi. 2001. Long Sentence Partitioning using Structure Analysis for Machine Translation. In *Proceedings of the Sixth Natural Language Processing Pacific Rim Symposium*, pages 646–652.

Katsuhito Sudoh, Kevin Duh, Hajime Tsukada, Tsutomu Hirao, and Masaaki Nagata. 2010. Divide and Translate: Improving Long Distance Reordering in Statistical Machine Translation. In *Proceedings of the Joint 5th Workshop on Statistical Machine Translation and MetricsMATR*, pages 418–427.

Peng Xu, Jaeho Kang, Michael Ringgaard, and Franz Och. 2009. Using a Dependency Parser to Improve SMT for Subject-Object-Verb Languages. In *proceedings of the 2009 Annual Conference of the North American Chapter of the Association for Computational Linguistics*, pages 245–253.